Decrypting the Threat Landscape: A Comprehensive Guide to Cybersecurity

Table of Content

Chapter 1: Understanding the Digital Battlefield

- Definition and scope of the digital battlefield.
- Evolution of the digital environment and its impact on security.
- Types of cyber threats and their characteristics.
- Understanding the motives behind cyber attacks.
- Identification and importance of critical infrastructure in the digital context.
- Vulnerabilities and potential targets within critical infrastructure.
- Linking cybersecurity to national security.
- Key threats faced by nations in the digital space.
- Examination of state-sponsored cyber activities.
- The use of cyber tools as part of geopolitical strategies.

Chapter 2: Unveiling Cyber Threat Actors: Who's Behind the Screen?

- Definition and classification of cyber threat actors.
- Motivations driving various threat actors.
- Understanding the involvement of nation-states in cyber operations.
- Examples of state-sponsored cyber attacks.
- Examining hacktivism and ideological cyber threats.
- Case studies illustrating hacktivist activities.
- Overview of cybercrime syndicates and their operations.
- Economic motives driving cybercriminals.
- Definition of insider threats and their impact.
- Strategies for mitigating risks posed by insiders.

Chapter 3: Fortifying the Gates: Building Robust Cyber Defenses

- Definition and goals of cyber defense.
- The evolving nature of cyber threats and the need for proactive measures.
- The importance of risk assessment in cybersecurity.
- Strategies for identifying and prioritizing cybersecurity risks.
- Overview of established cybersecurity frameworks.
- Tailoring frameworks to organizational needs.
- Securing network infrastructure against cyber threats.
- Implementing firewalls, intrusion detection/prevention systems, and secure network configurations.
- Protecting individual devices and endpoints from cyber threats.
- The role of endpoint security solutions.

Chapter 4: Data Breaches and Beyond: Navigating the Aftermath

- Definition and common causes of data breaches.
- The impact of data breaches on organizations and individuals.
- Strategies for timely detection of data breaches.
- Legal and ethical considerations in notifying affected parties.
- Conducting a thorough forensic analysis after a data breach.
- The role of digital forensics in identifying the scope and perpetrators.
- Compliance requirements following a data breach.
- Potential legal consequences for organizations.
- Crafting effective communication strategies during and after a data breach.
- Managing public relations and reputation damage.

Chapter 5: The Human Factor: Psychology in Cybersecurity

- The role of human behavior in cybersecurity.
- Cognitive biases and decision-making in the context of cyber threats.
- Definition and examples of social engineering attacks.
- Recognizing and mitigating the impact of social engineering.
- Examining the tactics used in phishing and spear phishing attacks.
- Strategies for educating users and reducing susceptibility.
- Psychological factors contributing to insider threats.
- Building awareness and resilience against insider attacks.
- Designing effective security training programs for employees.
- Measuring the success of awareness initiatives.

Chapter 6: Emerging Technologies and Cybersecurity: A Symbiotic Evolution

- Definition and scope of emerging technologies in the digital landscape.
- The rapid evolution of technological innovations.
- Applications of AI and ML in threat detection and analysis.
- Challenges and ethical considerations in AI-driven cybersecurity.
- How blockchain enhances security in digital transactions.
- Potential applications of blockchain in cybersecurity.
- Security risks associated with the proliferation of IoT devices.
- Strategies for securing IoT networks and devices.
- The impact of quantum computing on traditional cryptographic methods.
- Post-quantum cryptography as a countermeasure.

Chapter 7: Global Cybersecurity Challenges: A Cross-Border Perspective

- The interconnected nature of cybersecurity challenges on a global scale.
- The need for international cooperation in addressing cyber threats.
- Examples of cyber threats that transcend national borders.
- Challenges in attributing and responding to cross-border attacks.
- Overview of existing international laws and treaties related to cybersecurity.
- Gaps and challenges in the current legal framework.
- The role of diplomacy in addressing cyber conflicts.
- Case studies illustrating diplomatic efforts in cybersecurity.
- Successful examples of international cooperation in cybersecurity.
- Barriers and challenges to effective collaboration.

Chapter 8: The Future of Cybersecurity: Trends and Projections

- Acknowledging the dynamic nature of the cybersecurity landscape.
- The importance of anticipating and preparing for future challenges.
- Projected advancements in AI and automation for cyber defense.
- The integration of AI into offensive cyber capabilities.
- Predicting future trends in cyber threats.
- The emergence of new threat vectors and attack methods.
- The adoption and evolution of zero-trust security models.
- Benefits and challenges associated with implementing zero-trust.
- Anticipated changes in cybersecurity regulations.
- The impact of regulatory shifts on organizations.

Introduction

In an era defined by rapid technological progress, the digital landscape has transformed into a dynamic arena, serving both as a playground for innovation and a battleground for cybersecurity. "Decrypting the Threat Landscape: A Comprehensive Guide to Cybersecurity" emerges as an indispensable companion, offering an illuminating journey through the intricate realm of digital security. Beyond being a mere manual, this book stands as a revelation, a guide empowering individuals and organizations to not only comprehend but also effectively counter and conquer the relentless and ever-evolving challenges posed by cybersecurity threats.

As we traverse the virtual landscape, the narrative unfolds with a deep dive into the multifaceted nature of the digital battlefield. The introductory chapters lay the groundwork, dissecting the significance of the interconnected world and framing it as the stage upon which modern conflicts play out. The narrative emphasizes how, with each stride in technological prowess, new threats emerge from the shadows, necessitating a comprehensive understanding of the threat landscape.

"Decrypting the Threat Landscape" strategically navigates through critical junctures of cybersecurity, dedicating chapters to unveil the elusive figures behind the screen – cyber threat actors. It meticulously explores their motivations, tactics, and the intricate web of cyber warfare. Moving beyond the shadows, the guide pivots to the proactive aspect of cybersecurity in the third chapter, "Fortifying the Gates: Building Robust Cyber Defenses." Here, the focus shifts to the development of resilient defense mechanisms, crucial in safeguarding against the ever-looming digital threats.

The aftermath of cyber incidents is dissected in Chapter 4, "Data Breaches and Beyond: Navigating the Aftermath," shedding light on the intricate process of dealing with and recovering from data breaches. As the narrative unfolds, attention turns to the often underestimated human factor in cybersecurity. Chapter 5, aptly titled "The Human Factor: Psychology in Cybersecurity," delves into the psychological aspects shaping both defenders and attackers in the digital realm.

Chapter 6 propels the reader into the future with "Emerging Technologies and Cybersecurity: A Symbiotic Evolution," exploring how the rapid evolution of technology shapes the landscape and, in turn, influences cybersecurity measures. The global perspective takes center stage in Chapter 7, "Global Cybersecurity Challenges: A Cross-Border Perspective," providing insights into the challenges that transcend geographical boundaries and demand international collaboration.

Anticipating the road ahead, Chapter 8 unfolds "The Future of Cybersecurity: Trends and Projections," where the guide peers into forthcoming developments, preparing readers for the dynamic shifts on the horizon. As the journey culminates, the guide ventures into the ethical and legal dimensions of cybersecurity in Chapter 9, providing a nuanced understanding of the complex landscape governed by laws and ethical considerations.

In its concluding chapter, "Cybersecurity Governance and Risk Management: Strategies for Resilience," the guide ties together the threads of governance and risk management, emphasizing the need for adaptive strategies to foster resilience in the face of ever-evolving threats. "Decrypting the Threat Landscape" thus stands not merely as a guide but as a comprehensive narrative, equipping its readers to navigate, decipher, and ultimately triumph over the challenges embedded in the intricate world of cybersecurity.

Chapter 1: Understanding the Digital Battlefield

Definition and scope of the digital battlefield.

The digital battlefield, within the expansive landscape of contemporary technology, encapsulates a multifaceted arena where the forces of innovation and security engage in a perpetual struggle for dominance. In essence, it represents the virtual space where individuals, organizations, and nations interact, collaborate, and, inevitably, contend with the evolving challenges posed by the interconnected world. The scope of the digital battlefield extends far beyond traditional notions of conflict, encompassing not only military engagements but also economic, political, and societal activities deeply intertwined with the digital realm.

At its core, the definition of the digital battlefield hinges on the transformative impact of technology on the nature of human interactions and power dynamics. It is not confined to a specific geographic location but rather spans the entirety of the internet, encompassing networks, devices, and the vast expanse of cyberspace. This virtual battleground is characterized by its intangible nature, where the stakes are often high but the terrain is invisible, existing in the intricate web of data flows, digital communications, and the infrastructure that underpins our technologically driven world.

The scope of the digital battlefield is broad and continually expanding as technological advancements introduce new frontiers and complexities. Beyond the conventional domains of military operations, the digital battlefield incorporates economic systems, critical infrastructure, and even the very fabric of social connectivity. Cybersecurity, therefore, becomes paramount in this context, serving as the armor that shields against an array of threats, from malicious actors seeking to exploit vulnerabilities for financial gain to state-sponsored entities engaging in espionage or acts of sabotage.

The actors on this digital stage are diverse and elusive, ranging from individual hackers motivated by personal gain to sophisticated state-sponsored groups with strategic geopolitical objectives. Unveiling the identities and motives of these cyber threat actors is a persistent challenge, contributing to the elusive and dynamic nature of the digital battlefield. This dynamicity is further accentuated by the rapid pace of technological evolution, with each advancement presenting new opportunities for innovation but simultaneously exposing novel vulnerabilities that can be exploited.

As technology permeates every facet of modern life, the digital battlefield becomes integral to not only military strategies but also economic competitiveness and the functioning of democratic institutions. It involves the protection of sensitive information, the assurance of secure communication channels, and the preservation of privacy in an era where personal and organizational data are invaluable commodities. The implications of success or failure in this digital struggle extend far beyond the virtual realm, influencing geopolitical power dynamics, economic stability, and societal well-being.

Understanding the digital battlefield necessitates a holistic approach that transcends traditional boundaries. It involves acknowledging the interconnectedness of global systems, recognizing the interdependencies of critical infrastructure, and appreciating the intricate web of relationships that define the digital age. The scope of the digital battlefield, therefore, demands a comprehensive and adaptive cybersecurity strategy that goes beyond mere defense and incorporates proactive measures to anticipate, counter, and mitigate the evolving threats that characterize this complex and dynamic landscape. In navigating the digital battlefield, the imperative lies not only in protecting against immediate threats but also in fostering resilience and innovation to thrive in the ever-shifting terrain of the interconnected world.

Evolution of the digital environment and its impact on security.

The evolution of the digital environment stands as a testament to the relentless march of technological progress, reshaping the very fabric of our interconnected world and introducing profound implications for security. The journey begins with the inception of the digital era, marked by the advent of computers and the gradual integration of electronic systems into various facets of human life. This initial phase laid the groundwork for the digitization of information, offering newfound efficiency but also introducing vulnerabilities that were previously unimaginable.

The proliferation of the internet in the late 20th century marked a transformative leap, turning the digital environment into a global network of interconnected systems. As the world became increasingly reliant on the internet for communication, commerce, and information exchange, the scope and complexity of the digital environment expanded exponentially. The evolution from isolated computer systems to a globally connected web laid the foundation for a dynamic, borderless landscape where information flowed seamlessly across geographical boundaries.

With this interconnectedness came the emergence of the World Wide Web, a platform that democratized access to information but also introduced a new paradigm of cyber threats. The digital environment evolved into a vast repository of data, and as individuals, businesses, and governments embraced digital technologies, the value of this data skyrocketed. Consequently, securing this valuable commodity became a paramount concern, giving rise to the field of cybersecurity.

The evolution of the digital environment witnessed the rise of e-commerce, online banking, and digital communication platforms, fundamentally altering the way individuals and organizations conducted their affairs. While these advancements brought unprecedented convenience, they also presented lucrative targets for malicious actors seeking financial gain or exploiting sensitive information for various motives. Cybersecurity, once a niche concern, became an essential aspect of safeguarding the digital landscape against an array of threats, ranging from individual hackers to organized cybercriminal networks.

The proliferation of mobile devices further accelerated the evolution of the digital environment, turning it into an omnipresent force in daily life. Smartphones and tablets became ubiquitous, providing users with constant connectivity and access to a myriad of services. This mobile revolution, while enhancing convenience, introduced a new dimension of security challenges. Mobile devices became prime targets for cyber attacks, and the need to secure not just traditional computer systems but also a diverse array of connected devices became a pressing imperative.

As society embraced the Internet of Things (IoT), the digital environment continued its evolution into a vast ecosystem of interconnected devices, from smart home appliances to industrial machinery. The interconnectivity of these devices, while offering unprecedented efficiency and automation, also created a sprawling attack surface for cyber adversaries. Security vulnerabilities in one device could potentially cascade into widespread disruptions, underscoring the importance of securing the entire ecosystem.

The evolution of the digital environment also intersected with the rise of cloud computing, transforming the way data was stored, processed, and accessed. Cloud services offered scalability and flexibility but introduced new considerations for data security and privacy. Organizations shifted from traditional, on-premises infrastructure to cloud-based solutions, necessitating a paradigm shift in cybersecurity strategies to adapt to this dynamic and distributed computing environment.

In recent years, the digital environment has witnessed the integration of artificial intelligence (AI) and machine learning (ML) into cybersecurity practices. These technologies, while providing innovative tools for threat detection and response, also present a double-edged sword, as malicious actors seek to exploit AI for more sophisticated and evasive attacks. The evolving arms race between cybersecurity measures and advanced threats underscores the dynamic nature of the digital landscape.

The impact of the evolving digital environment on security extends beyond the realms of technology. It has profound implications for privacy, individual rights, and the geopolitical landscape. The digitization of information has transformed data into a valuable commodity, leading to debates on privacy rights, data ownership, and the ethical use of technology. Nation-states engage in cyber operations that blur the lines between traditional warfare and digital conflict, redefining the nature of security in the 21st century.

In conclusion, the evolution of the digital environment has been a transformative journey, reshaping the way we live, work, and interact. From the early days of isolated computer systems to the interconnected, mobile, and IoT-driven landscape of today, the digital environment has become an integral part of the human experience. As technology continues to advance, so too will the security challenges evolve, demanding a proactive and adaptive approach to safeguard the digital realm against emerging threats and vulnerabilities. The narrative of the digital environment and security is an ongoing saga, marked by innovation, resilience, and the perpetual quest to strike a balance between progress and protection in an ever-evolving digital frontier.

Types of cyber threats and their characteristics.

The landscape of cyber threats is as diverse as the digital environment itself, encompassing a spectrum of malicious activities perpetrated by individuals, criminal organizations, and state-sponsored entities. Among the myriad types of cyber threats, malware emerges as a pervasive and adaptable adversary. Malicious software, or malware, takes various forms, including viruses, worms, trojans, and ransomware, each designed to infiltrate systems, compromise data integrity, or disrupt operations. Viruses attach themselves to legitimate programs, replicating and spreading when the infected program is executed, while worms self-replicate and spread independently. Trojans disguise themselves as legitimate software but carry malicious payloads, and ransomware encrypts data, demanding payment for its release.

Phishing, another prevalent cyber threat, capitalizes on social engineering to manipulate individuals into divulging sensitive information such as passwords or financial details. Often disguised as trustworthy entities through emails or fraudulent websites, phishing attacks exploit human vulnerabilities, emphasizing the significance of cybersecurity awareness and education. Spear phishing targets specific individuals or organizations with tailored and sophisticated messages, making it a potent tool for cybercriminals seeking valuable data or unauthorized access.

Distributed Denial of Service (DDoS) attacks represent a category of cyber threats that aim to overwhelm a target's online services, rendering them unavailable to users. By flooding the target with an excessive volume of traffic or exploiting vulnerabilities in network infrastructure, DDoS attacks disrupt normal operations, causing financial losses and tarnishing the target's reputation. Advanced Persistent Threats (APTs) are characterized by long-term and targeted campaigns, often orchestrated by nation-states or well-funded groups. APTs involve sophisticated tactics, techniques, and procedures, enabling attackers to maintain undetected access, gather intelligence, and execute strategic objectives over an extended period.

Exploiting vulnerabilities in software and systems, zero-day attacks target undisclosed and unpatched weaknesses. These attacks are particularly challenging to defend against because security measures are not yet in place when the vulnerability is exploited. Similarly, drive-by downloads occur when users unintentionally download malicious code by visiting compromised websites, emphasizing the importance of regularly updating software and employing robust web security measures. Man-in-the-Middle (MitM) attacks intercept and manipulate communications between two parties, enabling attackers to eavesdrop, alter data, or inject malicious content. Wi-Fi eavesdropping, session hijacking, and DNS spoofing are common techniques employed in MitM attacks.

Cross-Site Scripting (XSS) and Cross-Site Request Forgery (CSRF) are web-based attacks that exploit vulnerabilities in websites or web applications. XSS involves injecting malicious scripts into web pages viewed by other users, compromising their data or session information. CSRF, on the other hand, leverages a user's authenticated session to perform unauthorized actions on their behalf without their consent. Ransomware attacks have surged in prevalence, with cybercriminals encrypting victims' data and demanding payment for its release. The sophistication of ransomware has evolved, targeting individuals, businesses, and even critical infrastructure, posing significant financial and operational risks.

Cryptojacking represents a stealthy form of cyber threat wherein attackers exploit victims' computing resources to mine cryptocurrencies without their knowledge. This type of attack can degrade system performance, increase energy consumption, and incur additional costs for affected individuals or organizations. Internet of Things (IoT) devices, with their increasing prevalence, have become targets for cyber threats. Insecure IoT devices can be exploited to launch attacks, compromise networks, or invade user privacy, emphasizing the need for robust security measures in the rapidly expanding IoT ecosystem.

While the aforementioned threats are diverse, the common thread among them is the continuous evolution and adaptation exhibited by malicious actors. Cyber threats are dynamic, often responding to advancements in technology and security measures. The characteristics of cyber threats underscore the necessity for a multifaceted and proactive cybersecurity strategy that includes regular updates, user education, robust access controls, and continuous monitoring. As the digital landscape evolves, understanding the diverse array of cyber threats becomes paramount for individuals, businesses, and governments alike, in order to fortify defenses and mitigate the risks inherent in the interconnected world.

Understanding the motives behind cyber attacks.

The motives behind cyber attacks are as diverse and dynamic as the digital landscape itself, reflecting the multifaceted nature of the individuals, groups, and entities that engage in these activities. One of the primary motivations driving cyber attacks is financial gain. Cybercriminals often target individuals and organizations to extract valuable information such as financial credentials, personal data, or intellectual property that can be monetized on the dark web. This profit-centric motive underpins a wide array of cyber threats, including phishing, ransomware, and identity theft, where the end goal is to exploit vulnerabilities for financial benefit.

Beyond financial motivations, ideological or political reasons serve as compelling factors behind many cyber attacks. State-sponsored cyber espionage, for instance, involves governments seeking to gain a competitive advantage by infiltrating the networks of other nations to gather intelligence, monitor political opponents, or gain insights into military capabilities. Hacktivism represents another dimension of cyber attacks rooted in ideology, where individuals or groups leverage digital means to promote a particular political or social agenda, often through disruptive actions or information warfare.

Cyber attacks are also frequently motivated by espionage, whether for economic, military, or industrial purposes. Nation-states and corporate entities alike may engage in cyber espionage to gain access to proprietary technologies, trade secrets, or sensitive government information. The quest for a strategic advantage on the global stage often drives these actors to employ sophisticated cyber tools and techniques to infiltrate and exfiltrate valuable data without detection.

A desire for disruption and chaos serves as a motive for some cyber attacks, with the goal of destabilizing political, economic, or societal structures. Terrorist organizations, for instance, may resort to cyber attacks as a means to create fear, compromise critical infrastructure, or undermine public trust. Cyber attacks with disruptive motives can target a wide range of sectors, including energy, healthcare, and transportation, amplifying the potential impact on individuals and society at large.

Espionage and disruption are not the only motives; revenge and retaliation also play a role in driving cyber attacks. Individuals or groups may resort to hacking as a form of retribution against perceived adversaries, seeking to damage reputations, leak sensitive information, or compromise digital assets. This motive is often intertwined with personal vendettas or conflicts, amplifying the emotional and psychological dimensions of cyber attacks.

An emerging and concerning motive behind cyber attacks is cyber warfare, where nation-states leverage digital means as an extension of traditional military strategies. The goal in cyber warfare is not only to gather intelligence but also to incapacitate the adversary's critical infrastructure, disrupt communications, and compromise military capabilities. This evolving landscape poses significant challenges to the traditional norms and rules of engagement in armed conflicts, necessitating a reevaluation of international norms and agreements in the realm of cyber warfare.

In addition to financial, ideological, espionage, disruption, revenge, and warfare motives, the sheer thrill of cyber exploits motivates some individuals. Often referred to as "script kiddies" or amateur hackers, these individuals engage in cyber attacks for the excitement, challenge, and notoriety that hacking activities can bring. Their motives may lack the strategic intent seen in more sophisticated attacks, but their actions can still inflict harm and create vulnerabilities in digital systems.

Understanding the motives behind cyber attacks is crucial for developing effective cybersecurity strategies. As motives evolve and new threats emerge, the cybersecurity landscape becomes increasingly complex. It requires a comprehensive and adaptive approach that combines technological solutions, user education, and international cooperation to address the diverse motivations that drive cyber attacks. By comprehending the underlying motives, cybersecurity professionals, policymakers, and individuals alike can better anticipate, prevent, and respond to the ever-evolving challenges posed by malicious actors in the digital realm.

Identification and importance of critical infrastructure in the digital context.

The identification and safeguarding of critical infrastructure have become paramount in the digital context, as society's essential functions and services increasingly rely on interconnected digital systems. Critical infrastructure encompasses a diverse array of sectors, including energy, transportation, healthcare, finance, and telecommunications, each playing a vital role in the functioning of modern societies. In the digital age, these sectors have undergone a profound transformation, integrating advanced technologies to enhance efficiency, connectivity, and accessibility. The identification of critical infrastructure within the digital context involves recognizing the systems, networks, and assets that are indispensable for the stability, security, and prosperity of a nation.

In the realm of energy, digital technologies have revolutionized the management and control of power grids. Smart grids, enabled by advanced sensors and communication systems, optimize energy distribution, enhance resilience, and support the integration of renewable energy sources. The identification of critical energy infrastructure extends beyond power generation to include oil and gas facilities, where digital control systems and networks play a crucial role in extraction, refining, and distribution processes. Disruptions to these systems can have cascading effects, impacting not only energy supply but also the broader economy and societal well-being.

Transportation systems, another vital component of critical infrastructure, have embraced digital technologies for efficiency, safety, and connectivity. Intelligent transportation systems rely on digital networks to manage traffic, enhance logistics, and facilitate communication between vehicles. Air traffic control, maritime navigation, and railway operations all depend on intricate digital infrastructures, making their identification and protection essential. Disruptions to transportation systems can result in economic losses, logistical challenges, and compromise public safety.

In the healthcare sector, the digitalization of medical records, diagnostic tools, and treatment protocols has significantly improved patient care and operational efficiency. However, it has also rendered healthcare infrastructure vulnerable to cyber threats. The identification of critical healthcare infrastructure involves recognizing the interconnected nature of digital medical systems, including electronic health records, medical devices, and telemedicine platforms. Cyber-attacks on healthcare infrastructure can have life-threatening consequences, compromising patient data, disrupting medical services, and undermining public trust.

The financial sector, a cornerstone of modern economies, relies extensively on digital systems for banking operations, electronic transactions, and financial communications. The identification of critical financial infrastructure involves acknowledging the digital platforms that facilitate monetary transactions, stock exchanges, and global financial networks. Cyber threats targeting financial infrastructure can result in significant economic losses, erode public confidence in financial institutions, and pose systemic risks to the stability of the financial system.

Telecommunications infrastructure serves as the backbone of the digital age, enabling global connectivity, information exchange, and digital communication. The identification of critical telecommunications infrastructure encompasses the vast networks of fiber optics, satellites, and wireless communication systems that underpin modern connectivity. Disruptions to telecommunications infrastructure can impede emergency communications, hinder information flow, and compromise the functioning of other critical sectors.

The importance of critical infrastructure in the digital context extends beyond individual sectors to the concept of "cyber-physical systems." These systems integrate digital technologies with physical processes, blurring the lines between the virtual and physical worlds. Industrial control systems (ICS) in manufacturing, for instance, rely on digital networks to automate and optimize production processes. The identification of critical infrastructure in the context of cyber-physical systems involves recognizing the interdependence of digital technologies and physical operations, emphasizing the need for robust cybersecurity measures to prevent disruptions and potential physical consequences.

The growing interconnectedness of critical infrastructure has heightened the importance of securing the supply chain, as many digital systems rely on components and services from various vendors. The identification of critical infrastructure must, therefore, encompass not only the immediate assets of a particular sector but also the broader ecosystem of suppliers, service providers, and interconnected networks. Cyber threats targeting the supply chain can introduce vulnerabilities that, if exploited, may propagate across multiple sectors, amplifying the potential impact of an attack.

The digitalization of critical infrastructure brings about significant benefits but also introduces new challenges and risks. Cyber threats targeting critical infrastructure have evolved in sophistication and scope, ranging from ransomware attacks on healthcare systems to advanced persistent threats against energy grids. The consequences of a successful cyber attack on critical infrastructure can extend beyond financial losses to include societal disruption, compromise of national security, and even potential loss of life.

The identification and protection of critical infrastructure in the digital context require a multi-faceted approach that combines technological solutions, regulatory frameworks, and international cooperation. Robust cybersecurity measures, including threat detection, incident response, and continuous monitoring, are essential to safeguarding critical digital systems. Regulatory bodies play a crucial role in establishing standards and frameworks to ensure the resilience and security of critical infrastructure, fostering a culture of compliance and accountability.

International cooperation is vital in addressing the transnational nature of cyber threats targeting critical infrastructure. Information sharing, collaboration on cybersecurity best practices, and the development of norms and agreements enhance the collective ability to identify, prevent, and respond to cyber attacks. Cybersecurity exercises, simulations, and continuous improvement initiatives contribute to building resilience within critical infrastructure sectors, preparing organizations to withstand and recover from cyber incidents.

In conclusion, the identification and importance of critical infrastructure in the digital context underscore the integral role these systems play in the functioning of modern societies. As digital technologies continue to advance, the interconnectedness of critical infrastructure increases, necessitating a comprehensive and adaptive approach to cybersecurity. The protection of critical infrastructure is not only a matter of economic and operational resilience but also a fundamental element in ensuring the safety, security, and well-being of nations in the digital age.

Vulnerabilities and potential targets within critical infrastructure.

Within the intricate web of critical infrastructure, vulnerabilities and potential targets abound, presenting a complex landscape where the interplay of digital technologies and physical processes creates points of susceptibility. One prominent vulnerability lies in the reliance on interconnected and often outdated legacy systems. Many critical infrastructure sectors, such as energy and manufacturing, still utilize legacy systems that were not designed with modern cybersecurity considerations in mind. These outdated systems may lack essential security features, making them susceptible to exploitation by malicious actors seeking entry points into critical networks.

Moreover, the increasing integration of Industrial Control Systems (ICS) and Supervisory Control and Data Acquisition (SCADA) systems within critical infrastructure introduces vulnerabilities. These systems, designed to automate and optimize physical processes, often operate in a realm where cybersecurity was not initially a primary concern. As these digital control systems become more interconnected with enterprise networks and the internet, they become potential targets for cyber attacks. Vulnerabilities in ICS and SCADA systems could be exploited to manipulate physical processes, disrupt operations, or cause equipment failures with cascading consequences.

The human factor also emerges as a significant vulnerability within critical infrastructure. Insider threats, whether intentional or unintentional, pose risks that can compromise sensitive information or grant unauthorized access to critical systems. Employees with privileged access or individuals with knowledge of operational processes may inadvertently contribute to vulnerabilities through actions such as clicking on malicious links in phishing emails or neglecting cybersecurity best practices. Insider threats can be particularly challenging to mitigate, as they may not be driven solely by malicious intent but can also result from human error or negligence.

The growing reliance on third-party vendors and the global supply chain introduces additional vulnerabilities within critical infrastructure. Many organizations within these sectors depend on external suppliers for components, software, and services. If a vendor's cybersecurity measures are lacking, it creates a potential avenue for attackers to compromise the supply chain and introduce vulnerabilities into critical systems. The interconnected nature of supply chains amplifies the potential impact of a cyber attack, as a compromise in one part of the chain can propagate across multiple sectors.

The convergence of information technology (IT) and operational technology (OT) within critical infrastructure creates a nexus of vulnerabilities. Historically, IT and OT systems operated in separate domains, but the increasing digitization of operational processes has led to their integration. While this convergence offers operational benefits, it also introduces new attack surfaces and potential vulnerabilities. Cyber attackers may exploit weaknesses in IT systems to gain access to OT networks, where they can manipulate physical processes or disrupt critical operations.

Furthermore, the ubiquity of internet-connected devices and the Internet of Things (IoT) introduces vulnerabilities within critical infrastructure. Smart sensors, actuators, and IoT devices are increasingly integrated into industrial processes, providing real-time data and enhancing automation. However, these devices often lack robust security features, making them susceptible to compromise. If attackers gain control over IoT devices within critical infrastructure, they can manipulate data, disrupt operations, or use these devices as entry points into broader networks.

The importance of communication networks to critical infrastructure introduces vulnerabilities that, if exploited, can have cascading effects. The reliance on internet connectivity, wireless communication, and interconnected networks makes communication infrastructure a potential target. Cyber attacks on communication networks can disrupt the flow of information between critical systems, impede emergency communications, and hinder the coordination of response efforts during incidents. Disruptions to communication networks can exacerbate the impact of cyber attacks on critical infrastructure by impeding situational awareness and response capabilities.

The financial sector, a vital component of critical infrastructure, is susceptible to cyber threats that can have wide-ranging consequences. Cyber attackers may target financial institutions with the intent of financial gain, disrupting financial transactions, or undermining public confidence in the banking system. Digital banking platforms, online payment systems, and financial trading platforms represent potential targets for cyber attacks, as their compromise could lead to financial losses, economic instability, and erosion of trust in the financial sector.

Healthcare infrastructure, especially with the increasing digitization of medical records and the adoption of telemedicine, is vulnerable to cyber threats that can compromise patient data and disrupt healthcare services. Cyber attacks on healthcare infrastructure can have life-threatening consequences, affecting patient care, medical research, and the overall functioning of healthcare systems. The potential for unauthorized access to medical records, manipulation of treatment protocols, and disruption of critical medical devices poses significant risks to the integrity and availability of healthcare services.

Transportation systems, including air traffic control, maritime navigation, and railway operations, are potential targets for cyber attacks that can result in disruptions, safety hazards, and economic losses. Cybersecurity vulnerabilities within transportation infrastructure may be exploited to manipulate traffic control systems, disrupt logistics, or compromise the safety of passengers and cargo. The interconnectedness of transportation networks amplifies the potential impact of cyber attacks, as disruptions in one segment of the transportation sector can have cascading effects across the entire system.

In conclusion, the identification of vulnerabilities and potential targets within critical infrastructure is essential for developing effective cybersecurity strategies. The convergence of digital technologies with physical processes introduces a dynamic and multifaceted landscape of vulnerabilities that malicious actors may exploit. Recognizing the interdependencies between sectors, the reliance on outdated systems, the human factor, supply chain vulnerabilities, the convergence of IT and OT, and the growing prevalence of IoT devices underscores the complex nature of securing critical infrastructure in the digital age. Addressing these vulnerabilities requires a holistic and adaptive approach, encompassing robust cybersecurity measures, regulatory frameworks, international cooperation, and continuous improvement initiatives to enhance the resilience and security of critical infrastructure.

Linking cybersecurity to national security.

Linking cybersecurity to national security is a fundamental recognition of the interconnected and digitized nature of modern societies. In the 21st century, cyberspace has become an integral component of a nation's critical infrastructure, economic systems, and governmental functions. The increasing dependence on digital technologies for communication, commerce, and governance has made nations more vulnerable to cyber threats, elevating the importance of cybersecurity in safeguarding national security interests. The linkage between cybersecurity and national security extends beyond the protection of sensitive information to encompass the preservation of economic stability, public safety, and the integrity of democratic institutions.

In the context of national security, cyberspace serves as both a domain of opportunity and a battleground. States leverage cyberspace for intelligence gathering, military operations, and economic espionage. At the same time, it has become a domain where malicious actors, ranging from cybercriminals to state-sponsored entities, exploit vulnerabilities to compromise systems, disrupt operations, and potentially inflict significant harm. Recognizing the strategic implications of cyber threats, nations integrate cybersecurity into their national security doctrines, emphasizing the need to protect critical infrastructure, defend against cyber attacks, and deter adversaries in the digital realm.

Critical infrastructure, a linchpin of national security, relies heavily on digital systems that control essential services such as energy, transportation, healthcare, and finance. The compromise of critical infrastructure through cyber attacks poses not only economic risks but also threats to public safety and societal well-being. The interconnectedness of critical infrastructure sectors further magnifies the potential impact of cyber threats, as disruptions in one sector may have cascading effects across others, underscoring the need for robust cybersecurity measures to fortify the resilience of national infrastructure.

Economic stability is intimately tied to the cybersecurity posture of a nation. In an era where economies are increasingly driven by digital technologies, the compromise of financial systems, theft of intellectual property, and economic espionage through cyber means can have profound consequences. Nations recognize that the protection of economic assets in cyberspace is essential for sustaining prosperity and competitiveness on the global stage. Cybersecurity measures become instrumental in safeguarding intellectual property, preserving economic data integrity, and ensuring the secure flow of financial transactions, all of which are critical to national economic security.

The democratic processes and institutions that form the foundation of many nations are not immune to the impact of cyber threats. Elections, political campaigns, and government operations are increasingly digitized, making them susceptible to interference, disinformation campaigns, and cyber attacks. Cybersecurity, therefore, assumes a role in preserving the integrity of democratic systems, ensuring the confidentiality of sensitive political communications, and guarding against attempts to manipulate public opinion through malicious cyber activities. The protection of democratic institutions in cyberspace becomes an integral aspect of national security strategies.

Military operations and national defense strategies have undergone a profound transformation with the integration of cyberspace into the domain of warfare. Cyber capabilities have become essential tools for intelligence gathering, strategic planning, and even offensive operations. Nations recognize the need to develop robust cyber capabilities to defend against cyber attacks from adversaries and to deter potential threats. The linkage between cybersecurity and national defense involves not only protecting military networks but also ensuring the resilience of critical infrastructure that supports defense operations.

The attribution challenge in cyberspace adds a layer of complexity to national security considerations. Unlike traditional forms of warfare, where the origin of an attack is often more readily identifiable, cyber attacks can be launched from anywhere in the world with a degree of anonymity. Nation-states must navigate the complexities of attributing cyber attacks to specific actors, whether they are cybercriminals, hacktivists, or state-sponsored entities. Developing effective mechanisms for attribution is crucial for formulating appropriate responses and deterrent measures, linking cybersecurity to the broader realm of national security strategy.

International cooperation and collaboration become imperative in addressing the global nature of cyber threats. Nations recognize that the interconnectedness of cyberspace means that an attack on one country's critical infrastructure can have implications for others. Therefore, forging international agreements, sharing threat intelligence, and developing norms of responsible behavior in cyberspace become integral components of national security strategies. Cybersecurity is not solely a national concern; it is a shared global challenge that requires coordinated efforts to enhance collective resilience against cyber threats.

The emergence of hybrid threats, where cyber capabilities are integrated with traditional military and geopolitical strategies, further reinforces the link between cybersecurity and national security. Adversarial nations may employ cyber means to achieve strategic objectives without resorting to open conflict, using cyber attacks to disrupt economies, manipulate public opinion, or undermine the stability of rival nations. Nations recognize the need for comprehensive cybersecurity strategies that align with broader national security interests to address the evolving landscape of hybrid threats.

As artificial intelligence, quantum computing, and other advanced technologies continue to reshape the digital landscape, nations acknowledge the imperative of staying at the forefront of innovation while concurrently securing these technologies against potential exploitation. The linkage between cybersecurity and national security extends to the preservation of technological leadership, ensuring that advancements in critical areas are not compromised or co-opted by adversaries seeking strategic advantages in the digital realm.

In conclusion, linking cybersecurity to national security is an acknowledgment of the evolving nature of threats in the digital age. Cyberspace has become a domain where economic, political, military, and societal interests intersect, making the protection of digital assets and infrastructure integral to a nation's overall security posture. The identification and mitigation of cyber threats, the fortification of critical infrastructure, and the integration of cybersecurity into national defense strategies collectively contribute to the resilience of nations in the face of an ever-evolving and interconnected digital landscape. The linkage between cybersecurity and national security underscores the recognition that securing the digital realm is not just a matter of technological defense but an imperative for safeguarding the broader interests and well-being of nations in the modern era.

Key threats faced by nations in the digital space.

In the rapidly evolving digital landscape, nations face a myriad of complex and interconnected threats that extend beyond traditional security paradigms. Cyber threats have become pervasive, impacting economic stability, national security, and the very fabric of modern societies. One key threat is the persistent risk of state-sponsored cyber attacks. Nation-states, seeking strategic advantages and influence, engage in sophisticated cyber operations to compromise the networks of other countries. These attacks may involve espionage, intellectual property theft, or attempts to disrupt critical infrastructure, blurring the lines between traditional geopolitical rivalries and digital conflict.

Cyber espionage is a prevalent and persistent threat that nations grapple with in the digital space. State actors, driven by political, economic, or military motives, conduct intelligence-gathering operations through cyber means. By infiltrating the networks of foreign governments, organizations, or institutions, cyber espionage enables the collection of sensitive information, military intelligence, and trade secrets. The covert nature of cyber espionage poses challenges in attribution, as state-sponsored entities often employ advanced techniques to conceal their identities and intentions.

Ransomware has emerged as a formidable threat, affecting nations, businesses, and individuals alike. Malicious actors deploy ransomware to encrypt critical data or systems, demanding payment for their release. The scale and sophistication of ransomware attacks have increased, with some targeting critical infrastructure, government agencies, or healthcare systems. The disruptive impact of ransomware extends beyond financial losses to include operational disruptions, compromised data integrity, and potential harm to public safety.

Nation-states face the ongoing challenge of defending critical infrastructure against cyber attacks. The interconnected nature of digital systems in sectors such as energy, transportation, and healthcare makes critical infrastructure an attractive target for malicious actors. Cyber attacks on critical infrastructure can result in widespread disruptions, economic losses, and compromise national security. State-sponsored entities may seek to exploit vulnerabilities in infrastructure to gain strategic advantages or as part of hybrid warfare strategies.

The proliferation of disinformation campaigns represents a potent threat to nations' social fabric and democratic institutions. State-sponsored or politically motivated actors engage in spreading false narratives, manipulating public opinion, and undermining trust in institutions through online platforms. The weaponization of information in the digital space poses challenges to the integrity of elections, political discourse, and societal cohesion, requiring nations to develop strategies for countering disinformation while upholding principles of free expression.

The evolving threat landscape includes the rise of advanced persistent threats (APTs), characterized by prolonged and targeted cyber campaigns. APTs are often associated with nation-state actors conducting strategic cyber operations with specific objectives, such as economic espionage or gaining long-term access to sensitive networks. The sophisticated tactics, techniques, and procedures employed by APTs make them challenging to detect and mitigate, emphasizing the need for continuous vigilance and adaptive cybersecurity measures.

The Internet of Things (IoT) introduces vulnerabilities that nations must address to ensure the security of connected devices. As the number of IoT devices proliferates in critical sectors such as healthcare, manufacturing, and smart cities, they become potential targets for cyber attacks. Insecure IoT devices can be exploited to launch large-scale botnet attacks, compromise networks, or invade user privacy, underscoring the importance of robust security measures and regulatory frameworks to mitigate IoT-related threats.

Supply chain vulnerabilities pose significant risks to nations as they rely on a global ecosystem of suppliers and service providers. Malicious actors may target the supply chain to introduce compromised components, software, or services into critical systems. The compromise of the supply chain can have cascading effects, amplifying the impact of cyber attacks on national security, critical infrastructure, and economic stability. Strengthening supply chain security involves collaboration, transparency, and diligence in verifying the integrity of components and services.

State-sponsored disinformation campaigns, often fueled by political motives, challenge the information integrity of nations. These campaigns involve the deliberate spread of false or misleading information to influence public opinion, sway elections, or create discord within societies. The weaponization of disinformation requires nations to invest in media literacy, enhance digital resilience, and establish mechanisms for detecting and countering the dissemination of false narratives.

Emerging technologies, such as artificial intelligence (AI) and quantum computing, introduce both opportunities and risks in the digital space. AI can be leveraged for innovative cybersecurity solutions, but it also presents challenges as malicious actors explore AI-driven tactics for cyber attacks. Quantum computing, while promising advancements in cryptography, poses a threat to current encryption standards, requiring nations to stay ahead in developing quantum-resistant cryptographic solutions to protect sensitive information.

The increasing sophistication of cybercriminal networks poses a persistent threat to nations' cybersecurity. Cybercriminals engage in a range of activities, from financial fraud and theft to selling illicit goods and services on the dark web. The fluid and decentralized nature of cybercrime makes it challenging for law enforcement to combat, necessitating international collaboration, legislative frameworks, and advanced cybersecurity measures to deter and prosecute cybercriminals.

Nations face the challenge of managing the human factor in cybersecurity, recognizing that individuals can be both targets and vectors of cyber attacks. Insider threats, whether intentional or unintentional, pose risks to national security. Employees with privileged access may inadvertently contribute to vulnerabilities through actions such as falling victim to phishing attacks or neglecting cybersecurity best practices. Addressing the human factor involves education, training, and awareness programs to foster a cybersecurity culture within organizations and society at large.

As nations navigate the complex digital landscape, they must grapple with the multifaceted and dynamic nature of cyber threats. The interconnectedness of global systems, the strategic use of cyber capabilities by state actors, and the continuous evolution of cyber threats underscore the importance of a comprehensive and adaptive approach to cybersecurity. Nations must invest in technological innovation, international cooperation, regulatory frameworks, and cybersecurity resilience to effectively mitigate the diverse threats posed in the digital space. The proactive and collaborative efforts of nations are crucial to building cyber defenses that safeguard national interests, uphold democratic values, and ensure the security and well-being of societies in the digital age.

Examination of state-sponsored cyber activities.

An examination of state-sponsored cyber activities delves into the complex realm where nations leverage digital capabilities to pursue strategic objectives, advancing their interests in the global landscape. State-sponsored cyber activities represent a sophisticated form of geopolitical maneuvering, where cyber capabilities are integrated into traditional statecraft to gather intelligence, conduct espionage, and exert influence. One hallmark of state-sponsored cyber activities is the strategic intent behind the actions, often orchestrated by intelligence agencies or military entities seeking a competitive advantage, economic gains, or the advancement of national security objectives. These activities transcend mere cybercrime, involving coordinated and well-funded efforts that are deeply embedded in the geopolitical strategies of nation-states.

Espionage, a longstanding practice in the world of intelligence, has undergone a profound transformation with the integration of cyberspace into the domain of statecraft. State-sponsored cyber espionage involves the targeted and clandestine collection of sensitive information from foreign governments, organizations, or individuals. Advanced Persistent Threats (APTs), which are characterized by stealth, persistence, and tailored targeting, are often associated with state-sponsored cyber espionage campaigns. Nations seek to gain insights into the military capabilities, economic strategies, and political intentions of adversaries, using cyber means to infiltrate networks and exfiltrate valuable intelligence without detection.

Cyber activities by nation-states extend beyond traditional intelligence gathering to the realm of economic espionage. State-sponsored entities leverage cyber capabilities to target businesses, research institutions, and industries to steal intellectual property, trade secrets, and proprietary technologies. The stolen information may be used to advance the economic interests of the sponsoring nation, giving it a competitive edge in industries such as technology, pharmaceuticals, or defense. Economic espionage through cyberspace underscores the integration of cyber capabilities into broader strategies aimed at enhancing national economic competitiveness.

Strategic cyber operations also involve the potential to disrupt or manipulate critical infrastructure, signaling a shift towards the militarization of cyberspace. State-sponsored entities recognize the inherent vulnerabilities within the interconnected networks that control energy, transportation, and healthcare systems. Cyber attacks on critical infrastructure can have profound consequences, ranging from widespread operational disruptions and economic losses to compromising national security. State-sponsored cyber activities in this domain are characterized by the development of offensive capabilities to target adversary infrastructure strategically, possibly as part of broader military or geopolitical strategies.

Political influence campaigns, often driven by state-sponsored actors, leverage cyberspace to shape narratives, manipulate public opinion, and influence political outcomes. Disinformation, propaganda, and the spread of false narratives become tools in the digital arsenal of nations seeking to undermine adversaries or advance their geopolitical agendas. The strategic use of social media, online platforms, and information warfare in state-sponsored influence campaigns underscores the fusion of cyber capabilities with psychological operations, challenging the democratic processes and institutions of targeted nations.

The concept of hybrid warfare encompasses state-sponsored cyber activities that integrate cyber capabilities with traditional military strategies. Hybrid threats involve a combination of conventional warfare, irregular warfare, and cyber operations to achieve strategic objectives. State-sponsored entities may use cyber attacks as a means to weaken adversary defenses, disrupt communication networks, or compromise critical infrastructure in preparation for or in conjunction with conventional military operations. Hybrid warfare exemplifies the blurring of boundaries between physical and digital conflict, presenting nations with multifaceted challenges in responding to complex and adaptive threats.

Attribution, or the ability to accurately identify the source of cyber attacks, poses a significant challenge in the realm of state-sponsored cyber activities. State-sponsored entities employ sophisticated techniques to obfuscate their identities, utilizing proxy servers, false flags, and advanced malware to muddy the waters of attribution. The complexity of cyberspace, where actors can operate with a high degree of anonymity, makes it challenging for targeted nations to definitively attribute cyber attacks to specific states. The attribution challenge underscores the need for robust capabilities in cybersecurity forensics, threat intelligence, and international cooperation to effectively identify and respond to state-sponsored cyber activities.

State-sponsored cyber activities are not confined to a select few powerful nations; an increasing number of states are developing and deploying cyber capabilities to advance their interests. The democratization of cyber capabilities has expanded the landscape of potential actors, with both large and small nations engaging in state-sponsored cyber activities. This proliferation introduces a layer of unpredictability, as states with varying levels of technical sophistication and strategic motivations contribute to the dynamic and contested nature of cyberspace.

The international community grapples with establishing norms, rules of engagement, and diplomatic frameworks to address state-sponsored cyber activities. The absence of clear boundaries in cyberspace complicates efforts to deter malicious behavior and hold nations accountable for their actions. Multilateral initiatives, such as the Tallinn Manual and the Budapest Convention, seek to provide guidelines for responsible state behavior in cyberspace, but the evolution of state-sponsored cyber activities necessitates ongoing dialogues and diplomatic efforts to establish norms that align with the evolving geopolitical landscape.

Countermeasures against state-sponsored cyber activities involve a combination of technological innovation, cybersecurity resilience, and international cooperation. Nations invest in the development of advanced cybersecurity capabilities to detect, mitigate, and respond to cyber threats effectively. Cybersecurity resilience, encompassing strategies for securing critical infrastructure, protecting sensitive data, and fostering a cyber-aware culture, becomes a linchpin in mitigating the impact of state-sponsored cyber activities. International cooperation involves sharing threat intelligence, coordinating responses, and establishing norms to deter and hold accountable nations engaged in malicious cyber behavior.

The increasing integration of artificial intelligence (AI) and machine learning into state-sponsored cyber activities adds a layer of complexity to the threat landscape. AI-driven cyber capabilities enhance the speed, sophistication, and adaptability of attacks, making it imperative for nations to advance their own AI capabilities for cyber defense. The use of AI in state-sponsored cyber activities raises concerns about the potential for autonomous cyber weapons, where machines make decisions in real-time, challenging traditional notions of human control and accountability in conflict.

In conclusion, an examination of state-sponsored cyber activities reveals a landscape where nations leverage digital capabilities for intelligence, economic gains, military objectives, and geopolitical influence. The integration of cyberspace into traditional statecraft represents a paradigm shift in the way nations pursue their interests, introducing new challenges and complexities. State-sponsored cyber activities encompass a spectrum of strategic operations, from espionage and economic espionage to the militarization of cyberspace and hybrid warfare. The dynamic and contested nature of cyberspace, coupled with the challenges of attribution and the proliferation of cyber capabilities, underscores the need for adaptive cybersecurity strategies, international cooperation, and diplomatic efforts to navigate the evolving landscape of state-sponsored cyber activities.

The use of cyber tools as part of geopolitical strategies.

The use of cyber tools as part of geopolitical strategies has emerged as a defining feature of the contemporary global landscape, where digital capabilities are integrated into the broader realm of statecraft to advance national interests, exert influence, and gain strategic advantages. Geopolitical strategies in the digital age extend beyond traditional military and diplomatic domains, incorporating cyberspace as a dynamic and contested arena where nations engage in covert operations, intelligence gathering, economic competition, and even acts of warfare. This paradigm shift reflects the recognition that power projection and influence are increasingly intertwined with a nation's ability to leverage cyber tools effectively in pursuit of its geopolitical objectives.

One key aspect of the use of cyber tools in geopolitical strategies is cyber espionage, where nations deploy sophisticated digital capabilities to gather intelligence and insights into the activities, capabilities, and intentions of other states. State-sponsored entities engage in targeted and covert cyber operations to infiltrate the networks of foreign governments, military organizations, and private industries, aiming to gain a strategic advantage in the geopolitical arena. The clandestine nature of cyber espionage allows nations to conduct intelligence gathering without the need for traditional spies on the ground, enabling a new dimension of covert information warfare.

Economic competition in the digital age is intricately linked to the use of cyber tools as part of geopolitical strategies. Nations recognize the strategic importance of gaining an edge in critical industries, technological innovation, and economic dominance. State-sponsored cyber activities include economic espionage, where cyber capabilities are harnessed to steal intellectual property, trade secrets, and proprietary technologies from rival nations or industries. The stolen information provides a competitive advantage, allowing nations to leapfrog in technological innovation, enhance their economic competitiveness, and potentially undermine the economic stability of adversary states.

The militarization of cyberspace represents a significant evolution in geopolitical strategies, as nations integrate cyber tools into their military doctrines and operational plans. Cyber capabilities have become essential components of military arsenals, offering new avenues for disrupting adversary infrastructure, conducting electronic warfare, and gaining strategic advantages in conflict scenarios. State-sponsored entities develop offensive cyber capabilities, enabling them to target critical infrastructure, military networks, and communication systems in times of crisis or war. The blending of cyber capabilities with traditional military strategies marks a paradigm shift in the nature of warfare, where the digital realm becomes a contested domain for achieving military objectives.

The concept of hybrid warfare further underscores the integration of cyber tools into broader geopolitical strategies. Hybrid warfare involves the combination of conventional military tactics, irregular warfare, information operations, and cyber capabilities to achieve strategic objectives. State-sponsored entities leverage cyber tools as force multipliers in hybrid warfare scenarios, using them to disrupt adversary communications, manipulate public opinion, and undermine the cohesion of targeted societies. The fluid and adaptive nature of hybrid warfare challenges traditional notions of conflict, requiring nations to develop comprehensive strategies that encompass the full spectrum of geopolitical tools, including cyber capabilities.

Political influence campaigns conducted through cyberspace have become a prominent feature of geopolitical strategies. State-sponsored actors leverage social media platforms, online news outlets, and information warfare techniques to shape narratives, spread propaganda, and influence political outcomes in targeted nations. The strategic use of disinformation, fake news, and online manipulation becomes a means of sowing discord, destabilizing political systems, and shaping public opinion in ways that align with the interests of the sponsoring nation. The weaponization of information in the digital space underscores the importance of narrative control as a key element of geopolitical influence.

The use of cyber tools in geopolitical strategies is not confined to offensive operations; defensive cyber capabilities also play a crucial role in safeguarding national interests. Nations invest in cybersecurity measures to protect critical infrastructure, secure sensitive information, and defend against cyber threats from rival states. Cybersecurity resilience becomes a linchpin in geopolitical strategies, as nations strive to mitigate the impact of cyber attacks, enhance their ability to detect and respond to threats, and fortify their critical digital assets against potential adversaries.

The attribution challenge poses a significant complexity in the use of cyber tools as part of geopolitical strategies. State-sponsored entities often employ advanced techniques to obfuscate their identities, using proxy servers, false flags, and deceptive tactics to conceal the source of cyber attacks. The difficulty in accurately attributing cyber incidents to specific nations complicates the development of effective deterrence mechanisms and responses. The attribution challenge underscores the need for advanced cybersecurity forensics, international cooperation in sharing threat intelligence, and the establishment of norms for responsible state behavior in cyberspace.

International norms and rules of engagement in cyberspace are still evolving as nations grapple with the implications of the use of cyber tools in geopolitical strategies. Efforts such as the Tallinn Manual and the Budapest Convention aim to provide guidelines for responsible state behavior in cyberspace, but the dynamic and contested nature of the digital realm poses challenges in establishing clear boundaries. Diplomatic efforts are underway to develop international norms that balance the rights and responsibilities of states in cyberspace, seeking to prevent the escalation of cyber conflict and promote stability in the global digital landscape.

The development and deployment of advanced technologies, including artificial intelligence (AI) and quantum computing, add new dimensions to the use of cyber tools in geopolitical strategies. AI-driven cyber capabilities enhance the speed, adaptability, and sophistication of cyber operations, creating challenges in defensive measures and attribution. Quantum computing introduces the potential for breaking current encryption standards, requiring nations to stay ahead in developing quantum-resistant cryptographic solutions to protect sensitive information from potential adversaries.

In conclusion, the use of cyber tools as part of geopolitical strategies reflects a paradigm shift in the way nations pursue their interests in the digital age. Cyberspace has become a dynamic and contested arena where intelligence gathering, economic competition, military operations, and influence campaigns intersect. State-sponsored cyber activities encompass a spectrum of strategic operations, from covert espionage and economic competition to the militarization of cyberspace and hybrid warfare. The evolving nature of cyberspace, coupled with the challenges of attribution, the proliferation of cyber capabilities, and the need for international norms, underscores the complexity of navigating the digital landscape in the pursuit of geopolitical objectives. Nations must adapt their strategies, invest in cybersecurity resilience, and engage in diplomatic efforts to shape the evolving norms that govern state behavior in the complex and interconnected world of cyberspace.

Chapter 2: Unveiling Cyber Threat Actors: Who's Behind the Screen?

Definition and classification of cyber threat actors.

Cyber threat actors, also known as adversaries or malicious entities, encompass a diverse range of individuals, organizations, or nation-states that engage in activities aimed at exploiting vulnerabilities in information systems, networks, and computer infrastructures. These actors can be classified into various categories based on their motives, skills, and the extent of their resources. One primary classification distinguishes between state-sponsored and non-state actors. State-sponsored threat actors are typically affiliated with government entities and conduct cyber operations to achieve political, military, or economic objectives. They often possess significant resources, advanced capabilities, and operate with a high level of sophistication, engaging in cyber espionage, sabotage, or strategic disruption.

Non-state threat actors, on the other hand, encompass a broader spectrum and include financially motivated cybercriminals, hacktivists, and ideological or politically motivated groups. Cybercriminals aim to derive financial gain through activities such as ransomware attacks, data breaches, or identity theft. Their primary motivation is economic, and they exploit vulnerabilities for monetary rewards. Hacktivists, driven by ideological or political beliefs, seek to advance their causes through cyber means, often engaging in website defacements, distributed denial-of-service (DDoS) attacks, or data leaks to promote their agenda or protest against perceived injustices.

Another classification criterion involves distinguishing between insider and outsider threat actors. Insiders, such as disgruntled employees or individuals with authorized access to an organization's systems, pose a unique challenge as they can exploit their privileged positions to compromise data, conduct sabotage, or facilitate unauthorized access. Outsiders, on the other hand, encompass individuals or groups who lack legitimate access and attempt to compromise systems from external positions, utilizing various techniques such as phishing, malware, or social engineering.

Furthermore, threat actors can be categorized based on their level of sophistication, ranging from script kiddies with limited technical skills who use pre-existing tools and exploits, to advanced persistent threats (APTs) that employ advanced techniques, zero-day vulnerabilities, and custom malware. APTs are often associated with state-sponsored actors seeking long-term access to sensitive information or critical infrastructure. Cyber mercenaries represent another subset of threat actors, offering their services for hire to conduct cyber operations on behalf of clients, whether for espionage, sabotage, or other malicious purposes.

The motivation behind cyber attacks is a crucial factor in classifying threat actors. Economic espionage, state-sponsored cyber-espionage, cybercrime for financial gain, hacktivism, and cyberterrorism are common motives. Understanding the motives helps in developing effective strategies for detection, prevention, and response. Moreover, threat actors can be categorized based on their targets, such as individuals, organizations, critical infrastructure, or governments. The nature of the target often provides insights into the motivations and potential impact of the cyber threats.

Attribution of cyber attacks to specific threat actors is challenging due to the evolving tactics, techniques, and procedures (TTPs) employed to obfuscate their identities. Threat intelligence, forensic analysis, and collaboration between private sector entities, government agencies, and international organizations are essential for accurately identifying and attributing cyber threat actors. As the cyber landscape continues to evolve, the classification of threat actors remains a dynamic and critical aspect of cybersecurity efforts, shaping the development of strategies to mitigate and counteract the ever-growing threat landscape.

Motivations driving various threat actors.

The motivations driving various threat actors in the realm of cybersecurity are multifaceted, reflecting a complex interplay of political, economic, ideological, and personal factors. State-sponsored threat actors, often associated with governments or intelligence agencies, are primarily motivated by geopolitical objectives. These entities engage in cyber espionage to gather intelligence, monitor adversaries, and gain strategic advantages in areas such as military planning, economic competition, or diplomatic negotiations. The acquisition of sensitive information through sophisticated cyber operations serves as a means to enhance a nation's security and global influence.

Non-state threat actors, including cybercriminals, are primarily motivated by financial gain. The monetization of cyber activities, such as ransomware attacks, data breaches, and identity theft, serves as a lucrative incentive for these individuals or organized crime groups. The digital landscape provides a fertile ground for exploiting vulnerabilities in systems and networks, allowing cybercriminals to amass substantial profits through extortion, cryptocurrency theft, or the sale of stolen data on underground markets.

Hacktivists, driven by ideological or political motivations, leverage cyberspace to advance their causes or express dissent. These threat actors engage in cyber operations to protest perceived injustices, promote specific ideologies, or draw attention to social and political issues. Hacktivism manifests in activities like website defacements, distributed denial-of-service (DDoS) attacks, or data leaks, aiming to disrupt or manipulate information in alignment with their beliefs.

Another category of threat actors includes insider threats, individuals with authorized access to systems who exploit their privileged positions for personal gain, revenge, or ideological reasons. Insiders may leak sensitive information, facilitate unauthorized access, or sabotage systems, posing unique challenges for organizations in terms of trust and security. Understanding the motives of insiders is crucial for implementing effective security measures to mitigate the risks associated with internal threats.

Cyber mercenaries represent a distinct category of threat actors motivated by financial incentives to provide cyber services for hire. These mercenaries offer their expertise to conduct cyber operations on behalf of clients, which can range from corporations seeking competitive advantages to governments outsourcing cyber capabilities. The motivations of cyber mercenaries often align with financial gain, presenting a unique challenge for attribution due to the diverse range of clients and objectives they serve.

In the context of hacktivism, the motivations can span a wide spectrum, encompassing social justice, human rights, political activism, or opposition to specific policies. The anonymity afforded by the digital realm empowers hacktivists to express dissent without fear of direct physical reprisals, making cyberspace an attractive medium for those seeking to effect change or raise awareness on global issues.

The motivations behind cyber terrorism, a subset of threat actors with the intent to cause fear, disruption, or harm through cyber means, are often rooted in extremist ideologies. Cyber terrorists may target critical infrastructure, government systems, or public services to instill fear, disrupt societal functions, or advance their political or ideological agenda. The interconnectedness of modern societies amplifies the potential impact of cyber terrorism, emphasizing the importance of cybersecurity measures to safeguard against such threats.

In conclusion, the motivations driving various threat actors in the cyber domain are diverse and dynamic. Understanding these motivations is essential for developing effective cybersecurity strategies that address the specific motives, tactics, and objectives of different threat actors. As the cyber landscape continues to evolve, an adaptive and comprehensive approach to cybersecurity is crucial to mitigate the ever-growing range of cyber threats driven by geopolitical tensions, economic interests, ideological beliefs, and personal motives.

Understanding the involvement of nation-states in cyber operations.

The involvement of nation-states in cyber operations has become a defining feature of the contemporary geopolitical landscape, shaping the dynamics of international relations, warfare, and espionage. Nations have recognized the strategic advantages offered by cyberspace, leading to the development of sophisticated capabilities for both offensive and defensive cyber operations. State-sponsored cyber activities are diverse, ranging from intelligence gathering and surveillance to acts of cyber espionage, sabotage, and warfare.

One primary motivation driving nation-states to engage in cyber operations is the pursuit of strategic advantage and national security. Cyberspace provides a unique arena for states to conduct operations that can yield valuable intelligence, monitor adversaries, and influence global events. The ability to gather information clandestinely through cyber means allows states to enhance their situational awareness, improve decision-making processes, and gain a competitive edge in geopolitical arenas. The concept of "cyber power" has emerged, emphasizing a nation's ability to leverage cyberspace for political, military, and economic advantage.

Cyber espionage is a prevalent form of state-sponsored cyber activity, wherein nations seek to acquire sensitive information from other states, organizations, or individuals. This information may include military plans, economic strategies, technological advancements, or diplomatic communications. State-sponsored cyber espionage allows nations to bypass traditional intelligence-gathering methods, operating in the digital realm with a degree of anonymity and deniability. The stolen information can be used to inform policy decisions, shape negotiation strategies, or gain insights into the capabilities and intentions of other nations.

The integration of cyber capabilities into military doctrines has transformed the nature of warfare, giving rise to the concept of "cyber warfare" as a complementary domain alongside traditional land, air, and sea operations. Nation-states invest in developing offensive cyber capabilities to disrupt or disable an adversary's critical infrastructure, communications networks, and military systems. Cyber attacks can be executed with precision, offering a means to incapacitate or degrade an opponent's capabilities without resorting to traditional kinetic methods. The strategic implications of cyber warfare have prompted nations to bolster their cyber defenses while simultaneously exploring offensive capabilities as a deterrent or means of retaliation.

The attribution challenge remains a significant aspect of state-sponsored cyber operations. Nation-states often employ sophisticated techniques to conceal their involvement, utilizing proxies, false-flag operations, or leveraging the global nature of the internet to obfuscate the origin of cyber attacks. The difficulty in attributing cyber incidents to specific states complicates the development of an effective international framework for accountability and response. Attribution is further complicated by the presence of non-state actors and cyber mercenaries who may conduct operations on behalf of states, blurring the lines between state-sponsored and independent cyber activities.

The economic realm is also a focal point for nation-states engaged in cyber operations. Economic espionage, conducted through cyber means, allows states to gain a competitive advantage by stealing intellectual property, trade secrets, and proprietary information from foreign companies. This stolen information can be used to boost domestic industries, advance technological innovation, or weaken economic rivals. Economic motivations drive states to invest in cyber capabilities that can facilitate industrial espionage, economic intelligence gathering, and the theft of valuable intellectual assets.

In addition to offensive cyber activities, nation-states recognize the importance of defensive capabilities to safeguard their own critical infrastructure and sensitive information. The increasing interconnectedness of global networks means that vulnerabilities in one nation's systems can have cascading effects on others. As a result, states invest in cybersecurity measures to protect against cyber attacks and ensure the resilience of their critical infrastructure, including energy grids, financial systems, and communication networks.

The evolving landscape of international norms and rules in cyberspace is a reflection of the challenges posed by nation-state involvement in cyber operations. Efforts to establish norms of behavior in cyberspace, such as the Tallinn Manual and the United Nations Group of Governmental Experts on Developments in the Field of Information and Telecommunications in the Context of International Security (UN GGE), aim to define responsible state behavior in cyberspace and discourage actions that could escalate tensions or lead to conflict.

In conclusion, the involvement of nation-states in cyber operations has become a central aspect of modern geopolitics. The motivations driving state-sponsored cyber activities encompass national security, strategic advantage, economic interests, and intelligence gathering. The integration of cyber capabilities into military doctrines and the challenges of attribution underscore the complex nature of state-sponsored cyber operations. As cyberspace continues to shape global affairs, the development of international norms and frameworks becomes crucial to manage the risks and consequences associated with state engagement in the digital domain.

Examples of state-sponsored cyber attacks.

State-sponsored cyber attacks have become prominent tools in the arsenals of nations seeking to advance their strategic, political, or economic objectives in the interconnected world of cyberspace. Several notable examples underscore the breadth and sophistication of these operations. One such instance is the Stuxnet worm, a highly sophisticated malware believed to be jointly developed by the United States and Israel. Discovered in 2010, Stuxnet was designed to target Iran's nuclear facilities, specifically its uranium enrichment program. The worm demonstrated unprecedented capabilities, such as the ability to manipulate programmable logic controllers (PLCs) in industrial systems, causing physical damage to Iran's centrifuges. Stuxnet marked a paradigm shift by showcasing the potential for cyber attacks to impact critical infrastructure and disrupt a nation's strategic capabilities.

The NotPetya ransomware attack in 2017 is another notable example, attributed to Russia by various cybersecurity experts and governments, although Russia denies involvement. NotPetya initially targeted Ukraine, spreading through a compromised software update for a tax accounting system. However, its impact extended far beyond Ukraine, affecting multinational corporations, banks, and critical infrastructure worldwide. NotPetya demonstrated the potential for state-sponsored cyber attacks to have unintended global consequences, as the malware's rapid spread highlighted the interconnected nature of the digital ecosystem.

China's involvement in state-sponsored cyber activities has been a subject of international scrutiny. The cyber espionage campaign known as APT1 or Operation Aurora, linked to China's People's Liberation Army, targeted numerous American corporations, particularly those in the defense and technology sectors. The attackers sought to steal intellectual property and gain insights into the targeted companies' strategic plans. The operation underscored China's pursuit of economic and technological advantages through cyber means, raising concerns about the theft of sensitive information for economic espionage.

In 2014, North Korea was accused of orchestrating the cyber attack on Sony Pictures Entertainment. The attack, widely known as the Sony Pictures hack, resulted in the compromise of sensitive corporate data, employee information, and unreleased films. The motivation behind the attack was attributed to North Korea's displeasure with the film "The Interview," which depicted a fictional assassination plot against North Korea's leader. The incident highlighted how state-sponsored cyber attacks could be used as a tool for political retaliation and censorship.

The Russian government's interference in the 2016 United States presidential election showcased the potential impact of cyber operations on democratic processes. Russian hackers, allegedly affiliated with the Russian military intelligence agency GRU, conducted phishing campaigns, disseminated disinformation through social media, and infiltrated election-related systems. While the direct manipulation of voting machines was not confirmed, the incident highlighted the broader issue of information warfare and the use of cyber means to influence political outcomes in foreign nations.

Iran's cyber capabilities came to the fore with the Stuxnet incident, but the country has since been involved in various cyber activities. One notable example is the Shamoon malware, which first emerged in 2012 and resurfaced in subsequent years. Shamoon targeted energy companies in the Middle East, particularly in Saudi Arabia, and was designed to overwrite data and render systems inoperable. While attribution is challenging, many experts believe Iran to be behind these attacks. The incidents underscored the potential use of cyber attacks as a tool for geopolitical influence and economic disruption.

The 2015 cyber attack on Ukraine's power grid demonstrated the potential for state-sponsored cyber attacks to impact critical infrastructure directly. The attackers, widely believed to be associated with Russia, used malware to compromise the control systems of power distribution stations, leading to widespread power outages. The incident marked one of the first instances where a cyber attack was used to disrupt essential services on a large scale, showcasing the vulnerabilities of critical infrastructure to digital threats.

More recent examples include the SolarWinds supply chain attack discovered in 2020, attributed to Russian state-sponsored hackers. The attackers compromised the software supply chain of Solar-Winds, a prominent IT management software provider, to distribute a trojanized update. This resulted in the infiltration of numerous government agencies and private organizations, allowing the perpetrators to conduct extensive espionage activities. The SolarWinds incident exemplified the sophistication of supply chain attacks and their potential to compromise high-value targets indirectly.

These examples collectively highlight the diverse motivations and tactics employed by nation-states in the realm of state-sponsored cyber attacks. The incidents underscore the need for robust cybersecurity measures, international cooperation, and the development of norms and agreements to address the challenges posed by cyber operations in an increasingly interconnected world. As technology continues to advance, the landscape of state-sponsored cyber activities will likely evolve, necessitating ongoing efforts to understand, mitigate, and respond to the ever-growing threats in cyberspace.

Examining hacktivism and ideological cyber threats.

Hacktivism, a portmanteau of "hacking" and "activism," represents a form of cyber threat driven by ideological or political motivations. Unlike conventional cybercrime, hacktivism involves the use of hacking techniques to promote a specific social or political agenda. The motivations behind hacktivism are diverse and can include issues related to human rights, freedom of expression, social justice, environmental concerns, or opposition to government policies. Hacktivists leverage their technical skills to conduct online actions that raise awareness, protest, or disrupt digital platforms. One

of the defining characteristics of hacktivism is the fusion of technological expertise with ideological fervor, creating a unique intersection between activism and cybersecurity.

The methods employed by hacktivists vary widely and can range
from relatively simple website defacements to more sophisticated
attacks on critical infrastructure. Distributed Denial of Service
(DDoS) attacks, a common tactic among hacktivists, involve overwhelming a target's online services with traffic, rendering them tem-
porarily inaccessible. The goal is not necessarily to steal data or profit
financially but to disrupt the normal functioning of a targeted system, often as a means of protest or as a form of digital civil disobedi-
ence. The Anonymous collective is a notable example of a hacktivist
group that gained global attention for its involvement in various operations, utilizing DDoS attacks and other tactics to advance its causes.

One prominent episode in hacktivist history was Operation Payback, initiated by Anonymous in 2010. The operation began as a
response to attempts to shut down The Pirate Bay, a file-sharing
website. Anonymous orchestrated DDoS attacks against organizations perceived as adversaries of internet freedom, including those
involved in anti-piracy efforts. The campaign expanded to target financial institutions, government agencies, and corporations, reflecting a broadening of hacktivist objectives beyond a single issue. Operation Payback demonstrated the agility and decentralized nature
of hacktivist movements, as well as their ability to rapidly shift focus
and tactics in response to evolving circumstances.

While hacktivism is often associated with loosely organized
groups like Anonymous, it can also involve more structured entities
with specific geopolitical agendas. The Syrian Electronic Army
(SEA) is an example of a hacktivist group with clear ideological motives aligned with the Syrian government. The SEA emerged during
the Syrian Civil War and conducted cyber operations to support the

Assad regime. The group engaged in tactics such as website defacements, social media account takeovers, and spreading propaganda. The SEA exemplifies how hacktivism can be harnessed as a tool in broader geopolitical conflicts, blurring the lines between state-sponsored and ideologically driven cyber threats.

Another dimension of ideological cyber threats involves the intersection of hacktivism with extremism, terrorism, or radical ideologies. Terrorist organizations and extremist groups have increasingly turned to the internet as a platform for recruitment, propaganda dissemination, and coordination of activities. The overlap between hacktivism and extremism can lead to the emergence of cyber threats that seek to advance radical ideologies or support acts of violence. The challenge for cybersecurity experts and law enforcement is to distinguish between hacktivism driven by political or social concerns and malicious cyber activities rooted in violent extremism.

The phenomenon of hacktivism also extends to issues of privacy and surveillance. Groups and individuals concerned about intrusive surveillance practices by governments or corporations may resort to hacking as a means to expose perceived violations of privacy. Whistleblower platforms like WikiLeaks, while not directly engaged in hacking, serve as outlets for the dissemination of sensitive information obtained through cyber means. The leaking of classified documents by whistleblowers can be seen as a form of hacktivism aimed at transparency and accountability, raising ethical questions about the balance between national security and citizens' right to information.

The motivations behind hacktivism are often intertwined with broader societal issues. The rise of hacktivist movements can be seen as a response to perceived injustices, government overreach, or corporate malfeasance. The use of digital tools to amplify dissent reflects a changing landscape where the internet becomes a battleground for ideological struggles. The Arab Spring, for example, witnessed the use of hacktivist tactics to support pro-democracy movements, illustrating the potential of digital activism to influence political change.

However, the ethical considerations surrounding hacktivism are complex. While hacktivists may view their actions as a form of digital protest against oppressive regimes or corporate wrongdoing, their methods can have unintended consequences. DDoS attacks, for instance, can impact not only the targeted organizations but also the users who depend on those services. The fine line between hacktivism and cybercrime raises questions about the legality and morality of certain actions undertaken in the name of ideological causes.

As hacktivism continues to evolve, the landscape is characterized by both individual actors and organized groups employing increasingly sophisticated techniques. The use of social media platforms, encrypted communication channels, and advanced hacking tools amplifies the impact of hacktivist campaigns. The Cat-and-Mouse game between hacktivists and cybersecurity professionals underscores the need for organizations and governments to adapt their security measures continually.

In conclusion, hacktivism represents a dynamic and multifaceted phenomenon that merges technology with ideology. The motivations driving hacktivist movements span a spectrum of issues, from civil liberties and human rights to geopolitical conflicts and environmental concerns. As hacktivism intersects with state-sponsored cyber activities, extremism, and issues of privacy, it challenges traditional notions of security and activism. Balancing the right to digital protest with the potential risks and consequences remains a critical challenge in the evolving landscape of ideological cyber threats. Understanding the motivations, tactics, and implications of hacktivism is essential for policymakers, cybersecurity professionals, and society at large as they navigate the complex interplay between technology, ideology, and activism in the digital age.

Case studies illustrating hacktivist activities.

Case studies provide in-depth insights into specific instances of hacktivist activities, shedding light on the motivations, tactics, and impacts of these digital campaigns. One prominent case is the Operation Payback orchestrated by the hacktivist collective Anonymous in 2010. Triggered by the attempts to shut down The Pirate Bay, a file-sharing website, Operation Payback initially focused on retaliation against entities involved in anti-piracy efforts. Anonymous employed Distributed Denial of Service (DDoS) attacks, disrupting the online services of organizations perceived as adversaries of internet freedom. As the campaign evolved, targets broadened to include financial institutions, government agencies, and corporations. Operation Payback showcased the decentralized nature of hacktivist movements, with participants joining efforts spontaneously to protest perceived injustices. The case highlighted how hacktivism could swiftly adapt and broaden its scope, demonstrating the impact of digital activism on a global scale.

In 2011, the hacktivist collective LulzSec gained notoriety for a series of high-profile cyber attacks. One of their notable targets was Sony Pictures, where they breached the company's network, compromising sensitive data, including user information and unreleased films. LulzSec's motivations were rooted in a blend of anarchic humor and opposition to corporate and governmental entities. Their attacks extended beyond Sony to include PBS, Nintendo, and even the CIA. LulzSec's short-lived but impactful campaign underscored the challenge of attribution in hacktivist cases, as the group operated under the banner of anonymity, making it difficult for authorities to identify and apprehend the perpetrators. The case exemplified the disruptive potential of hacktivist groups with diverse agendas.

The Syrian Electronic Army (SEA) represents a unique case where hacktivism aligns closely with state-sponsored cyber activities. Emerging during the Syrian Civil War, the SEA conducted cyber operations in support of the Assad regime. The group engaged in tactics such as website defacements, social media account takeovers, and spreading pro-government propaganda. Notable incidents include the compromise of the Associated Press's Twitter account, where false information about an attack on the White House was disseminated, causing temporary panic in financial markets. The SEA's activities showcased the convergence of hacktivism and geopolitical conflicts, blurring the lines between state-sponsored and ideologically driven cyber threats. The case highlighted how hacktivism could become entwined with broader geopolitical narratives and state interests.

The hacktivist group GhostSec gained attention for its activities against online platforms associated with the Islamic State (ISIS). Formed as an offshoot of Anonymous, GhostSec focused on countering online recruitment efforts by ISIS through cyber means. In one case, GhostSec identified and reported Twitter accounts associated with ISIS, leading to the suspension of thousands of profiles. The group utilized a combination of hacking, social media monitoring, and information sharing to disrupt ISIS's online presence. The case of GhostSec exemplifies hacktivism aimed at countering extremist ideologies and leveraging digital tools to contribute to global security efforts. It illustrates how hacktivist groups can emerge with specific missions to counter perceived threats to society.

The 2016 U.S. presidential election brought hacktivism to the forefront with allegations of Russian interference. Russian-sponsored hacktivist groups, notably Fancy Bear and Cozy Bear, were accused of conducting cyber operations to influence the election. The groups targeted the Democratic National Committee (DNC), releasing sensitive emails through platforms like WikiLeaks, with the aim of undermining the credibility of the election process. The case underscored the potential of hacktivism to impact democratic processes and raised concerns about the manipulation of information for political ends. It highlighted the intersection of state-sponsored cyber activities and hacktivism in the context of broader geopolitical objectives.

In 2017, the hacktivist group APT34, believed to have ties to the Iranian government, gained attention for its cyber espionage activities. APT34 targeted individuals and organizations, particularly in the Middle East, with the goal of stealing sensitive information related to geopolitical and national security matters. The group employed tactics such as spear-phishing campaigns, malware deployment, and social engineering to compromise its targets. The case of APT34 illustrates the blend of state-sponsored cyber activities with hacktivist motives, as the group aimed to advance Iran's geopolitical interests through digital means. The case underscores the complexity of attribution in the realm of cyber threats.

The hacktivist group AntiSec, an amalgamation of Anonymous and LulzSec members, gained prominence in 2011 for its cyber operations against law enforcement agencies. In one high-profile case, AntiSec breached the systems of the cybersecurity firm HBGary Federal, exposing internal documents and emails. The attack was a response to HBGary Federal's CEO boasting about his ability to unmask members of Anonymous. AntiSec's activities exemplified the retaliatory nature of hacktivism and its potential to target entities seen as adversaries of digital freedom. The case also highlighted the vulnerability of even cybersecurity-focused organizations to determined hacktivist campaigns.

The rise of hacktivist movements intersecting with political and social issues was evident in the aftermath of the 2014 shooting of Michael Brown in Ferguson, Missouri. The hacktivist group, loosely associated with Anonymous, targeted law enforcement agencies in protest against perceived police brutality and racial injustice. The group engaged in DDoS attacks, website defacements, and leaks of sensitive information to draw attention to the social and political issues surrounding the incident. The Ferguson case exemplifies how hacktivism can emerge as a response to events with broader societal implications, leveraging digital tools to amplify voices and promote social change.

In 2020, hacktivist activities surged in response to the global Black Lives Matter protests. Various hacktivist groups, including Anonymous, engaged in operations against government websites, law enforcement agencies, and organizations perceived as obstructing the protests. DDoS attacks, data leaks, and defacements were used as tactics to support the movement. The case demonstrated how hacktivism can align with social justice causes, mobilizing digital resources to protest against systemic issues and amplify the voices of marginalized communities.

The case studies presented showcase the diverse nature of hacktivist activities, ranging from campaigns driven by geopolitical motivations to those rooted in social justice causes. These examples underscore the adaptability and fluidity of hacktivist movements, capable of shifting focus and tactics in response to evolving issues. The cases also highlight the challenges associated with attribution, as hacktivist groups often operate in the shadows, leveraging anonymity to avoid direct identification. As hacktivism continues to evolve, its impact on political, social, and cybersecurity landscapes remains a complex and dynamic area of study. Understanding the motivations and tactics of hacktivist groups is crucial for developing effective cybersecurity strategies and addressing the broader societal implications of digital activism.

Overview of cybercrime syndicates and their operations.

Cybercrime syndicates represent a sophisticated and evolving facet of the digital underworld, comprising organized groups with the expertise and resources to execute complex and lucrative cybercriminal operations. These syndicates operate in the shadows of the internet, leveraging advanced technologies and exploiting vulnerabilities to engage in a broad spectrum of illicit activities for financial gain. The motivations that drive cybercrime syndicates are diverse, encompassing financial rewards, geopolitical objectives, and the theft of sensitive information for various purposes, including extortion, identity theft, and corporate espionage.

One of the defining features of cybercrime syndicates is their organizational structure, which often mirrors that of legitimate businesses. These groups are composed of specialists with distinct roles, ranging from skilled hackers and malware developers to money launderers and individuals responsible for maintaining infrastructure and operational security. This division of labor allows cybercrime syndicates to function efficiently and carry out multifaceted operations with a level of sophistication that poses significant challenges to law enforcement and cybersecurity professionals.

Financially motivated cybercrime syndicates often focus on lucrative activities such as online fraud, ransomware attacks, and the theft of financial information. The advent of digital currencies, like Bitcoin, has provided these groups with a means to launder money and receive payments in a decentralized and pseudonymous manner, adding a layer of complexity to tracking financial transactions. Ransomware attacks, in particular, have become a favored tactic, where cybercriminals encrypt victims' data and demand a ransom for its release. These operations are often carried out with precision, targeting high-profile entities such as corporations, government agencies, and critical infrastructure.

Nation-states sometimes employ cybercrime syndicates or mercenaries to achieve geopolitical objectives, blurring the lines between state-sponsored and criminal cyber activities. These state-affiliated syndicates engage in cyber espionage, intellectual property theft, and disruptive attacks on adversaries' critical infrastructure. The motivation behind these operations extends beyond financial gain to include geopolitical influence, military advantage, and the pursuit of national interests in the digital realm. The challenge of attribution in these cases is significant, as the involvement of cybercrime syndicates provides states with plausible deniability.

The emergence of dark web marketplaces has facilitated the collaboration and coordination of cybercrime syndicates, providing a platform for the exchange of hacking tools, stolen data, and services. These marketplaces operate on encrypted networks, allowing cybercriminals to communicate and transact anonymously. The commodification of cybercrime services on the dark web has lowered the entry barriers for aspiring cybercriminals, enabling them to purchase sophisticated tools and expertise without possessing advanced technical skills. This trend has contributed to the proliferation of cybercrime and the diversification of tactics employed by syndicates.

Cybercrime syndicates are also known for their involvement in identity theft, where personal and financial information is stolen to commit fraud. This may involve the creation of fake identities, the opening of fraudulent financial accounts, or the unauthorized use of credit card information. The widespread data breaches experienced by major corporations and institutions have provided cybercriminals with vast repositories of sensitive information, enabling them to conduct large-scale identity theft operations.

The collaboration between cybercrime syndicates and other criminal organizations, such as drug cartels or human trafficking networks, has further amplified the scope and impact of cybercrime. These alliances leverage digital tools for money laundering, communication, and operational security, creating a convergence of traditional and cyber-enabled criminal activities. The interplay between these groups complicates law enforcement efforts and underscores the need for a holistic approach to combating transnational organized crime in the digital age.

The realm of cybercrime syndicates extends beyond individual actors to encompass large-scale operations targeting specific industries or sectors. For example, the financial sector frequently falls victim to sophisticated cyber attacks orchestrated by syndicates seeking to compromise banking systems, conduct fraudulent transactions, or manipulate financial markets. Similarly, the healthcare industry has become a prime target for cybercriminals aiming to exploit vulnerabilities in medical systems, steal patient data, or deploy ransomware to disrupt critical healthcare services.

The growing prevalence of cybercrime-as-a-service models has further fueled the expansion of cybercrime syndicates. These models allow less technically proficient criminals to access and utilize advanced cyber tools and services without developing the skills themselves. This commercialization of cybercrime democratizes access to sophisticated hacking capabilities, widening the pool of potential threat actors and contributing to the increasingly complex landscape of digital threats.

Advanced Persistent Threats (APTs) orchestrated by cybercrime syndicates demonstrate a sustained and stealthy approach to cyber operations. APTs often involve long-term campaigns targeting specific organizations or individuals with the goal of exfiltrating sensitive information or maintaining persistent access to networks. These operations require a high degree of sophistication, combining advanced technical capabilities with social engineering tactics to infiltrate and navigate complex network infrastructures.

Law enforcement agencies, cybersecurity firms, and international organizations face significant challenges in combating cybercrime syndicates. The transnational nature of these organizations allows them to operate across jurisdictional boundaries, making it difficult for authorities to pursue and apprehend perpetrators. The dynamic and adaptive nature of cyber threats requires a collaborative and coordinated global response, emphasizing information sharing, threat intelligence cooperation, and the development of international norms and agreements.

In conclusion, cybercrime syndicates represent a formidable and dynamic force in the digital landscape, with motivations ranging from financial gain to geopolitical influence. These organized groups leverage advanced technologies, collaborate on dark web platforms, and exploit vulnerabilities to conduct a wide array of illicit activities. The evolving nature of cyber threats, coupled with the interconnectedness of the digital world, underscores the need for proactive and adaptive measures to mitigate the impact of cybercrime syndicates. As technology continues to advance, the landscape of cyber threats will inevitably evolve, necessitating ongoing efforts to understand, counter, and prevent the multifaceted operations of cybercrime syndicates.

Economic motives driving cybercriminals.

The economic motives driving cybercriminals form a complex web of incentives that underpin a wide array of illicit activities in the digital realm. At the core of these motives lies the pursuit of financial gain, propelling cybercriminals to exploit vulnerabilities, steal sensitive information, and engage in various forms of online fraud. Cybercrime has evolved into a lucrative industry, with actors ranging from individual hackers to sophisticated criminal organizations motivated by the prospect of substantial profits. One of the prevailing economic drivers is the monetization of stolen data, a commodity that holds significant value on the dark web. Personal information, including credit card details, social security numbers, and login credentials, serves as a digital currency for cybercriminals, enabling them to engage in identity theft, financial fraud, and other illicit activities.

Ransomware attacks exemplify the economic motivation that fuels cybercrime. In these attacks, malicious actors encrypt victims' data and demand a ransom in exchange for its release. The payment is often requested in cryptocurrency, providing a level of anonymity for the cybercriminals. The economic calculus behind ransomware is evident in the extortion model: cybercriminals target individuals, businesses, or even critical infrastructure, disrupting operations and demanding payment for the restoration of access to crucial data or systems. The success of ransomware campaigns has led to a proliferation of variants and a surge in ransomware-as-a-service models, where less technically proficient individuals can purchase or lease ransomware tools to conduct their own extortion operations.

Financially motivated cybercriminals also exploit vulnerabilities in online payment systems and banking infrastructure. Online fraud, including credit card fraud, account takeover attacks, and phishing schemes, allows cybercriminals to directly access victims' funds or make unauthorized transactions. The global nature of e-commerce and online banking facilitates cross-border cybercrime, making it challenging for law enforcement to track and apprehend perpetrators. Money mules, individuals recruited by cybercriminals to transfer and launder illicitly obtained funds, play a crucial role in facilitating the economic aspects of online fraud.

The sale of illicit goods and services on underground marketplaces is another avenue through which cybercriminals generate economic gains. These marketplaces operate on the dark web, providing a platform for the trade of stolen data, hacking tools, drugs, counterfeit documents, and various cybercrime services. Cryptocurrencies, with their decentralized and pseudonymous nature, have become the preferred method of transaction on these platforms, allowing cybercriminals to monetize their activities while maintaining a degree of anonymity. The economic ecosystem of underground marketplaces creates a self-sustaining cycle, where cybercriminals can reinvest their profits into acquiring more sophisticated tools or expanding their criminal enterprises.

Corporate espionage, driven by economic motives, involves cybercriminals infiltrating organizations to steal proprietary information, trade secrets, or intellectual property. Competing businesses or nation-states seeking a competitive advantage may employ cybercriminals to gain access to research and development data, product plans, or strategic information. The economic value of the stolen intellectual assets lies in their potential to confer a competitive edge or expedite innovation for the perpetrators or their clients. The theft of intellectual property through cyber espionage can have far-reaching economic consequences, affecting industries, economies, and global competitiveness.

The rise of cryptocurrency-related cybercrime highlights the economic appeal of exploiting decentralized digital currencies. Cryptocurrencies, such as Bitcoin, provide cybercriminals with a means to conduct financial transactions with a level of anonymity that traditional banking systems do not offer. Cryptocurrency theft, including hacking of cryptocurrency exchanges, fraudulent Initial Coin Offerings (ICOs), and cryptojacking (illicit use of computing power to mine cryptocurrencies), has become prevalent. The economic motivations behind cryptocurrency-related cybercrime are driven by the potential for direct financial gains, as well as the attractiveness of a decentralized financial system that operates outside traditional regulatory frameworks.

Economic motives also manifest in the realm of business email compromise (BEC) attacks, where cybercriminals compromise email accounts to impersonate executives, employees, or trusted partners. These attacks often target businesses involved in financial transactions, with the goal of diverting funds or obtaining sensitive financial information. BEC attacks rely on social engineering techniques to manipulate individuals into transferring money or disclosing financial details. The economic impact of successful BEC attacks can be significant, leading to financial losses, reputational damage, and operational disruptions for targeted organizations.

The economic ecosystem of cybercrime is sustained by the development and sale of hacking tools and services. Malware-as-a-Service (MaaS) and various exploit kits are commercially available on the dark web, allowing cybercriminals to access sophisticated tools without the need for advanced technical skills. The economic model of MaaS democratizes cybercrime, enabling individuals with malicious intent to participate in a thriving marketplace where hacking tools are commodified and accessible. The underground economy of cybercrime services creates a symbiotic relationship between tool developers, service providers, and end-users, contributing to the expansion and professionalization of cybercriminal activities.

The expansion of the Internet of Things (IoT) has introduced new economic opportunities for cybercriminals. IoT devices, often characterized by limited security features, are targeted for various purposes, including the creation of botnets for Distributed Denial of Service (DDoS) attacks and the exploitation of vulnerabilities for financial gain. The economic incentive for compromising IoT devices lies in their potential to be weaponized at scale, allowing cybercriminals to conduct large-scale attacks, disrupt online services, or engage in extortion campaigns against device manufacturers or service providers.

The economic consequences of cybercrime extend beyond immediate financial losses to include broader societal impacts. Critical infrastructure, such as energy grids, transportation systems, and healthcare facilities, is increasingly targeted by cybercriminals seeking financial gain or aiming to disrupt essential services. The potential for economic disruption in the wake of successful cyber attacks on critical infrastructure poses a significant threat to national security and economic stability.

As cybercriminal tactics continue to evolve, the economic motivations driving their activities persist as a powerful force. The interconnected nature of the digital world, the proliferation of valuable data, and the rapid expansion of emerging technologies contribute to the ongoing appeal of cybercrime as a lucrative and relatively low-risk endeavor. Mitigating the economic impact of cybercrime requires a multifaceted approach, encompassing improved cybersecurity measures, international collaboration, regulatory frameworks, and public awareness campaigns to address the root causes and consequences of financially motivated cybercriminal activities. In navigating this evolving landscape, understanding the economic dynamics that drive cybercrime is essential for developing effective strategies to protect individuals, businesses, and the broader digital ecosystem from the pervasive threats posed by financially motivated cybercriminals.

Definition of insider threats and their impact.

Insider threats represent a multifaceted cybersecurity challenge characterized by the risk posed to an organization from individuals within its own ranks who exploit their authorized access and privileges to compromise security. These insiders may include employees, contractors, or business partners who, intentionally or unintentionally, act in ways that could jeopardize the confidentiality, integrity, or availability of sensitive information and critical systems. The scope of insider threats encompasses a spectrum of malicious activities, ranging from deliberate theft or unauthorized disclosure of data to unintentional actions that inadvertently lead to security breaches. Understanding the motivations, types, and impacts of insider threats is crucial for organizations seeking to implement effective strategies to mitigate and manage this pervasive and often underestimated risk.

One significant category of insider threats is the malicious insider—individuals within an organization who deliberately exploit their insider status to compromise security for personal gain, ideological reasons, or as a response to perceived grievances. Malicious insiders may include disgruntled employees seeking revenge, individuals coerced by external actors, or those motivated by financial incentives. Their actions can manifest in various ways, such as stealing sensitive data, selling proprietary information, or intentionally disrupting operations. The intentional nature of these threats poses a considerable risk, as malicious insiders often possess a deep understanding of the organization's systems and protocols, making their actions difficult to detect and prevent.

Another facet of insider threats involves unintentional actions by well-meaning individuals who, without malicious intent, inadvertently compromise security. These individuals may fall victim to phishing attacks, inadvertently click on malicious links, or mishandle sensitive information due to a lack of awareness or training. Unintentional insider threats highlight the importance of cybersecurity education and awareness programs within organizations to instill a culture of security and equip employees with the knowledge to recognize and avoid potential risks.

Insider threats can also emerge in the form of negligent or careless behavior, where individuals, whether due to oversight, lack of adherence to security policies, or inadequate training, compromise the organization's security posture. This category includes employees who may inadvertently expose sensitive data, mishandle credentials, or neglect security protocols, creating vulnerabilities that malicious actors could exploit. Negligent insiders may not have ill intentions, but their actions can still have severe consequences, underscoring the need for robust cybersecurity policies, continuous training, and monitoring mechanisms.

The impact of insider threats on organizations is multifaceted, encompassing financial, reputational, and operational ramifications. Financially, the theft or unauthorized disclosure of sensitive information can result in direct monetary losses, including the costs associated with incident response, forensic investigations, legal proceedings, and potential regulatory fines. Additionally, intellectual property theft by insiders can erode a company's competitive advantage, leading to economic repercussions as proprietary information falls into the hands of competitors or is sold on the black market.

Reputationally, insider threats pose a significant risk to an organization's standing in the eyes of its customers, partners, and the public. Breaches caused by insiders can erode trust and confidence in the organization, potentially leading to customer attrition and damage to brand reputation. Public disclosure of an insider-related incident can attract negative media attention, exacerbating the reputational fallout and impacting the organization's ability to attract and retain customers.

Operational disruptions caused by insider threats can result in downtime, loss of productivity, and damage to critical systems. Malicious insiders with privileged access may exploit their positions to manipulate or sabotage systems, disrupt services, or introduce malware, causing operational chaos and financial losses. The inadvertent actions of negligent or careless insiders can also lead to system outages, data loss, and disruptions to business continuity.

Insider threats are particularly challenging to detect and mitigate due to the inherent trust placed in individuals with authorized access to organizational resources. Traditional perimeter-based security measures may be insufficient in addressing the insider threat landscape, as malicious or negligent insiders often operate within the organization's trusted boundaries. Detection mechanisms that focus on anomalous behavior, such as deviations from typical access patterns or unusual data transfer activities, become essential in identifying potential insider threats.

The insider threat landscape further complicates cybersecurity efforts as organizations embrace remote work and cloud-based technologies. The expanded attack surface and the reliance on collaboration tools create new vectors for insider threats, necessitating a reevaluation of security strategies. Remote employees may inadvertently expose sensitive information or fall victim to social engineering attacks, while the shift to cloud services introduces challenges in monitoring and securing data across diverse and distributed environments.

Mitigating insider threats requires a holistic and proactive approach that combines technological solutions, policy frameworks, and a strong organizational culture of security. User behavior analytics, endpoint monitoring, and anomaly detection systems can help identify suspicious activities that may indicate insider threats. Role-based access controls, least privilege principles, and regular access reviews can limit the potential impact of insider threats by restricting individuals to only the resources necessary for their roles.

Employee training and awareness programs play a crucial role in addressing unintentional insider threats, fostering a security-conscious culture where individuals understand the risks and are equipped to make informed decisions. Cybersecurity policies should be clear, comprehensive, and regularly communicated to ensure that employees are aware of their responsibilities in safeguarding sensitive information.

In addition to technical and policy measures, organizations can implement continuous monitoring and auditing practices to identify and investigate potential insider threats. This includes monitoring network traffic, reviewing access logs, and implementing data loss prevention (DLP) tools to detect and prevent the unauthorized exfiltration of sensitive information.

Collaboration between human resources, information security, and legal departments is essential in developing a comprehensive insider threat program. Establishing clear procedures for responding to incidents, conducting thorough investigations, and, when necessary, taking appropriate disciplinary or legal action can help organizations effectively manage insider threats and minimize their impact.

As organizations navigate an increasingly complex and interconnected digital landscape, the awareness of insider threats as a significant cybersecurity risk is paramount. By acknowledging the various motivations and types of insider threats, organizations can tailor their strategies to address this multifaceted challenge effectively. The proactive integration of technology, policies, and a security-focused culture will contribute to building resilience against insider threats and safeguarding the confidentiality, integrity, and availability of sensitive information within organizational boundaries.

Strategies for mitigating risks posed by insiders.

Mitigating risks posed by insiders within an organizational context demands a multifaceted and strategic approach to safeguard sensitive information and maintain the integrity of operations. One pivotal facet involves cultivating a robust organizational culture that prioritizes trust, transparency, and ethical behavior. Fostering an environment where employees feel valued and acknowledged contributes to a sense of loyalty, diminishing the likelihood of disgruntlement and subsequent insider threats. Comprehensive background checks during the hiring process are paramount, enabling the identification of potential red flags in an individual's history that may indicate a proclivity for malicious actions.

Moreover, implementing stringent access controls is instrumental in restricting employees' access to sensitive data only to the extent necessary for their roles. This involves adopting a principle of least privilege, limiting permissions based on job responsibilities. Regularly reviewing and updating access permissions in tandem with employee role changes or departures ensures the continuous alignment of access levels with current job requirements. Advanced monitoring and auditing systems can be deployed to scrutinize user activities, enabling prompt detection of unusual behavior or unauthorized access. Additionally, raising employee awareness through training programs about the importance of data security, the consequences of insider threats, and reporting mechanisms creates a proactive defense against potential internal risks.

Incorporating technological solutions such as Data Loss Prevention (DLP) tools adds an extra layer of protection by identifying and preventing the unauthorized transmission of sensitive data. These tools can monitor, detect, and respond to potential data breaches in real time, curbing the impact of insider threats. Developing and enforcing a comprehensive incident response plan is crucial to minimize the damage in the event of a security breach, allowing for swift containment and resolution. Collaboration with external cybersecurity experts can further enhance an organization's ability to anticipate and counter insider threats through the infusion of external perspectives and cutting-edge knowledge.

Continuous employee monitoring, however, should be balanced with respect for privacy and legal considerations. Striking this delicate balance involves establishing clear communication channels to inform employees about the extent of monitoring practices, emphasizing their purpose in maintaining overall organizational security. Whistleblower protection programs can encourage employees to report suspicious activities without fear of retaliation, fostering an open and accountable organizational culture. Moreover, periodic security awareness training should be part of an ongoing education program, ensuring that employees remain vigilant and up-to-date on evolving cybersecurity threats.

To fortify defenses against insider threats, organizations can implement role-based access controls, segregating duties to minimize the risk of collusion among employees. This strategy limits the potential for malicious actors to exploit vulnerabilities by necessitating collaboration between multiple individuals. Additionally, regular security audits and vulnerability assessments can uncover and rectify weak points in an organization's security posture, reducing the likelihood of successful insider attacks. Collaboration with law enforcement agencies can be a valuable preventive measure, fostering a collaborative approach to identifying and neutralizing potential insider threats.

Furthermore, implementing user behavior analytics can help organizations identify abnormal patterns of behavior that may indicate a compromised or malicious insider. By leveraging machine learning algorithms, these tools can analyze vast amounts of data to detect deviations from established norms, triggering alerts for further investigation. Building a resilient cybersecurity infrastructure involves adopting a holistic approach that integrates people, processes, and technology. Cybersecurity policies and procedures should be regularly reviewed and updated to reflect the evolving threat landscape, ensuring that the organization remains adaptive and responsive to emerging challenges.

In conclusion, mitigating risks posed by insiders demands a comprehensive and dynamic strategy that encompasses organizational culture, technological solutions, employee training, and proactive monitoring. By establishing a culture of trust, implementing stringent access controls, leveraging advanced technologies, and fostering collaboration with external experts, organizations can significantly enhance their ability to thwart insider threats. Continuous education and awareness programs, coupled with a commitment to privacy and ethical considerations, form the bedrock of a resilient defense against internal risks. As the cybersecurity landscape evolves, organizations must remain vigilant and proactive, adapting their strategies to address emerging challenges and fortify their defenses against insider threats.

Chapter 3: Fortifying the Gates: Building Robust Cyber Defenses

Definition and goals of cyber defense.

Cyber defense, in the realm of information security, constitutes a multifaceted strategy and set of practices designed to safeguard computer systems, networks, and data from unauthorized access, attacks, and disruptions. At its core, cyber defense seeks to protect the confidentiality, integrity, and availability of digital assets, recognizing the interconnectedness of today's technology-driven landscape. The overarching goal of cyber defense is to create a robust and resilient security posture that can withstand a diverse range of cyber threats, ranging from malware and phishing attacks to more sophisticated and targeted intrusions.

One fundamental aspect of cyber defense involves establishing a secure perimeter around an organization's digital infrastructure. This entails deploying firewalls, intrusion detection systems, and other boundary defenses to monitor and control incoming and outgoing network traffic. By erecting this initial line of defense, organizations aim to filter out malicious activities and unauthorized access attempts, thus preventing potential threats from breaching the network.

Additionally, cyber defense extends beyond the perimeter, acknowledging the reality that determined adversaries may find ways to infiltrate network boundaries. Thus, the implementation of robust authentication mechanisms, including multi-factor authentication, plays a pivotal role in ensuring that only authorized individuals gain access to critical systems and sensitive information. Encryption technologies further enhance data protection by rendering intercepted information indecipherable to unauthorized entities, even if they manage to compromise the network.

An integral element of effective cyber defense is the continuous monitoring and analysis of network activities. Security information and event management (SIEM) systems enable organizations to detect and respond to anomalous behavior and potential security incidents in real time. Through the aggregation and correlation of log data from various sources, SIEM systems empower security teams to identify patterns indicative of malicious activities, allowing for swift intervention and mitigation.

As cyber threats evolve in sophistication, organizations increasingly recognize the need for proactive defense measures. Threat intelligence, encompassing information about the tactics, techniques, and procedures employed by cyber adversaries, becomes a critical asset in anticipating and countering potential attacks. By staying abreast of emerging threats and vulnerabilities, organizations can adapt their defense strategies to mitigate risks and bolster their security posture.

Collaboration and information-sharing within the cybersecurity community and across industries contribute to a collective defense against cyber threats. Engaging in partnerships, such as those with government agencies, industry alliances, and cybersecurity vendors, enables organizations to tap into a broader pool of knowledge and resources. Information-sharing platforms facilitate the dissemination of timely threat intelligence, empowering organizations to proactively fortify their defenses against emerging risks.

Cyber defense is not solely a technological endeavor; it also hinges on the human factor. Employee training and awareness programs are pivotal in cultivating a security-conscious organizational culture. Educating users about the risks of social engineering, phishing, and other deceptive tactics empowers them to recognize and thwart potential threats, reducing the likelihood of inadvertent security breaches.

Incident response planning is a crucial facet of cyber defense, ensuring that organizations have a structured and well-coordinated approach to handling security incidents when they occur. This involves establishing incident response teams, defining escalation procedures, and conducting regular drills to assess the efficacy of response plans. The ability to swiftly contain and mitigate the impact of a security incident is essential in minimizing potential damage and downtime.

As cyber threats become increasingly sophisticated and dynamic, the concept of cyber resilience emerges as an integral component of cyber defense. Cyber resilience involves not only preventing and detecting cyber threats but also ensuring the ability to recover quickly from incidents and adapt to changing circumstances. This resilience encompasses a holistic approach that integrates technology, processes, and people, with a focus on minimizing the impact of disruptions and maintaining essential functions.

In conclusion, cyber defense is a comprehensive and dynamic approach to protecting digital assets from a myriad of cyber threats. It encompasses technological measures, proactive threat intelligence practices, collaboration within the cybersecurity community, employee education, and robust incident response planning. The ultimate goal is to establish a resilient security posture that can adapt to the evolving threat landscape, withstand cyber attacks, and ensure the continued functionality and security of digital systems and data. As organizations navigate the complexities of the digital age, a strategic and holistic approach to cyber defense becomes imperative to safeguard against the ever-changing landscape of cyber threats.

The evolving nature of cyber threats and the need for proactive measures.

The evolving nature of cyber threats in today's interconnected and digitized world necessitates a paradigm shift in how organizations approach cybersecurity. As technology advances, so too do the tactics and techniques employed by malicious actors, demanding a proactive and adaptive stance to mitigate the risks posed by an ever-changing threat landscape. Cyber threats, once characterized by rela-

tively simple and opportunistic attacks, have evolved into highly sophisticated and targeted campaigns that exploit vulnerabilities across
various layers of digital infrastructure.

One prominent facet of this evolution is the rise of advanced
persistent threats (APTs), wherein threat actors employ sophisticated techniques to gain unauthorized access to systems and remain undetected for extended periods. APTs often involve a combination of
social engineering, zero-day exploits, and meticulous reconnaissance
to compromise high-value targets, such as government agencies, critical infrastructure, and large enterprises. The persistent and stealthy
nature of APTs underscores the need for proactive measures that go
beyond traditional security approaches.

The proliferation of ransomware represents another alarming dimension of cyber threats. Cybercriminals increasingly leverage ransomware to encrypt critical data, rendering it inaccessible until a ransom is paid. Noteworthy in its impact on both individuals and organizations, ransomware attacks have become more sophisticated,
with threat actors employing tactics such as double extortion, where
stolen data is threatened with public exposure unless additional payments are made. The dynamic nature of ransomware highlights the
imperative for proactive defenses that encompass robust backup
strategies, employee training, and advanced threat detection capabilities.

As the digital landscape expands, so does the attack surface, with
the Internet of Things (IoT) introducing new vulnerabilities. The
interconnectedness of IoT devices, ranging from smart home appliances to industrial control systems, creates a vast and intricate web
of potential entry points for cyber attackers. Proactively addressing
IoT security requires a comprehensive approach, including device authentication, encryption, and ongoing monitoring to detect and respond to anomalous activities. The integration of IoT devices into
organizational networks necessitates a heightened focus on ensur-

ing their security to prevent them from becoming conduits for cyber threats.

Social engineering, a longstanding method in the cyber attacker's toolkit, continues to evolve and adapt to exploit human vulnerabilities. Phishing attacks, for example, have become more sophisticated, often incorporating highly convincing email lures and leveraging psychological manipulation techniques. The increasing use of artificial intelligence (AI) in crafting targeted and personalized phishing campaigns underscores the need for proactive user education and awareness programs. Organizations must cultivate a culture of cybersecurity awareness to empower employees to recognize and resist social engineering attempts.

The expansive use of cloud services and the adoption of remote work practices further amplify the complexity of the cybersecurity landscape. Cloud environments offer numerous benefits, but they also introduce unique security challenges, including misconfigured settings, unauthorized access, and data exposure. Proactive measures in this context involve implementing robust cloud security frameworks, conducting regular assessments, and leveraging tools that provide visibility into cloud infrastructure. As remote work becomes a persistent feature of modern workplaces, organizations must fortify their defenses against cyber threats targeting remote endpoints and communication channels.

The rapid development of technology, while driving innovation and efficiency, also introduces risks through emerging threats such as supply chain attacks. Cyber attackers recognize the interconnected nature of modern ecosystems and exploit vulnerabilities in the supply chain to compromise trusted software or hardware components. Proactively mitigating supply chain risks involves thorough vetting of third-party vendors, implementing secure development practices, and incorporating mechanisms for detecting and responding to potential compromises within the supply chain.

To address the evolving nature of cyber threats, threat intelligence becomes a critical component of proactive cybersecurity measures. Organizations must actively gather, analyze, and apply intelligence about emerging threats and vulnerabilities to anticipate and counteract potential attacks. Collaboration within the cybersecurity community, sharing threat intelligence through Information Sharing and Analysis Centers (ISACs) and other platforms, strengthens the collective ability to stay ahead of evolving threats. Proactive threat intelligence practices enable organizations to adjust their defenses in real-time, adapting to the dynamic tactics employed by cyber adversaries.

Machine learning and artificial intelligence have emerged as powerful tools in the realm of cybersecurity, offering the capability to analyze vast datasets and identify patterns indicative of malicious activities. Proactive measures involving AI-driven threat detection and response enhance an organization's ability to detect and thwart cyber threats in real-time. These technologies can autonomously identify anomalies, predict potential security incidents, and automate responses, thereby augmenting the speed and efficacy of cyber defenses.

In conclusion, the evolving nature of cyber threats demands a proactive and adaptive approach to cybersecurity. Organizations must recognize the dynamic landscape they operate in and continually reassess and fortify their defenses. This requires a combination of advanced technologies, threat intelligence practices, user education, and collaboration within the cybersecurity community. By embracing proactive measures that anticipate and counteract emerging threats, organizations can enhance their resilience against the evolving tactics of cyber adversaries, ultimately safeguarding their digital assets and maintaining the trust of stakeholders in an increasingly interconnected world.

The importance of risk assessment in cybersecurity.

The importance of risk assessment in cybersecurity is paramount in the contemporary digital landscape, where organizations face an ever-expanding array of threats and vulnerabilities. A risk assessment serves as the foundational pillar upon which effective cybersecurity strategies are built, offering a systematic and comprehensive approach to identifying, analyzing, and mitigating potential risks that could compromise the confidentiality, integrity, and availability of digital assets. In essence, it serves as a proactive mechanism for organizations to understand their unique threat landscape, assess the potential impact of various risks, and make informed decisions about resource allocation and security measures.

One fundamental aspect of risk assessment lies in its ability to provide a holistic view of an organization's cybersecurity posture. By conducting a thorough analysis of the entire IT infrastructure, including networks, systems, applications, and data, organizations can pinpoint vulnerabilities and weaknesses that might be exploited by malicious actors. This comprehensive understanding enables informed decision-making regarding the allocation of resources to areas that pose the greatest risk, allowing organizations to prioritize and address the most critical security concerns.

Furthermore, risk assessments facilitate the identification of assets and their respective values, aiding organizations in categorizing information based on its sensitivity and importance. This classification informs the development of targeted protective measures, ensuring that the most critical and valuable assets receive heightened security measures. This approach is particularly crucial in environments where limited resources necessitate a strategic and risk-based allocation of cybersecurity investments.

Risk assessments also play a pivotal role in compliance and regulatory adherence. Many industries and jurisdictions mandate adherence to specific cybersecurity standards and regulations, necessitating organizations to conduct regular risk assessments as part of their compliance efforts. By identifying and addressing potential risks proactively, organizations not only enhance their cybersecurity posture but also demonstrate a commitment to regulatory compliance, mitigating legal and reputational risks associated with non-compliance.

One of the key advantages of risk assessment is its role in fostering a culture of continuous improvement within an organization's cybersecurity practices. Cyber threats are dynamic and ever-evolving, making it imperative for organizations to continually reassess their risk landscape. Regular risk assessments enable organizations to adapt their cybersecurity strategies in response to emerging threats, technological advancements, and changes in the business environment. This iterative process of assessment, mitigation, and improvement is essential for maintaining resilience in the face of an ever-changing threat landscape.

Risk assessments also provide a mechanism for informed decision-making at the executive level. By presenting a clear picture of potential risks and their associated impacts, cybersecurity professionals can effectively communicate the importance of specific security measures to organizational leadership. This facilitates a more nuanced understanding of the risks faced by the organization, enabling executives to make strategic decisions about cybersecurity investments, resource allocations, and risk tolerance.

Moreover, risk assessments contribute to incident preparedness by identifying potential scenarios and vulnerabilities that could lead to security incidents. By anticipating potential risks, organizations can develop and implement effective incident response plans that enable swift and coordinated responses in the event of a security breach. This proactive approach minimizes the impact of incidents, reduces downtime, and helps in preserving the organization's reputation.

The collaborative nature of risk assessments is another compelling aspect. Involving key stakeholders from various departments, including IT, legal, compliance, and business units, fosters a cross-functional understanding of cybersecurity risks. This collaborative approach ensures that risk assessments consider not only technical vulnerabilities but also legal, regulatory, and business risks. It encourages a shared responsibility for cybersecurity across the organization, breaking down silos and promoting a unified front against potential threats.

Furthermore, risk assessments provide a basis for third-party risk management. As organizations increasingly rely on third-party vendors and service providers, understanding the cybersecurity risks associated with these relationships becomes critical. Through risk assessments, organizations can evaluate the security practices of their vendors, assess the potential impact of third-party vulnerabilities, and establish criteria for selecting and managing external partners. This proactive approach helps mitigate the risks associated with third-party dependencies and strengthens the overall cybersecurity ecosystem.

In conclusion, the importance of risk assessment in cybersecurity cannot be overstated. It serves as a linchpin in the development of effective cybersecurity strategies, providing organizations with a systematic and informed approach to identifying, analyzing, and mitigating potential risks. From providing a comprehensive view of the threat landscape to fostering a culture of continuous improvement and aiding in compliance efforts, risk assessments play a pivotal role in enhancing an organization's cybersecurity resilience. As organizations navigate the complexities of the digital age, the proactive identification and mitigation of risks through robust risk assessment practices become imperative for safeguarding digital assets and maintaining the trust of stakeholders.

Strategies for identifying and prioritizing cybersecurity risks.

Developing effective strategies for identifying and prioritizing cybersecurity risks is paramount in the dynamic and ever-evolving landscape of digital threats. One crucial approach to this challenge involves conducting a comprehensive risk assessment, a systematic process that encompasses the identification, analysis, and evaluation of potential risks to an organization's information systems and assets. In essence, risk identification is the foundational step in understanding the multifaceted landscape of cybersecurity threats. This involves a thorough examination of an organization's digital infrastructure, encompassing networks, systems, applications, and data, to pinpoint vulnerabilities and weaknesses that could be exploited by malicious actors.

In the quest for robust risk identification, organizations often leverage various tools and methodologies. Vulnerability assessments, for instance, provide a targeted examination of systems and applications to uncover known vulnerabilities. These assessments involve the use of automated scanning tools, supplemented by manual testing, to identify weaknesses that may be exploited by cyber attackers. Regular vulnerability assessments offer a proactive means of identifying and addressing potential risks before they can be leveraged to compromise security.

Penetration testing represents another potent strategy for identifying cybersecurity risks. Unlike vulnerability assessments, penetration tests involve simulated attacks on an organization's systems to evaluate their resistance to real-world threats. By mimicking the tactics of malicious actors, penetration testing provides valuable insights into an organization's security posture, helping identify vulnerabilities that may not be evident through automated scanning alone. This proactive approach allows organizations to understand potential points of weakness and prioritize remediation efforts accordingly.

In addition to technical assessments, organizations benefit from engaging in threat intelligence gathering. By monitoring and analyzing information about current and emerging cyber threats, organizations can proactively identify risks that may target specific industries, technologies, or vulnerabilities. Threat intelligence enables organizations to stay ahead of evolving threats, enhancing their ability to prepare for and mitigate risks before they materialize. This proactive stance is particularly critical in a landscape where threat actors continually adapt their tactics to exploit new vulnerabilities.

Beyond technical assessments, a comprehensive risk identification strategy encompasses examining organizational processes, policies, and human factors. This involves evaluating employee awareness, training programs, and security culture to identify potential gaps that could expose the organization to risks. Human error, often a significant contributor to cybersecurity incidents, can be mitigated through targeted training and awareness initiatives that empower employees to recognize and respond effectively to potential threats.

Once risks are identified, the next critical step involves prioritization. Not all risks are created equal, and resources are finite, necessitating a strategic approach to focus efforts on mitigating the most critical threats. One widely adopted method for prioritizing cybersecurity risks is the use of risk matrices. These matrices assess the likelihood and impact of identified risks, assigning a risk score that guides prioritization efforts. Risks with higher scores, indicative of greater potential impact and likelihood, are addressed with a higher priority, ensuring that resources are allocated where they can have the most significant impact on overall cybersecurity resilience.

Additionally, organizations often turn to risk-based frameworks such as the National Institute of Standards and Technology (NIST) Cybersecurity Framework or the ISO/IEC 27001 standard. These frameworks provide structured approaches to identifying, assessing, and managing cybersecurity risks. They offer organizations a set of guidelines and best practices for developing risk management processes that align with their specific industry and regulatory requirements. By adhering to established frameworks, organizations can systematically identify and prioritize risks, ensuring a comprehensive and structured approach to cybersecurity risk management.

Contextualizing risks within the organizational context is another key aspect of prioritization. This involves considering the specific goals, objectives, and mission of the organization to determine the impact of potential risks on its overall operations. Risks that directly threaten critical business functions or sensitive information are accorded higher priority, aligning risk management efforts with the broader strategic goals of the organization. This contextual understanding ensures that cybersecurity risk management is not seen in isolation but is integrated into the overarching business strategy.

Furthermore, organizations can prioritize risks by considering external factors, including industry benchmarks, regulatory requirements, and threat landscapes. Benchmarking against industry standards and compliance frameworks helps organizations align their risk management practices with established norms and expectations. Understanding the regulatory landscape is crucial for prioritizing risks that could result in legal and compliance repercussions. Additionally, staying informed about emerging threats in the broader threat landscape allows organizations to prioritize risks that align with current and evolving cyber threats.

Collaboration and communication are integral components of effective risk prioritization. Involving key stakeholders from different departments, including IT, legal, compliance, and business units, ensures a comprehensive understanding of the potential impact of risks across the organization. Regular communication channels, such as risk committees or cross-functional teams, facilitate ongoing discussions about risk priorities and enable the organization to adapt its risk management strategy in response to changing circumstances.

A risk's potential impact on confidentiality, integrity, and availability of data is a crucial consideration in prioritization efforts. Risks that could compromise sensitive information, disrupt critical operations, or undermine the trust of stakeholders are typically accorded higher priority. This triad of considerations ensures a balanced approach to risk prioritization, addressing risks that pose the greatest threat to the organization's overall security and resilience.

In conclusion, developing effective strategies for identifying and prioritizing cybersecurity risks is fundamental to building a resilient defense against the myriad threats that organizations face. A comprehensive risk assessment, incorporating technical assessments, threat intelligence, and an understanding of human factors, forms the bedrock of risk identification. Prioritizing risks involves leveraging risk matrices, contextualizing risks within the organizational landscape, adhering to established frameworks, considering external factors, and fostering collaboration. By adopting a systematic and strategic approach to risk management, organizations can allocate resources judiciously, address the most critical threats, and enhance their overall cybersecurity resilience in the face of an ever-evolving threat landscape.

Overview of established cybersecurity frameworks.

Established cybersecurity frameworks serve as foundational structures that organizations can leverage to build robust and effective cybersecurity programs. These frameworks provide a systematic approach to identifying, assessing, and managing cybersecurity risks, offering guidelines, best practices, and standards to enhance an organization's overall security posture. One of the widely recognized cybersecurity frameworks is the National Institute of Standards and Technology (NIST) Cybersecurity Framework. Developed by NIST in response to an executive order from the U.S. government, this framework provides a risk-based approach to managing cybersecurity, consisting of five core functions: Identify, Protect, Detect, Respond, and Recover. The Identify function involves understanding and managing cybersecurity risks, while the Protect function focuses on implementing safeguards to ensure the security and resilience of critical infrastructure. The Detect function emphasizes continuous monitoring and timely detection of cybersecurity events, while the Respond function involves an organized response to incidents. Finally, the Recover function aims to restore capabilities and services after an incident, emphasizing the importance of resilience in the face of cyber threats.

Another influential framework is the ISO/IEC 27001 standard, which provides a globally recognized set of requirements for establishing, implementing, maintaining, and continually improving an information security management system (ISMS). This framework adopts a process-based approach, guiding organizations through risk assessment and treatment, security policy development, and the implementation of controls to ensure the confidentiality, integrity, and availability of information assets. ISO/IEC 27001 is known for its adaptability to various organizational sizes, industries, and risk profiles, making it a versatile framework that aligns with different regulatory and compliance requirements.

The Center for Internet Security (CIS) Controls, formerly known as the SANS Critical Security Controls, is another impactful framework designed to help organizations prioritize and implement essential cybersecurity measures. Consisting of 20 controls organized into three categories – Basic, Foundational, and Organizational – the CIS Controls offer a practical and risk-based approach to cybersecurity. These controls cover areas such as inventory and control of hardware assets, continuous vulnerability assessment and remediation, secure configuration, and data protection, providing a comprehensive framework for organizations to establish a strong cyber-security foundation.

In the healthcare sector, the Health Insurance Portability and Accountability Act (HIPAA) Security Rule establishes standards for the protection of electronic protected health information (ePHI). While not a comprehensive cybersecurity framework, HIPAA's security requirements guide healthcare organizations in implementing measures to safeguard patient data. The Security Rule includes administrative, physical, and technical safeguards, addressing aspects like risk analysis, access controls, encryption, and incident response. Compliance with HIPAA is essential for healthcare entities to ensure the privacy and security of patient information.

The Payment Card Industry Data Security Standard (PCI DSS) is a framework specifically tailored for organizations that handle credit card transactions. Developed by the Payment Card Industry Security Standards Council (PCI SSC), PCI DSS outlines security requirements to protect cardholder data. This framework includes measures such as secure network configurations, encryption, access controls, and regular security testing. Compliance with PCI DSS is mandatory for organizations involved in processing credit card payments, and adherence to its provisions is crucial for maintaining the trust of customers and stakeholders.

The International Electrotechnical Commission (IEC) 62443 series of standards focuses on industrial automation and control systems (IACS) cybersecurity. These standards, commonly referred to as the IEC 62443 series, provide a comprehensive framework for securing critical infrastructure in sectors such as energy, manufacturing, and transportation. The IEC 62443 framework addresses the unique challenges of IACS cybersecurity, offering guidelines for implementing security measures tailored to the specific needs of industrial control systems. It includes aspects such as network segmentation, access control, and incident response, aiming to enhance the resilience of industrial systems against cyber threats.

In the realm of risk management, the Committee of Sponsoring Organizations of the Treadway Commission (COSO) developed the Enterprise Risk Management (ERM) Framework. While not exclusive to cybersecurity, the COSO ERM Framework provides a holistic approach to managing risks across an organization. It emphasizes the integration of risk management into the organization's overall governance and strategy, fostering a culture of risk-aware decision-making. Within the context of cybersecurity, the COSO ERM Framework encourages organizations to align cybersecurity risks with broader enterprise risk management efforts, ensuring that cybersecurity is integrated into the organization's overall risk management framework.

The Cybersecurity Maturity Model Certification (CMMC) is a framework developed by the U.S. Department of Defense (DoD) to enhance the cybersecurity practices of organizations within the defense industrial base. CMMC builds upon existing frameworks, including NIST SP 800-171, and introduces a tiered approach with five maturity levels. Each level corresponds to the implementation of specific cybersecurity practices and processes, ranging from basic cyber hygiene to advanced capabilities. CMMC aims to strengthen the cybersecurity posture of defense contractors and subcontractors, ensuring the protection of sensitive information and reducing the risk of cyber threats within the defense supply chain.

The Information Technology Infrastructure Library (ITIL) is a set of practices for IT service management that, while not exclusive to cybersecurity, provides valuable guidance for organizations seeking to align IT services with business needs. ITIL includes a comprehensive set of best practices for service design, transition, operation, and improvement. In the context of cybersecurity, ITIL principles can be applied to establish effective cybersecurity processes, incident response procedures, and ongoing service improvement initiatives. By adopting ITIL practices, organizations can enhance the efficiency and effectiveness of their cybersecurity operations while aligning with broader business objectives.

These established cybersecurity frameworks collectively contribute to the development of a structured and proactive approach to cybersecurity. Organizations often tailor their cybersecurity programs by integrating elements from multiple frameworks, aligning with their industry, regulatory requirements, and specific risk profiles. While the selection of a framework depends on various factors, including organizational goals and compliance obligations, the overarching objective is to establish a resilient cybersecurity posture that addresses current and emerging threats. As the cybersecurity landscape continues to evolve, these frameworks provide valuable guidance for organizations seeking to navigate the complexities of securing their digital assets and maintaining the trust of stakeholders.

Tailoring frameworks to organizational needs.

Tailoring cybersecurity frameworks to organizational needs is a crucial and dynamic process that involves customizing established frameworks to align with an organization's unique characteristics, risk profile, industry requirements, and strategic objectives. While cybersecurity frameworks provide a solid foundation for addressing common cybersecurity challenges, their generic nature necessitates adaptation to the specific context and nuances of individual organizations. This tailoring process is not a one-size-fits-all endeavor; rather, it requires a thoughtful and strategic approach that considers the organization's size, industry sector, regulatory environment, technological landscape, and overall risk tolerance.

One fundamental aspect of tailoring cybersecurity frameworks involves conducting a thorough assessment of the organization's current cybersecurity posture. This assessment encompasses an analysis of existing policies, procedures, technologies, and personnel capabilities. By understanding the organization's strengths, weaknesses, and areas of improvement, stakeholders gain valuable insights into which aspects of a framework are directly applicable and where adjustments may be needed. This self-assessment forms the basis for a targeted and effective tailoring process.

Organizations often grapple with a myriad of regulatory and compliance requirements specific to their industry. Therefore, tailoring a cybersecurity framework involves integrating these industry-specific mandates into the overall cybersecurity strategy. For instance, healthcare organizations must align their cybersecurity practices with the Health Insurance Portability and Accountability Act (HIPAA) requirements, while financial institutions navigate the intricacies of the Gramm-Leach-Bliley Act (GLBA) or Payment Card Industry Data Security Standard (PCI DSS). By incorporating industry-specific compliance measures into the framework, organizations can ensure not only regulatory adherence but also a more robust defense against industry-relevant threats.

Tailoring also requires a meticulous consideration of the organization's risk appetite and risk tolerance. Different organizations have varying levels of comfort with risk, influenced by factors such as business objectives, stakeholder expectations, and the nature of their operations. Tailoring cybersecurity frameworks involves adjusting the framework's recommendations to align with the organization's risk appetite. For example, an organization with a low risk tolerance may prioritize stringent access controls and encryption measures, while a more risk-tolerant organization may place greater emphasis on incident response and recovery capabilities.

Customization extends to the technology landscape, encompassing the organization's existing infrastructure, applications, and emerging technologies. Cybersecurity frameworks often provide general guidelines on implementing technical controls, and tailoring involves aligning these controls with the organization's specific technological environment. This may include integrating security measures into legacy systems, addressing vulnerabilities in proprietary applications, and adapting controls to accommodate emerging technologies such as cloud computing, Internet of Things (IoT) devices, and artificial intelligence. By tailoring technical controls to the organization's technology stack, the framework becomes more relevant and effective in mitigating potential risks.

Furthermore, organizational culture and employee behavior play pivotal roles in cybersecurity effectiveness. Tailoring frameworks involves considering the human element and crafting policies and awareness programs that resonate with the organization's workforce. For instance, an organization with a highly mobile workforce may emphasize mobile device security measures and remote access controls, while a company with a culture of collaboration might prioritize user education on secure communication and data sharing practices. Addressing the human factor ensures that cybersecurity measures are not only technically robust but also align with the organization's unique workplace dynamics.

Budgetary constraints often influence an organization's ability to implement certain cybersecurity measures. Tailoring frameworks involves a pragmatic assessment of resource availability and the prioritization of cybersecurity investments based on the organization's financial capacity. This may include phased implementation plans, resource allocation to high-impact areas, and a focus on cost-effective solutions. By tailoring the framework to the organization's budgetary constraints, cybersecurity initiatives become more feasible, sustainable, and aligned with overall financial objectives.

An integral aspect of tailoring cybersecurity frameworks is the recognition that organizations evolve over time. Mergers, acquisitions, organizational restructuring, and changes in business strategies can significantly impact the cybersecurity landscape. Therefore, a tailored framework is dynamic and adaptable, capable of accommodating organizational changes seamlessly. Regular reviews and updates ensure that the framework remains relevant, responsive to emerging threats, and aligned with the organization's evolving needs. This iterative approach to tailoring enables organizations to stay ahead of the curve and proactively address cybersecurity challenges in a rapidly changing business environment.

Collaboration among various stakeholders within the organization is essential for successful tailoring. Engaging with key departments, such as IT, legal, compliance, and business units, fosters a cross-functional understanding of cybersecurity needs. Tailoring a framework involves soliciting input from these stakeholders to ensure that the framework reflects the diverse perspectives and priorities within the organization. Regular communication channels, such as cybersecurity committees or working groups, facilitate ongoing discussions about the effectiveness of tailored measures, areas for improvement, and adjustments based on emerging risks or organizational changes.

Moreover, organizations often find value in adopting a hybrid approach by integrating multiple cybersecurity frameworks. This approach allows organizations to leverage the strengths of different frameworks, creating a more comprehensive and adaptive cybersecurity strategy. For instance, an organization may combine elements of the NIST Cybersecurity Framework with ISO/IEC 27001 standards to address specific industry requirements while maintaining a risk-based approach. The hybrid approach enables organizations to tailor their cybersecurity measures to a greater extent, drawing upon the best practices and guidelines from multiple sources.

In conclusion, tailoring cybersecurity frameworks to organizational needs is a dynamic and strategic process that involves a comprehensive understanding of the organization's unique context, challenges, and priorities. By conducting a thorough self-assessment, aligning with industry-specific requirements, considering risk tolerance, addressing technology landscapes, accommodating budget constraints, and fostering a culture of cybersecurity, organizations can tailor frameworks to enhance their overall security posture. This iterative and collaborative approach ensures that cybersecurity measures remain relevant, adaptive, and aligned with the organization's evolving needs, ultimately contributing to a resilient defense against the ever-evolving landscape of cyber threats.

Securing network infrastructure against cyber threats.

Securing network infrastructure against cyber threats is a complex and multifaceted challenge that requires a comprehensive and strategic approach. Network infrastructure forms the backbone of an organization's digital operations, encompassing routers, switches, firewalls, servers, and various interconnected devices. As cyber threats continue to evolve in sophistication and diversity, organizations must implement robust measures to safeguard their network infrastructure from potential vulnerabilities and attacks.

One foundational element of network security is the establishment of secure network perimeters. Firewalls, both at the network and host levels, play a crucial role in monitoring and controlling incoming and outgoing network traffic. Configured with stringent rules, firewalls act as a barrier against unauthorized access and potential cyber threats. Intrusion Prevention Systems (IPS) further enhance network security by actively monitoring and analyzing network traffic for signs of malicious activity, automatically blocking or mitigating threats in real-time.

Secure access controls are paramount in fortifying network infrastructure. Implementing strict access policies ensures that only authorized individuals can access specific resources within the network. This involves deploying robust authentication mechanisms such as multi-factor authentication (MFA) to strengthen user verification. Role-based access controls (RBAC) further refine access privileges based on users' roles within the organization, limiting exposure to sensitive data and critical systems.

Encryption is a fundamental technology for securing data in transit across network infrastructure. The use of protocols such as Transport Layer Security (TLS) and Secure Sockets Layer (SSL) ensures that data exchanged between devices remains confidential and integral. This encryption is particularly crucial for protecting sensitive information, such as financial transactions and confidential communications, from interception by malicious actors.

Vulnerability management is an ongoing process that is integral to securing network infrastructure. Regular assessments and scans identify potential weaknesses in the network, including outdated software, misconfigurations, and known vulnerabilities. Timely patching and updates mitigate these risks, reducing the likelihood of exploitation by cyber threats. Additionally, organizations can employ intrusion detection systems (IDS) and vulnerability scanners to continuously monitor the network for signs of vulnerabilities and potential security incidents.

Network segmentation is a strategic measure that limits the lateral movement of cyber threats within the network. By dividing the network into isolated segments, organizations can contain the impact of a potential breach and prevent the unrestricted spread of malicious activities. This segmentation is particularly relevant in large networks where different departments or functions have distinct security requirements.

An essential aspect of securing network infrastructure is continuous monitoring and logging. Security Information and Event Management (SIEM) systems aggregate and analyze log data from various network devices and applications. Through real-time monitoring, SIEM systems enable the detection of anomalous behavior and potential security incidents. Analysis of log data provides valuable insights into network activities, aiding in the identification of patterns indicative of cyber threats.

Implementing robust endpoint security measures is crucial, considering that endpoints such as computers, laptops, and mobile devices serve as potential entry points for cyber threats. Endpoint protection solutions, including antivirus software, endpoint detection and response (EDR) tools, and mobile device management (MDM) systems, fortify the security of devices connected to the network. Regular updates, patching, and security configurations further contribute to endpoint resilience.

Network visibility is a cornerstone of effective cybersecurity. Organizations must have a clear understanding of the devices, applications, and users connected to their network. Network monitoring tools provide real-time insights into network traffic, helping identify abnormal patterns or suspicious activities. This visibility is essential for promptly detecting and responding to potential security incidents, reducing the dwell time of cyber threats within the network.

A proactive defense against cyber threats involves leveraging threat intelligence. By staying abreast of the latest cyber threats, attack vectors, and adversary tactics, organizations can tailor their network security measures to address specific risks. Threat intelligence feeds, information sharing platforms, and collaboration within the cybersecurity community contribute to a collective defense against emerging threats, enhancing the organization's ability to anticipate and counteract potential attacks.

Security awareness and training programs are vital components of securing network infrastructure. Human error remains a significant factor in cybersecurity incidents, and educating employees about potential threats, phishing attacks, and best security practices is crucial. Employees should be aware of the risks associated with social engineering tactics and be equipped to recognize and report potential security incidents promptly.

Incident response planning is a cornerstone of resilience in the face of cyber threats. Organizations must develop and regularly test incident response plans to ensure a swift and coordinated response in the event of a security incident. This involves defining roles and responsibilities, establishing communication protocols, and conducting simulations to assess the efficacy of the response plan. A well-prepared incident response capability minimizes the impact of security incidents and facilitates a quick return to normal operations.

The adoption of Zero Trust Architecture (ZTA) represents a paradigm shift in network security. ZTA assumes that no entity, whether internal or external, should be trusted by default. Instead, trust is continuously verified based on various factors such as user authentication, device health, and contextual information. This approach minimizes the attack surface and limits the lateral movement of cyber threats, enhancing overall network security.

As organizations increasingly migrate to cloud environments, securing cloud infrastructure becomes a critical consideration. Cloud security involves implementing robust identity and access management (IAM) controls, encrypting data in transit and at rest, and configuring secure cloud architectures. Cloud security measures should align with organizational policies and extend the principles of network security to cloud-based resources.

Collaboration and information-sharing within the cybersecurity community contribute to a collective defense against cyber threats. Engaging with industry-specific Information Sharing and Analysis Centers (ISACs), participating in threat intelligence sharing programs, and collaborating with cybersecurity vendors and researchers enhance the organization's situational awareness. By tapping into a broader pool of knowledge and expertise, organizations can strengthen their network security posture.

Regulatory compliance is a critical consideration in securing network infrastructure. Many industries are subject to specific regulations and data protection laws that mandate the implementation of cybersecurity measures. Compliance with regulations such as the General Data Protection Regulation (GDPR), the Health Insurance Portability and Accountability Act (HIPAA), or the Payment Card Industry Data Security Standard (PCI DSS) ensures that organizations meet legal requirements and maintain the trust of stakeholders.

In conclusion, securing network infrastructure against cyber threats demands a holistic and adaptive approach that encompasses technological measures, user awareness, proactive defense strategies, and compliance considerations. As cyber threats evolve in complexity and scale, organizations must continually reassess and enhance their network security measures. By integrating the principles of defense in depth, continuous monitoring, threat intelligence, and collaboration, organizations can build a resilient network infrastructure capable of withstanding the dynamic and persistent nature of modern cyber threats.

Implementing firewalls, intrusion detection/prevention systems, and secure network configurations.

Implementing firewalls, intrusion detection/prevention systems (IDS/IPS), and secure network configurations is a foundational strategy in fortifying an organization's cybersecurity posture. Firewalls serve as the initial line of defense, strategically positioned to monitor and control incoming and outgoing network traffic based on predetermined security rules. These rules, often configured to allow or deny specific types of traffic, create a barrier that mitigates the risk of unauthorized access and potential cyber threats. Firewalls, whether hardware-based appliances or software solutions, act as sentinels that analyze data packets, apply rule sets, and make decisions to either permit or block traffic, forming a crucial component in the protection of an organization's network infrastructure.

In parallel, intrusion detection and prevention systems contribute significantly to the proactive defense of network environments. IDS/IPS are designed to detect and respond to suspicious or malicious activities within the network. Intrusion detection systems passively monitor network traffic, analyzing patterns and behaviors to identify anomalies that may indicate a potential security incident. On the other hand, intrusion prevention systems take a more active role by not only detecting but also responding to threats. They can automatically block or mitigate suspicious activities in real-time, reducing the window of opportunity for cyber adversaries. The implementation of IDS/IPS enhances the organization's ability to promptly detect and respond to a wide range of cyber threats, from known attack patterns to emerging risks.

Secure network configurations form a critical aspect of the overall cybersecurity strategy, ensuring that network devices and systems are configured with optimal security settings. This involves the meticulous configuration of routers, switches, servers, and other network components to adhere to security best practices. Security baselines, often derived from industry standards or frameworks like the Center for Internet Security (CIS) Controls, guide the secure configuration process. By systematically configuring devices with the principle of least privilege, organizations limit unnecessary access and potential attack surfaces. Secure configurations also involve regular audits and assessments to verify adherence to security policies, ensuring that any deviations are promptly identified and remediated.

Firewalls, IDS/IPS, and secure network configurations collectively contribute to a defense-in-depth strategy, where multiple layers of security controls work in concert to protect against a spectrum of cyber threats. The implementation of firewalls, strategically positioned at network perimeters and segment boundaries, provides a fundamental barrier against unauthorized access. The integration of IDS/IPS enhances the organization's ability to detect and respond to threats that may bypass the initial firewall defenses, offering a proactive layer that actively monitors and mitigates potential risks within the network. Simultaneously, secure network configurations solidify the infrastructure's resilience by reducing the attack surface, enforcing access controls, and maintaining a consistent security posture.

Firewalls, as part of their role, distinguish between different types of network traffic and apply policies accordingly. Stateful inspection firewalls, for example, keep track of the state of active connections and make decisions based on the context of the traffic. This contextual awareness enables firewalls to allow or block traffic based on factors such as the source and destination addresses, ports, and the state of the connection. Additionally, next-generation firewalls (NGFW) incorporate advanced features such as intrusion prevention, application-layer filtering, and advanced threat detection, providing a more robust defense against modern cyber threats. Organizations often deploy firewalls not only at the network perimeter but also within internal network segments to create security zones and enforce access controls.

Intrusion detection systems operate based on predefined signatures, anomaly detection, or behavior analysis to identify potential security incidents. Signature-based detection involves comparing network traffic patterns against known attack signatures, while anomaly detection identifies deviations from established baselines. Behavior analysis, a more advanced approach, evaluates patterns of behavior within the network to identify suspicious activities. When an IDS detects potential threats, it generates alerts, enabling cybersecurity teams to investigate and respond to security incidents promptly. Intrusion prevention systems build upon this capability by taking automated actions, such as blocking malicious IP addresses or terminating suspicious connections, to actively mitigate threats in real-time.

Secure network configurations encompass a range of measures designed to minimize vulnerabilities and enforce security controls across network devices. This involves configuring routers and switches with access control lists (ACLs) to regulate traffic flow based on specified criteria. ACLs can restrict access to specific network resources, limit communication between segments, and define rules for permitted or denied traffic. Additionally, organizations implement Virtual LANs (VLANs) to segment networks logically, creating isolated broadcast domains and enhancing security by containing the impact of potential breaches. Regular audits of network configurations, adherence to security baselines, and the use of configuration management tools contribute to maintaining a secure and resilient network infrastructure.

The integration of firewalls, IDS/IPS, and secure network configurations is particularly crucial in preventing and mitigating common cyber threats. Distributed Denial of Service (DDoS) attacks, for instance, pose a significant risk to network availability. Firewalls equipped with DDoS protection features can detect and mitigate volumetric attacks, while intrusion prevention systems can identify and block malicious traffic patterns associated with DDoS attacks. Secure network configurations play a role by ensuring that devices and network resources are configured to withstand DDoS attacks, leveraging techniques such as rate limiting and traffic filtering.

Malware, another prevalent threat, often attempts to exploit vulnerabilities in networked systems. Firewalls equipped with malware detection capabilities can analyze incoming and outgoing traffic for known malware signatures or suspicious behavior. Intrusion detection systems can complement this defense by identifying indicators of compromise associated with malware activities. Secure network configurations contribute by ensuring that systems are hardened against common malware vectors, such as unpatched software vulnerabilities, unauthorized access points, and misconfigured devices.

The implementation of firewalls, IDS/IPS, and secure network configurations is instrumental in safeguarding sensitive data and meeting compliance requirements. In regulated industries such as healthcare and finance, organizations must adhere to stringent data protection standards. Firewalls with deep packet inspection capabilities can inspect encrypted traffic to detect potential threats or policy violations. IDS/IPS solutions contribute by monitoring for unauthorized access or data exfiltration attempts. Secure network configurations, aligned with regulatory frameworks such as the Health Insurance Portability and Accountability Act (HIPAA) or the Payment Card Industry Data Security Standard (PCI DSS), ensure that networked systems adhere to specific security controls and protect sensitive information.

The dynamic nature of cybersecurity threats necessitates continuous monitoring, updates, and adaptation of firewalls, IDS/IPS, and network configurations. Regularly updating firewall rule sets, intrusion detection signatures, and security configurations helps organizations stay ahead of emerging threats. Threat intelligence feeds, which provide information about new cyber threats and attack vectors, can be integrated into these systems to enhance their efficacy. Continuous monitoring and analysis of network traffic patterns enable organizations to identify evolving threats and adjust security controls accordingly, ensuring that the implemented measures remain effective against the evolving threat landscape.

In conclusion, the implementation of firewalls, intrusion detection/prevention systems, and secure network configurations is a fundamental strategy for enhancing the overall cybersecurity posture of organizations. These measures collectively create a robust defense-in-depth approach that protects against a spectrum of cyber threats, from unauthorized access to sophisticated malware attacks. By strategically positioning firewalls, deploying IDS/IPS, and configuring network devices securely, organizations establish a resilient foundation that not only safeguards their network infrastructure but also contributes to regulatory compliance and the protection of sensitive data. Continuous monitoring, updates, and adaptation ensure that these security measures remain effective in the face of the dynamic and persistent nature of modern cyber threats.

Protecting individual devices and endpoints from cyber threats.

Protecting individual devices and endpoints from cyber threats is a critical imperative in the contemporary digital landscape, where the ubiquity of connected devices exposes individuals to a myriad of potential risks. Individual devices, including computers, laptops, smartphones, tablets, and other Internet of Things (IoT) devices, serve as gateways to personal and sensitive information. The multifaceted nature of cyber threats, ranging from malware and phishing attacks to ransomware and data breaches, necessitates a comprehensive and proactive approach to endpoint security.

One fundamental aspect of safeguarding individual devices is the implementation of robust antivirus and antimalware solutions. These security tools are designed to detect, prevent, and remove malicious software that may compromise the integrity and functionality of devices. Antivirus software employs signature-based detection, behavioral analysis, and heuristics to identify known and unknown threats, providing a foundational layer of defense against a wide array of malware types. Regular updates and real-time scanning are essential to ensure that antivirus solutions remain effective in identifying and neutralizing evolving threats.

Endpoint protection extends beyond traditional antivirus measures to encompass advanced security solutions known as endpoint detection and response (EDR) systems. EDR solutions provide real-time monitoring, threat detection, and response capabilities, offering a more proactive and adaptive approach to endpoint security. By continuously analyzing endpoint activity, EDR systems can identify anomalous behavior indicative of potential security incidents. These solutions empower organizations and individuals to respond swiftly to emerging threats, minimizing the impact of cyber attacks and reducing the likelihood of successful breaches.

Secure and regular software updates represent a fundamental pillar of endpoint security. Operating systems, applications, and firmware must be promptly updated to patch known vulnerabilities and address security flaws. Cyber adversaries often exploit outdated software to gain unauthorized access or deploy malicious payloads. By enabling automatic updates or implementing a systematic update schedule, individuals can ensure that their devices benefit from the latest security patches, reducing the risk of exploitation and enhancing the overall resilience of their endpoints.

Implementing strong and unique passwords is a fundamental practice in protecting individual devices from unauthorized access. Weak or reused passwords represent a significant security vulnerability, as they can be easily exploited through techniques like password cracking or credential stuffing attacks. Utilizing complex passwords, incorporating a mix of uppercase and lowercase letters, numbers, and symbols, adds an additional layer of defense. Additionally, adopting password management tools assists in generating and securely storing complex passwords for various accounts, mitigating the risk of credential-related cyber threats.

Multi-factor authentication (MFA) serves as a powerful defense mechanism in augmenting the security of individual devices. MFA requires users to provide multiple forms of identification, typically a combination of something they know (password), something they have (a mobile device or authentication token), or something they are (biometric data). This multi-layered approach significantly enhances access controls, even in cases where passwords are compromised. The widespread adoption of MFA is pivotal in fortifying the security of endpoints, especially as cybercriminals increasingly target user credentials as a means of unauthorized access.

Securing individual devices necessitates a comprehensive approach to network security, considering that endpoints often connect to various networks, both wired and wireless. Utilizing virtual private networks (VPNs) adds an additional layer of protection by encrypting communication between the device and the network. VPNs are particularly valuable when accessing public Wi-Fi networks, which are often targeted by cybercriminals seeking to intercept sensitive data. Furthermore, individuals should configure firewalls on their devices to regulate incoming and outgoing network traffic, providing an additional defense against unauthorized access and potential cyber threats.

Phishing attacks, which leverage deceptive tactics to trick individuals into divulging sensitive information, represent a pervasive threat to endpoint security. Educating individuals about the characteristics of phishing emails, suspicious links, and fraudulent websites is crucial in empowering them to recognize and avoid phishing attempts. Security awareness training programs play a pivotal role in fostering a cybersecurity-conscious culture, ensuring that individuals remain vigilant against social engineering tactics that seek to exploit human vulnerabilities.

Endpoint security extends beyond traditional computing devices to encompass mobile devices, a ubiquitous aspect of modern life. Smartphones and tablets are susceptible to a range of cyber threats, including mobile malware, malicious apps, and device theft. Implementing security measures such as device encryption, screen lock passwords, and remote wiping capabilities adds an additional layer of protection to mobile endpoints. Mobile security applications provide antivirus and antimalware protection tailored to the unique characteristics of mobile platforms, safeguarding personal and business data stored on these devices.

Data backup is a fundamental aspect of endpoint security, serving as a last line of defense against ransomware and data loss incidents. Regularly backing up important data to secure and offline storage ensures that individuals can restore their information in the event of a cyber attack or device failure. Cloud-based backup solutions provide convenient and automated options for individuals to safeguard their data, minimizing the impact of data breaches and enhancing overall endpoint resilience.

Implementing endpoint security measures also requires a heightened focus on IoT devices, which are increasingly integrated into homes and workplaces. IoT devices, ranging from smart home appliances to industrial sensors, often lack robust security features and may serve as entry points for cyber attackers. Securing IoT devices involves changing default passwords, keeping firmware up to date, and segmenting IoT networks from critical infrastructure. Individuals must be cognizant of the security implications associated with IoT adoption and take proactive measures to mitigate potential risks.

Device management solutions, often utilized in enterprise environments, offer individuals the ability to centrally manage and secure their devices. Mobile device management (MDM) and endpoint management platforms enable individuals to enforce security policies, configure settings, and remotely monitor and manage devices. These solutions provide a centralized approach to endpoint security, particularly valuable in scenarios where individuals have multiple devices that require consistent security controls and configurations.

Collaboration and information-sharing within the cybersecurity community contribute to a collective defense against emerging threats. Individuals can benefit from threat intelligence feeds, online forums, and community-driven initiatives that provide insights into the latest cyber threats and attack techniques. By staying informed about evolving risks, individuals can adapt their endpoint security measures to address current and emerging challenges, enhancing their overall cybersecurity resilience.

Legal and regulatory considerations also play a role in individual endpoint security. Data protection laws, such as the General Data Protection Regulation (GDPR), impose obligations on individuals to protect the privacy and security of personal data. Understanding and complying with these regulations not only helps individuals avoid legal consequences but also reinforces a culture of responsible cybersecurity practices.

In conclusion, protecting individual devices and endpoints from cyber threats requires a multifaceted and proactive approach that encompasses technological measures, user awareness, and adherence to best practices. Robust antivirus solutions, endpoint detection and response systems, regular software updates, secure authentication practices, and network security measures collectively contribute to a resilient defense against a diverse range of cyber threats. Security education, collaboration within the cybersecurity community, and compliance with legal and regulatory requirements further enhance individual endpoint security. As cyber threats continue to evolve, individuals must remain vigilant, adapt their security measures accordingly, and actively contribute to a collective effort to create a more secure digital environment.

The role of endpoint security solutions.

Endpoint security solutions play a pivotal role in safeguarding organizations against a myriad of cyber threats by focusing on the protection of individual devices, such as computers, laptops, smartphones, and other endpoints connected to a network. As the digital landscape continues to evolve, with increased connectivity and a growing number of sophisticated cyber threats, the significance of robust endpoint security measures cannot be overstated. These solutions are designed to provide a comprehensive defense strategy that goes beyond traditional antivirus measures, addressing a broad spectrum of security challenges faced by organizations across various industries.

One fundamental aspect of endpoint security solutions is antivirus protection. Traditional antivirus software, a core component of endpoint security, employs signature-based detection to identify known malware and viruses. By maintaining a database of virus signatures, antivirus programs can recognize and block malicious code that matches these signatures, providing a foundational layer of defense against well-established threats. However, the evolving nature of cyber threats necessitates the integration of more advanced features into modern endpoint security solutions.

Endpoint Detection and Response (EDR) systems represent a significant advancement in endpoint security, offering real-time monitoring, threat detection, and response capabilities. EDR solutions provide organizations with the ability to proactively identify and mitigate security incidents by continuously analyzing endpoint activity. By monitoring processes, file changes, network connections, and user behavior, EDR systems can detect anomalies indicative of potential threats, such as malware infections, unauthorized access, or suspicious patterns. The proactive nature of EDR solutions enhances an organization's ability to respond swiftly to emerging threats, reducing the dwell time of cyber adversaries within the network.

Beyond traditional antivirus and EDR capabilities, modern endpoint security solutions often incorporate Behavioral Analysis. Behavioral analysis involves monitoring the behavior of applications and users to identify deviations from normal patterns. By establishing a baseline of typical behavior, these solutions can detect anomalous activities that may indicate the presence of malware, insider threats, or other security incidents. Behavioral analysis is particularly effective in identifying zero-day attacks and sophisticated threats that may not have known signatures.

Endpoint security solutions also emphasize the importance of Vulnerability Management. Regular software updates and patches are essential to addressing vulnerabilities in operating systems and applications. Endpoint security solutions facilitate the identification and remediation of vulnerabilities by conducting regular scans and assessments of endpoint devices. Automated vulnerability management ensures that devices are consistently updated with the latest security patches, minimizing the risk of exploitation by cyber adversaries seeking to capitalize on known weaknesses.

Secure Configuration Management is another critical aspect of endpoint security. Ensuring that individual devices are configured with optimal security settings helps reduce the attack surface and fortify defenses against potential threats. Security baselines, often derived from industry standards or frameworks, guide organizations in configuring endpoints with settings that align with best practices. Secure configurations involve implementing access controls, restricting unnecessary services, and enforcing encryption measures to enhance the overall resilience of endpoint devices.

The rise of Remote Work and Bring Your Own Device (BYOD) trends has added complexity to endpoint security. Mobile Device Management (MDM) and Mobile Security solutions have become integral components of endpoint security strategies. MDM solutions enable organizations to manage and secure mobile devices by enforcing policies, configuring settings, and remotely monitoring device activity. Mobile security solutions provide antivirus and anti-malware protection tailored to the unique characteristics of mobile platforms, ensuring that smartphones and tablets are safeguarded against evolving threats.

Encryption plays a crucial role in protecting sensitive data on endpoints. Full Disk Encryption (FDE) and File-Level Encryption help mitigate the risk of data breaches in the event of device loss or theft. Endpoint security solutions often include encryption features to secure data both at rest and in transit. By encrypting sensitive information, organizations can ensure that even if a device falls into the wrong hands, the data remains inaccessible without the appropriate decryption keys.

Endpoint security solutions address the growing threat landscape posed by Ransomware, a type of malware that encrypts a user's data and demands a ransom for its release. Behavioral analysis, threat intelligence integration, and real-time monitoring capabilities enable these solutions to detect and respond to ransomware attacks promptly. Some solutions also include features such as backup and recovery options to help organizations restore their data without succumbing to ransom demands.

Network-based threats are also within the purview of endpoint security solutions. Intrusion Prevention Systems (IPS) and Firewall Integration provide an additional layer of defense by monitoring and controlling network traffic. IPS solutions actively block or mitigate potential threats identified at the network level, preventing them from reaching individual endpoints. Integrating firewall capabilities into endpoint security solutions ensures that devices have an added layer of protection against unauthorized access and malicious network traffic.

The increasing sophistication of Phishing Attacks underscores the need for endpoint security solutions to incorporate Email Security features. Email remains a common vector for delivering malicious payloads and executing social engineering attacks. Endpoint security solutions with robust email security capabilities can scan email attachments, identify phishing attempts, and block malicious links before they reach the endpoint device. Educating users about phishing risks and incorporating awareness training further strengthens the organization's overall security posture.

Machine Learning and Artificial Intelligence are integral components of advanced endpoint security solutions. These technologies enable solutions to adapt to evolving threats by learning from patterns, anomalies, and historical data. Machine learning algorithms can identify new and unknown threats, enhancing the detection capabilities of endpoint security solutions. AI-driven features contribute to the automation of threat response, allowing organizations to respond swiftly to security incidents and minimize the impact of cyber threats.

Endpoint security solutions contribute significantly to Incident Response Planning. In the event of a security incident, these solutions provide organizations with the tools and capabilities needed to investigate and remediate the issue. Detailed logs, historical data, and real-time alerts generated by endpoint security solutions aid cybersecurity teams in understanding the scope of an incident, identifying the root cause, and implementing effective countermeasures. This proactive approach to incident response is essential in reducing the impact of security breaches and ensuring a swift return to normal operations.

Compliance with Regulatory Requirements is a key consideration in the deployment of endpoint security solutions. Many industries are subject to specific regulations that mandate the implementation of cybersecurity measures to protect sensitive data. Endpoint security solutions help organizations meet regulatory requirements by enforcing security controls, conducting regular assessments, and providing audit trails and reports. Compliance with standards such as the Health Insurance Portability and Accountability Act (HIPAA), the General Data Protection Regulation (GDPR), or the Payment Card Industry Data Security Standard (PCI DSS) is crucial for maintaining trust, avoiding legal consequences, and protecting the privacy of individuals.

The Collaboration and Integration capabilities of endpoint security solutions further enhance their effectiveness. Integration with Security Information and Event Management (SIEM) systems allows for centralized monitoring and analysis of security events across the organization. This collaboration ensures that endpoint security data is part of a holistic cybersecurity strategy, providing a comprehensive view of the threat landscape. Additionally, integration with threat intelligence feeds enables organizations to stay informed about emerging threats, ensuring that endpoint security measures are adaptive and proactive.

In conclusion, endpoint security solutions play a multifaceted and indispensable role in the overall cybersecurity posture of organizations. From traditional antivirus measures to advanced EDR systems, these solutions address the evolving nature of cyber threats faced by individual devices. By encompassing features such as behavioral analysis, vulnerability management, secure configuration, encryption, and network defense, endpoint security solutions provide a comprehensive defense strategy. The integration of machine learning, artificial intelligence, and collaboration capabilities further enhances their ability to detect, respond to, and mitigate cyber threats. As organizations navigate a dynamic and challenging threat landscape, investing in robust endpoint security solutions becomes imperative to protect sensitive data, maintain regulatory compliance, and ensure the resilience of digital assets.

Chapter 4: Data Breaches and Beyond: Navigating the Aftermath

Definition and common causes of data breaches.

A data breach is a cybersecurity incident in which unauthorized individuals gain access to sensitive or confidential information, leading to its exposure, theft, or compromise. These incidents pose significant threats to individuals, organizations, and, at times, entire industries, as they can result in financial losses, reputational damage, and legal consequences. The causes of data breaches are diverse, encompassing a range of technical vulnerabilities, human errors, and malicious activities that exploit weaknesses in an organization's security posture.

Technical vulnerabilities represent a common cause of data breaches, often stemming from weaknesses in software, hardware, or network configurations. Exploiting vulnerabilities in software applications and operating systems allows cyber attackers to gain unauthorized access to systems and databases. Failure to promptly apply security patches and updates to address known vulnerabilities increases the risk of exploitation. Additionally, misconfigurations in network devices, servers, and databases can create inadvertent entry points for attackers. Inadequate access controls, weak encryption, or improper security settings contribute to the exploitation of technical vulnerabilities, allowing unauthorized individuals to access and exfiltrate sensitive data.

Human errors play a significant role in data breaches, highlighting the critical importance of cybersecurity awareness and training. Inadvertent actions by employees, such as sending sensitive information to the wrong recipient, falling victim to phishing attacks, or improperly configuring security settings, can lead to data exposure. Negligence, lack of awareness, and insufficient training contribute to instances where individuals unintentionally compromise security measures. Social engineering tactics, including pretexting, baiting, and quid pro quo schemes, exploit human vulnerabilities to trick individuals into divulging sensitive information, providing cybercriminals with unauthorized access.

Malicious activities conducted by external attackers or insider threats represent another prevalent cause of data breaches. Cybercriminals employ various methods, including hacking, malware, and ransomware attacks, to infiltrate networks and exfiltrate data. Advanced Persistent Threats (APTs) involve sophisticated, long-term campaigns where attackers gain unauthorized access to systems and maintain a persistent presence to exfiltrate sensitive information over an extended period. Insider threats, whether intentional or unintentional, involve individuals within an organization exploiting their access to compromise data. Malicious insiders may steal information for personal gain, while unintentional insiders may unknowingly facilitate breaches through actions like sharing credentials or mishandling data.

Phishing attacks, a subset of social engineering tactics, are a common and effective means of initiating data breaches. Phishing involves the use of deceptive emails, messages, or websites to trick individuals into disclosing sensitive information, such as usernames, passwords, or financial details. Spear phishing targets specific individuals or organizations, often using personalized and highly convincing messages to increase the likelihood of success. The success of phishing attacks relies on exploiting human trust and manipulating individuals into taking actions that compromise the security of their data. As phishing techniques evolve, organizations must employ robust email security measures and continuously educate users to recognize and avoid phishing attempts.

Weak Authentication and Credential Management contribute significantly to data breaches, as compromised or stolen credentials provide unauthorized access to sensitive systems and information. Password-related vulnerabilities, including weak passwords, password reuse, and inadequate authentication mechanisms, create opportunities for attackers to gain unauthorized access. Credential stuffing attacks leverage usernames and passwords obtained from previous data breaches to gain unauthorized access to other accounts where individuals have reused credentials. Implementing strong authentication practices, such as multi-factor authentication (MFA), helps mitigate the risk associated with compromised credentials and enhances the overall security of authentication processes.

Insecure Application Development and Design contribute to data breaches when vulnerabilities exist in the software and applications that organizations use or develop. Flaws in code, inadequate input validation, and insecure data storage can be exploited by attackers to gain unauthorized access to sensitive information. Insecure Application Programming Interfaces (APIs) may expose data to unauthorized individuals if not properly secured. As organizations increasingly rely on custom or third-party applications, the security of these applications becomes critical in preventing data breaches. Implementing secure coding practices, conducting thorough security assessments, and regularly auditing applications contribute to reducing the risk of data breaches related to insecure development practices.

The proliferation of Bring Your Own Device (BYOD) and remote work trends introduces additional challenges in securing data. Mobile devices and remote access points may lack the same level of security controls as traditional corporate environments. Unsecured Wi-Fi networks, lost or stolen devices, and inadequate device encryption increase the risk of data breaches. Mobile malware poses a particular threat to devices, potentially compromising sensitive information stored on smartphones and tablets. Organizations must implement Mobile Device Management (MDM) solutions, enforce security policies, and educate users on secure mobile practices to mitigate the risks associated with the use of personal devices for work-related activities.

Insufficient Data Encryption is a contributing factor in data breaches, as unencrypted data is more susceptible to interception and unauthorized access. In transit, data should be encrypted to prevent eavesdropping during communication between devices and networks. Additionally, data at rest, stored on servers, databases, or endpoints, should be encrypted to protect it in the event of unauthorized access. Failure to implement robust encryption measures exposes sensitive information to potential compromise, especially when data is stored or transmitted across unsecured channels.

Supply Chain Vulnerabilities pose a growing risk to organizations, as interconnected ecosystems involve multiple third-party vendors and service providers. Cyber attackers may target supply chain partners to gain access to an organization's network or compromise the integrity of software and hardware components. Supply chain attacks, such as the compromise of software updates or the insertion of malicious components into hardware, can lead to widespread data breaches. Organizations must conduct thorough security assessments of their supply chain partners, implement secure development practices, and establish stringent security requirements for third-party components.

Inadequate Incident Response Planning and Preparedness can exacerbate the impact of data breaches. Organizations that lack comprehensive incident response plans may struggle to detect and contain security incidents promptly. A delayed or ineffective response allows attackers to persist within the network, increasing the extent of data exposure. Incident response planning involves defining roles and responsibilities, establishing communication protocols, conducting regular drills, and continuously improving response capabilities. Organizations must be prepared to swiftly identify, contain, eradicate, and recover from security incidents to minimize the impact of data breaches on both operational and reputational fronts.

In conclusion, data breaches result from a complex interplay of technical vulnerabilities, human errors, and malicious activities that exploit weaknesses in an organization's security infrastructure. Addressing the diverse causes of data breaches requires a comprehensive cybersecurity strategy that encompasses technical controls, user awareness and training, secure development practices, and incident response preparedness. As the threat landscape continues to evolve, organizations must remain vigilant, adapt their security measures accordingly, and implement a layered defense approach to safeguard sensitive information from unauthorized access and compromise.

The impact of data breaches on organizations and individuals.

Data breaches have profound and far-reaching impacts on both organizations and individuals, disrupting the delicate balance of trust, privacy, and security in the digital landscape. For organizations, the aftermath of a data breach is characterized by financial losses, reputational damage, legal consequences, and operational challenges. The financial repercussions often extend beyond immediate remediation efforts to include regulatory fines, legal settlements, and the costs associated with implementing enhanced security measures. The loss of customer trust and confidence can lead to decreased business, customer churn, and damage to brand equity, as individuals become wary of entrusting their sensitive information to an organization that has suffered a breach.

The reputational damage inflicted by a data breach is perhaps one of the most enduring and challenging aspects for organizations to address. The public perception of an organization's commitment to cybersecurity and data protection is significantly influenced by the manner in which it responds to and handles a data breach. News of a breach can spread rapidly, fueled by media coverage and social media, amplifying the negative impact on an organization's reputation. Stakeholders, including customers, partners, investors, and employees, may question the organization's ability to safeguard sensitive information, resulting in long-term consequences that extend beyond the immediate aftermath of the breach.

Legal consequences are a formidable aspect of the impact on organizations, particularly as data protection regulations become more stringent. Many jurisdictions have enacted laws governing the protection of personal data, imposing obligations on organizations to implement adequate security measures and notify affected individuals and regulatory authorities in the event of a breach. Non-compliance with these regulations can lead to significant fines and penalties, adding to the financial burden already incurred by the organization. Legal actions, including class-action lawsuits from affected individuals seeking compensation for damages, further compound the legal fallout from a data breach.

Operationally, organizations face challenges in restoring normalcy and trust after a data breach. Remediation efforts, such as identifying and closing security vulnerabilities, implementing enhanced security controls, and conducting forensic investigations, demand significant resources and time. The disruption to daily operations can be extensive, affecting productivity, business continuity, and the ability to deliver products or services. The need for transparent and effective communication during the recovery process is crucial to maintaining trust with stakeholders and minimizing the long-term impact on the organization's operations.

For individuals, the impact of a data breach is deeply personal and can have lasting consequences on privacy, financial security, and emotional well-being. The compromise of personal information, including names, addresses, social security numbers, and financial details, exposes individuals to the risk of identity theft, fraud, and unauthorized access to their accounts. The aftermath may involve the painstaking process of reclaiming one's identity, rectifying fraudulent transactions, and fortifying defenses against ongoing threats.

Financial security becomes a paramount concern for individuals affected by a data breach. Stolen financial information can be used to conduct unauthorized transactions, open fraudulent accounts, or engage in other forms of financial exploitation. Victims may face the arduous task of rectifying these unauthorized transactions, working with financial institutions, and repairing their credit histories. The financial toll extends beyond the immediate impact of the breach, potentially affecting an individual's ability to secure loans, mortgages, or lines of credit in the future.

Emotional distress is a less tangible but equally significant impact on individuals affected by data breaches. The violation of privacy and the sense of vulnerability resulting from the unauthorized exposure of personal information can lead to anxiety, stress, and a loss of trust in online platforms and services. Individuals may experience feelings of powerlessness and frustration as they navigate the aftermath of a breach, often grappling with the uncertainty of how their compromised information may be misused in the future.

In some cases, the impact on individuals goes beyond financial and emotional consequences to include potential harm to their physical well-being. Medical data breaches, for example, can compromise sensitive health information, leading to the unauthorized access and disclosure of individuals' medical histories, treatment plans, and other confidential healthcare details. The misuse of such information can have serious implications for an individual's health and well-being, creating ethical and legal challenges for healthcare organizations responsible for safeguarding this sensitive data.

The interconnected nature of the digital ecosystem means that the impact of data breaches on organizations and individuals is intertwined. Individuals, often customers or users of a breached organization's services, bear the brunt of the breach's consequences while simultaneously influencing the fate of the organization through their reactions and decisions. Organizations that prioritize transparency, effective communication, and robust security measures in the aftermath of a breach are more likely to rebuild trust and mitigate the long-term impact on both their operations and the individuals they serve.

Mitigating the impact of data breaches requires a proactive and holistic approach from both organizations and individuals. Organizations must invest in robust cybersecurity measures, including encryption, multi-factor authentication, and continuous monitoring, to fortify their defenses against evolving cyber threats. Regular security audits, employee training, and incident response planning contribute to a more resilient security posture. For individuals, practicing good cyber hygiene, such as using strong and unique passwords, enabling multi-factor authentication, and staying vigilant against phishing attempts, can enhance personal security in an interconnected digital landscape.

As the digital landscape continues to evolve, the specter of data breaches remains a persistent and dynamic challenge. Organizations and individuals alike must recognize the shared responsibility of protecting sensitive information and collaborate to foster a culture of cybersecurity awareness, resilience, and trust. By acknowledging the interconnectedness of their interests and taking proactive measures to address the impact of data breaches, organizations and individuals can contribute to a more secure and resilient digital ecosystem.

Strategies for timely detection of data breaches.

Timely detection of data breaches is a critical component of a robust cybersecurity strategy, allowing organizations to identify and respond to security incidents promptly, thereby mitigating the potential impact on sensitive information. One key strategy involves the implementation of Intrusion Detection Systems (IDS) and Intrusion Prevention Systems (IPS). These systems actively monitor network traffic, looking for patterns indicative of known threats or anomalous behavior that may signify a potential breach. By analyzing network packets in real-time, IDS and IPS solutions provide organizations with an early warning system, enabling swift response to emerging threats and minimizing the dwell time of malicious actors within the network.

Continuous monitoring of system logs and security events is another vital strategy for timely breach detection. Security Information and Event Management (SIEM) solutions aggregate and analyze log data from various sources, including servers, applications, and network devices. By correlating events and identifying patterns that may indicate a security incident, SIEM solutions enhance an organization's ability to detect breaches promptly. Real-time alerts and automated responses contribute to a proactive security posture, enabling organizations to investigate and respond to potential breaches in a timely manner.

User behavior analytics represents an advanced approach to breach detection, focusing on identifying deviations from normal patterns of user activity. By establishing baselines of typical behavior, organizations can leverage machine learning algorithms to detect anomalies that may signify a compromised account or insider threat. Anomalous patterns, such as unusual access times or atypical data transfer volumes, can trigger alerts, prompting further investigation. User behavior analytics provides a dynamic and adaptive method for detecting breaches, particularly those involving insider threats or compromised credentials.

Endpoint Detection and Response (EDR) solutions play a crucial role in the timely detection of data breaches at the individual device level. EDR solutions continuously monitor and analyze endpoint activities, including file changes, process executions, and network connections. By identifying unusual behavior or indicators of compromise, EDR solutions contribute to early breach detection.

Automated response capabilities further enhance an organization's ability to isolate compromised endpoints, contain the impact, and initiate remediation efforts swiftly.

Threat intelligence feeds offer a proactive strategy for timely breach detection by providing organizations with up-to-date information about emerging threats and attack vectors. Integrating threat intelligence feeds into security systems enables organizations to correlate indicators of compromise with known threat signatures. This proactive approach allows for the identification of potential breaches based on the latest threat intelligence, enhancing the organization's ability to detect and respond to threats before they manifest into full-fledged breaches.

Data loss prevention (DLP) solutions contribute to breach detection by monitoring and controlling the movement of sensitive data within an organization's network. These solutions use content inspection and contextual analysis to identify and prevent the unauthorized transfer or access of sensitive information. By setting policies that govern the permissible use and transmission of sensitive data, DLP solutions can generate alerts or block actions that may indicate a potential breach, facilitating timely intervention to prevent data exfiltration.

Implementing honeypots and decoy systems is a proactive strategy that involves creating simulated environments to attract and detect malicious activity. Honeypots, for instance, mimic vulnerable systems or enticing data to lure attackers. Any interaction with these decoy systems triggers alerts, providing organizations with early indicators of potential breaches. While not a direct part of the production environment, honeypots contribute valuable insights into the tactics, techniques, and procedures employed by adversaries, aiding in the refinement of detection capabilities.

Continuous vulnerability scanning and penetration testing are essential strategies for identifying potential weaknesses in an organization's systems and applications. By regularly assessing the security posture of networked assets, organizations can discover and remediate vulnerabilities before they are exploited in a data breach. Automated vulnerability scanners and ethical hacking through penetration tests contribute to a proactive and systematic approach to breach detection, allowing organizations to address potential entry points before they can be leveraged by malicious actors.

Security orchestration, automation, and response (SOAR) platforms enhance breach detection by automating incident response processes. These platforms integrate with various security tools, enabling automated workflows for incident detection, investigation, and containment. By orchestrating responses based on predefined playbooks, SOAR platforms streamline the incident response lifecycle, allowing organizations to detect and mitigate breaches more efficiently. Automation reduces the time required to respond to alerts, ensuring a swifter and more coordinated approach to breach detection and containment.

Implementing anomaly detection based on machine learning algorithms is a forward-looking strategy for timely breach detection. Machine learning models can analyze vast amounts of data to identify patterns and anomalies that may signify a security incident. By training models on historical data and continuously adapting to evolving threats, machine learning enhances the organization's ability to detect breaches, especially those involving novel or sophisticated attack techniques. Anomaly detection provides a dynamic and adaptive layer of defense, complementing traditional signature-based approaches.

Employee training and security awareness programs contribute to timely breach detection by empowering individuals to recognize and report suspicious activities. Human vigilance remains a critical element in the overall security posture, as employees are often the first line of defense against phishing attempts, social engineering, and other tactics employed by attackers. Educated and aware employees can serve as an additional layer of detection, helping organizations identify and respond to potential breaches at an early stage.

Incident response planning is a foundational strategy that ensures organizations are well-prepared to detect and respond to data breaches promptly. Establishing clear incident response protocols, defining roles and responsibilities, and conducting regular drills contribute to a well-coordinated and effective response to security incidents. The ability to detect breaches in a timely manner is closely linked to an organization's preparedness and agility in responding to security incidents, ensuring that the impact is minimized, and recovery efforts are initiated promptly.

Collaboration within the cybersecurity community and information-sharing initiatives contribute to timely breach detection. Threat intelligence-sharing platforms, industry forums, and collaboration with peer organizations enable the rapid dissemination of information about emerging threats and attack techniques. By staying informed about the latest developments in the threat landscape, organizations can adjust their detection capabilities to identify and respond to evolving breaches effectively.

In conclusion, timely detection of data breaches is a multifaceted challenge that requires a comprehensive and adaptive approach. Organizations must leverage a combination of technological solutions, proactive strategies, and human awareness to create a resilient defense against evolving cyber threats. From the implementation of intrusion detection systems to the integration of threat intelligence feeds and the use of advanced technologies like machine learning, organizations can enhance their breach detection capabilities. Moreover, a strong focus on employee training, incident response planning, and collaboration within the cybersecurity community ensures a holistic and proactive approach to detecting and mitigating the impact of data breaches.

Legal and ethical considerations in notifying affected parties.
The legal and ethical considerations surrounding the notification of affected parties in the aftermath of a data breach are complex and multifaceted, requiring a delicate balance between transparency, compliance with regulatory requirements, and the protection of individuals' rights. From a legal standpoint, many jurisdictions have enacted data breach notification laws that mandate organizations to inform affected parties when their personal information is compromised. Compliance with these laws is not only a legal obligation but also a critical component of maintaining trust and accountability in the handling of sensitive information. The European Union's General Data Protection Regulation (GDPR), for instance, imposes strict requirements on organizations to notify relevant supervisory authorities and affected individuals of data breaches without undue delay. Failure to comply with these legal obligations can result in significant fines and penalties, emphasizing the importance of understanding and adhering to the specific notification requirements outlined in applicable data protection laws.

Ethical considerations play a pivotal role in shaping the approach to notifying affected parties and extend beyond mere legal compliance. Ethical communication principles emphasize honesty, transparency, and respect for the individuals impacted by the breach. Organizations have an ethical obligation to communicate openly about the incident, providing clear and comprehensible information about the nature of the breach, the types of information compromised, and the potential risks faced by affected parties. This transparency allows individuals to make informed decisions about how to protect themselves in the aftermath of a breach. Ethical communication also involves acknowledging responsibility for the incident, demonstrating a commitment to remediation efforts, and offering support to affected parties, thereby fostering a sense of trust and accountability.

Balancing legal requirements and ethical considerations becomes particularly nuanced when determining the timing of breach notifications. Legal obligations often stipulate a timeframe within which organizations must notify affected parties and regulatory authorities. However, ethical considerations may prompt organizations to expedite notifications even if not legally required, especially if delaying notification could exacerbate the harm to individuals. The principle of minimizing harm to affected parties guides the ethical decision-making process, encouraging organizations to prioritize the timely communication of breaches to mitigate potential risks and allow individuals to take proactive measures to protect themselves.

The scope and content of breach notifications present additional legal and ethical considerations. Legal requirements typically prescribe the information that must be included in notifications, such as a description of the breach, the types of information compromised, and contact information for obtaining further details. Ethical considerations amplify these requirements, urging organizations to present information in a clear, understandable, and empathetic manner. Striking a balance between providing sufficient details to empower affected parties to respond effectively and avoiding unnecessary alarm or confusion requires careful consideration of the language, tone, and content of breach notifications.

The manner in which organizations choose to deliver breach notifications also raises legal and ethical considerations. While electronic notifications are often the most efficient means of reaching affected parties, legal requirements may specify alternative methods, such as postal mail or telephone calls. Ethical considerations extend to the accessibility and inclusivity of notification methods, recognizing that diverse groups of individuals may have different preferences and capabilities. Organizations must ensure that their chosen notification methods align with legal mandates while also taking into account the varied needs and circumstances of affected parties to facilitate effective communication.

Privacy considerations loom large in both legal and ethical dimensions when notifying affected parties of a data breach. Organizations must carefully navigate the disclosure of information about the breach while safeguarding the privacy and security of affected individuals. This involves providing sufficient information to enable affected parties to understand the nature of the breach and take necessary precautions without divulging unnecessary details that could compromise their privacy further. Ethical considerations underscore the importance of respecting individuals' privacy rights throughout the notification process, reinforcing the trust relationship between organizations and those they serve.

Anonymity and confidentiality considerations come into play when notifying affected parties, especially in situations where the breach involves sensitive or confidential information. Legal requirements may dictate the extent to which organizations can anonymize or de-identify information in breach notifications. Ethical considerations call for a careful balance between privacy protection and transparency, ensuring that affected parties receive meaningful information without unnecessary exposure of sensitive details that could exacerbate the impact of the breach on individuals.

The provision of support services for affected parties emerges as a crucial ethical consideration in the aftermath of a data breach. Legal requirements may mandate the inclusion of information about available support services in breach notifications. Ethical considerations go beyond mere compliance, urging organizations to proactively offer support to those impacted by the breach. This support may encompass identity theft protection services, credit monitoring, or guidance on securing personal information. Ethical responsibility extends to assisting affected parties in navigating the potential consequences of the breach, demonstrating a commitment to mitigating harm and fostering a sense of care and accountability.

Engaging with regulatory authorities is a legal requirement in many jurisdictions following a data breach, as organizations are often obligated to report incidents to relevant supervisory bodies. Ethical considerations come into play in the organization's approach to cooperation and transparency with regulatory authorities. Proactive and forthright communication with regulators, including timely and accurate reporting of the breach, demonstrates a commitment to accountability and may mitigate potential legal consequences. Ethical responsibility extends to collaborating with regulatory authorities to address the root causes of the breach, implement remediation measures, and contribute to the broader goal of enhancing cybersecurity practices across the industry.

International and cross-border considerations introduce additional legal and ethical complexities in the notification of affected parties. Organizations operating globally must navigate varying legal requirements across jurisdictions, each with its own data protection laws and breach notification mandates. Ethical considerations call for a commitment to providing consistent and equitable treatment to affected parties, irrespective of their geographic location. This involves navigating the intricate landscape of international data transfer regulations, respecting the privacy rights of individuals globally, and ensuring that breach notifications align with the diverse legal frameworks that may apply.

In conclusion, the legal and ethical considerations in notifying affected parties of a data breach are integral to maintaining trust, accountability, and respect for individuals' rights in the digital age. Organizations must navigate a complex landscape of legal mandates, ethical principles, and privacy considerations to strike the right balance between transparency and compliance. By prioritizing timely and transparent communication, respecting privacy rights, and proactively offering support to affected parties, organizations can fulfill their legal obligations while upholding the ethical standards necessary to preserve trust in the face of a data breach.

Conducting a thorough forensic analysis after a data breach.

Conducting a thorough forensic analysis after a data breach is a critical and intricate process that plays a pivotal role in understanding the scope, nature, and impact of the incident. Forensic analysis is not only instrumental in identifying the root causes of the breach but also in aiding organizations in implementing effective remediation measures and fortifying their cybersecurity defenses against future threats. The initial phase of forensic analysis involves the identification and isolation of affected systems and devices. This step is crucial for preventing further damage and ensuring the preservation of potential digital evidence. By isolating compromised systems, forensic investigators create a controlled environment for analysis, minimizing the risk of contaminating or altering critical data that may be instrumental in uncovering the details of the breach.

The acquisition of forensic evidence is a meticulous process that requires specialized tools and techniques. Forensic investigators use a variety of methods to collect and preserve digital evidence, ranging from memory and disk imaging to network traffic captures. These techniques aim to create a forensic snapshot of the compromised systems, capturing the state of memory, disk storage, and network communications at the time of the breach. This digital evidence serves as a foundation for subsequent analysis, enabling investigators to reconstruct the sequence of events, identify the methods used by attackers, and determine the extent of the compromise.

Timeline reconstruction is a key aspect of forensic analysis, allowing investigators to create a chronological sequence of events leading up to and following the data breach. This timeline provides insights into the tactics, techniques, and procedures employed by attackers, helping organizations understand the specific methods used to infiltrate systems, move laterally within the network, and exfiltrate sensitive data. The reconstruction of the timeline also aids in establishing the duration of the breach, shedding light on the dwell time of attackers within the compromised environment.

Analyzing system artifacts and logs is central to forensic investigations, offering valuable insights into the activities of both attackers and system users. Event logs, registry entries, and system artifacts can reveal unauthorized access, changes to configurations, and the execution of malicious code. Forensic investigators scrutinize these artifacts to identify the initial entry point of attackers, the lateral movement through the network, and any attempts to cover their tracks. This meticulous examination of system data is essential for building a comprehensive understanding of the breach and informing remediation efforts.

Malware analysis is a critical component of forensic analysis, especially in incidents involving malicious software or code. Forensic investigators dissect the malware to understand its functionality, capabilities, and objectives. This analysis provides insights into the tactics employed by attackers, whether it be data exfiltration, privilege escalation, or the establishment of persistent access. Understanding the characteristics of the malware enables organizations to enhance their threat intelligence, update security controls, and fortify their defenses against similar threats in the future.

Network forensics is an integral part of post-breach analysis, focusing on the examination of network traffic to identify patterns indicative of malicious activity. By scrutinizing network logs, packet captures, and communication patterns, investigators can trace the lateral movement of attackers, pinpoint compromised systems, and identify command and control infrastructure. Network forensics provides a holistic view of the breach, allowing organizations to understand how attackers navigated the network, communicated with external servers, and exfiltrated data.

User behavior analysis is instrumental in forensic investigations, especially when insider threats or compromised credentials are suspected. By examining user activity logs, authentication records, and access patterns, investigators can identify anomalous behavior that may signify unauthorized access or malicious activity. This analysis extends to privileged accounts and administrators, whose compromised credentials can grant attackers extensive access within the network. Understanding user behavior is crucial for mitigating the risks associated with compromised accounts and preventing similar incidents in the future.

Memory forensics is a specialized area of analysis that focuses on the examination of volatile memory (RAM) to uncover artifacts and indicators of compromise. Memory analysis provides real-time insights into the state of a system during the breach, revealing running processes, open network connections, and injected code. This level of granularity is essential for identifying sophisticated attack techniques, such as fileless malware or memory-resident exploits, which may evade traditional detection methods. Memory forensics contributes to a comprehensive understanding of the breach, enabling organizations to enhance their incident response and detection capabilities.

Hash analysis and file integrity checking are fundamental for verifying the integrity of system files and identifying malicious alterations. Forensic investigators use cryptographic hash functions to generate unique identifiers (hash values) for files and compare them with known good values. Any discrepancies indicate potential tampering or the presence of malicious files. Hash analysis not only aids in identifying compromised files but also in determining the extent of the breach by assessing the integrity of critical system components. This analysis is crucial for ensuring the reliability of forensic findings and supporting legal proceedings that may follow a data breach.

Communication with affected parties and stakeholders is an ethical and legal imperative in the aftermath of a data breach. Forensic investigators play a key role in providing accurate and timely information to organizations, regulatory authorities, and individuals impacted by the breach. Transparent communication about the forensic analysis process, findings, and remediation efforts is essential for maintaining trust, meeting legal obligations, and demonstrating accountability. Effective communication also involves providing guidance to affected parties on protective measures they can take, such as changing passwords or monitoring financial accounts, to mitigate the potential consequences of the breach.

Documentation and reporting are essential elements of forensic analysis, serving both legal and practical purposes. Investigators meticulously document their findings, methodologies, and the forensic analysis process to create a comprehensive forensic report. This report not only aids in legal proceedings, regulatory compliance, and internal reviews but also serves as a valuable resource for organizations to learn from the incident. Detailed documentation enables organizations to refine their cybersecurity practices, update policies and procedures, and implement measures to prevent similar incidents in the future.

Chain of custody is a foundational principle in forensic analysis, ensuring the integrity and admissibility of digital evidence in legal proceedings. Investigators meticulously document the handling, storage, and transfer of evidence, creating a chain of custody that establishes the authenticity and reliability of the forensic findings. Adhering to chain of custody protocols is essential for organizations seeking to leverage forensic evidence in legal proceedings, regulatory inquiries, or internal investigations. This meticulous approach enhances the credibility of the forensic analysis and supports the organization's efforts to hold perpetrators accountable.

Collaboration with law enforcement agencies is a critical aspect of forensic analysis, especially in cases where criminal activity is suspected. Forensic investigators work closely with law enforcement to share findings, provide expertise, and support criminal investigations. This collaboration extends to the exchange of threat intelligence, coordination of response efforts, and, when necessary, the pursuit of legal actions against the perpetrators. Engaging with law enforcement enhances the effectiveness of forensic analysis, contributes to the attribution of cybercriminals, and reinforces the collective effort to combat cybercrime.

Continuous improvement is an intrinsic aspect of forensic analysis, emphasizing the importance of learning from each incident to enhance cybersecurity resilience. Post-incident reviews, debriefings, and lessons learned sessions provide opportunities for organizations to reflect on the forensic analysis process, identify areas for improvement, and update their incident response plans. This iterative approach ensures that organizations evolve their cybersecurity practices based on the insights gained from forensic analysis, adapting to the dynamic and evolving nature of cyber threats.

In conclusion, conducting a thorough forensic analysis after a data breach is a multidimensional and dynamic process that involves technical expertise, legal compliance, ethical considerations, and collaboration with various stakeholders. Forensic investigators play a crucial role in uncovering the details of the breach, identifying the tactics used by attackers, and providing organizations with the insights needed to strengthen their cybersecurity defenses. From the initial isolation of affected systems to the meticulous examination of digital evidence and the collaboration with law enforcement, forensic analysis serves as a cornerstone in the broader effort to understand, respond to, and prevent data breaches in an increasingly interconnected and digital landscape.

The role of digital forensics in identifying the scope and perpetrators.

Digital forensics plays a pivotal role in the aftermath of a cyber incident, serving as a comprehensive investigative process aimed at identifying the scope of the breach and attributing it to specific perpetrators. In the wake of a cyber incident, the immediate objective of digital forensics is to understand the extent of the compromise by systematically examining digital evidence related to the incident. The scope encompasses a wide array of elements, including compromised systems, unauthorized access points, exfiltrated data, and the tactics employed by adversaries. Digital forensic investigators employ a methodical approach to reconstruct the sequence of events, enabling organizations to ascertain the full scope of the incident and make informed decisions regarding remediation efforts.

The identification of the scope begins with the isolation and analysis of affected systems. Digital forensic experts focus on preserving the integrity of potential evidence while gaining insights into the methods used by attackers to gain access and move laterally within the network. By scrutinizing system artifacts, logs, and memory data, investigators can uncover the footprint left by adversaries, identifying compromised systems and the specific tactics employed to infiltrate the organization's digital environment. This meticulous examination allows for a precise delineation of the breach's scope, guiding subsequent investigative efforts.

Network forensics emerges as a critical component in identifying the scope of a cyber incident. Digital forensic experts analyze network traffic, logs, and communication patterns to trace the pathways taken by attackers. This includes understanding how adversaries entered the network, navigated through different segments, and potentially exfiltrated sensitive data. By examining network artifacts and communication protocols, investigators gain insights into the lateral movement of attackers, helping to identify the compromised systems and the pathways through which the breach unfolded. Network forensics provides a panoramic view of the incident, offering a comprehensive understanding of the breach's scope within the organizational infrastructure.

The analysis of digital evidence extends beyond individual systems and network traffic to encompass memory forensics. Examining volatile memory (RAM) allows digital forensic investigators to uncover artifacts and indicators of compromise that may not be present in static data sources. Memory analysis provides real-time insights into the state of a system during the breach, enabling investigators to identify running processes, injected code, and other volatile elements that may signify malicious activity. This level of detail is instrumental in understanding the tactics employed by attackers and contributes to a nuanced comprehension of the breach's scope.

As part of the scope identification process, forensic investigators engage in timeline reconstruction, piecing together the chronological sequence of events that led to the cyber incident. This involves analyzing logs, timestamps, and digital artifacts to create a cohesive timeline of the breach. Timeline reconstruction is crucial for understanding the duration of the incident, the specific activities conducted by attackers at different stages, and the overall timeline of compromise. By establishing a temporal framework, investigators gain a more accurate and contextualized understanding of the scope, facilitating targeted remediation efforts.

Digital forensics also plays a pivotal role in identifying the perpetrators behind a cyber incident. Attribution, or the process of determining the individuals or entities responsible for the breach, is a complex endeavor that relies on a combination of technical analysis, threat intelligence, and sometimes collaboration with law enforcement agencies. Digital forensic experts analyze the tactics, techniques, and procedures (TTPs) employed by attackers to build a profile that may align with known threat actor groups or previously observed cybercriminal behavior. Attribution is a challenging aspect of digital forensics, often requiring a deep understanding of the threat landscape and the ability to correlate technical indicators with broader threat intelligence.

The examination of malware is a fundamental aspect of digital forensics that contributes significantly to identifying the perpetrators. Malware analysis involves dissecting the malicious software used in the attack to understand its functionality, origin, and potential affiliations. Digital forensic experts scrutinize the code, behavior, and characteristics of the malware to glean insights into the motives of the attackers and their methods. This analysis may reveal signatures, patterns, or code similarities that align with known threat actor groups or campaigns, aiding in the attribution process.

Network indicators also play a crucial role in attributing cyber incidents to specific perpetrators. By examining command and control servers, communication protocols, and patterns of network traffic, digital forensic investigators can identify patterns indicative of known threat actors or specific cybercriminal groups. Sophisticated attackers may use infrastructure that has been previously observed in other incidents, providing clues that contribute to the attribution process. Collaboration with threat intelligence providers and law enforcement agencies enhances the capacity to correlate network indicators with broader patterns of cyber threat activity.

The concept of "attribution beyond the code" involves looking beyond the technical aspects of an attack to consider other contextual elements that may aid in identifying the perpetrators. This includes the analysis of motives, geopolitical considerations, and the broader threat landscape. Attribution is not solely a technical challenge; it requires a multidisciplinary approach that considers geopolitical tensions, historical context, and the strategic objectives of potential threat actors. Digital forensic investigators, working in collaboration with threat intelligence analysts and geopolitical experts, can contribute to a holistic understanding of the perpetrators and their motivations.

Collaboration with law enforcement agencies is a key aspect of the attribution process within digital forensics. In cases where criminal activity is suspected, digital forensic experts work closely with law enforcement to share findings, provide expertise, and support legal proceedings. Law enforcement agencies may bring additional resources, investigative powers, and legal frameworks to bear on the attribution process. This collaboration enhances the overall effectiveness of digital forensics in identifying perpetrators and contributes to the pursuit of legal actions against cybercriminals.

False flag operations, in which attackers deliberately disguise their identity or employ deceptive techniques to mislead investigators, pose a challenge to digital forensics in the attribution process. Sophisticated threat actors may intentionally leave false clues, use tools associated with other groups, or manipulate digital evidence to obfuscate their true identity. Detecting and mitigating the impact of false flags requires a nuanced and careful analysis by digital forensic experts who must critically evaluate the evidence, cross-reference findings with threat intelligence, and consider the broader context of the cyber threat landscape.

Ethical and legal considerations are integral to the process of identifying the scope and perpetrators through digital forensics. Forensic investigators must adhere to legal and ethical standards in the collection, analysis, and handling of digital evidence. This includes obtaining proper authorization for accessing systems, preserving the chain of custody for evidence, and respecting individuals' privacy rights. The use of forensic tools and methodologies must align with legal requirements, and investigators must be prepared to testify about their findings in legal proceedings, emphasizing the importance of conducting digital forensics within a framework of legal and ethical guidelines.

In conclusion, digital forensics plays a central and multifaceted role in identifying the scope of a cyber incident and attributing it to specific perpetrators. From the meticulous examination of digital evidence on compromised systems and network traffic to the analysis of malware, timelines, and indicators of compromise, digital forensic experts contribute to a comprehensive understanding of the breach. Attribution, a complex process that involves technical analysis, threat intelligence, and collaboration with law enforcement, is a key objective in identifying the individuals or entities behind the cyber incident. As cyber threats continue to evolve, digital forensics remains an indispensable tool for organizations seeking to respond effectively to incidents, enhance their cybersecurity resilience, and contribute to the broader effort to combat cybercrime.

Compliance requirements following a data breach.

Compliance requirements following a data breach impose a multifaceted set of obligations on organizations, encompassing legal, regulatory, and industry-specific frameworks that guide the response, notification, and mitigation efforts in the aftermath of a security incident. One of the primary legal considerations is adherence to data protection laws, which vary across jurisdictions. The European Union's General Data Protection Regulation (GDPR), for example, mandates that organizations promptly notify the relevant supervisory authority and affected individuals when a data breach occurs, emphasizing transparency and accountability. Failure to comply with GDPR can result in substantial fines, making it imperative for organizations to have robust mechanisms in place to meet these legal obligations.

In the United States, a patchwork of state-level data breach notification laws further complicates compliance requirements. Most states have enacted legislation that requires organizations to notify affected individuals when their personal information is compromised. The timing, content, and method of notification often vary by state, necessitating a comprehensive understanding of the specific legal requirements applicable in each jurisdiction where the affected individuals reside. Federal laws, such as the Health Insurance Portability and Accountability Act (HIPAA) in the healthcare sector, impose additional notification and reporting obligations for breaches involving sensitive information.

Beyond legal obligations, regulatory compliance is a crucial aspect following a data breach. Many industries, such as finance, healthcare, and telecommunications, are subject to sector-specific regulations that mandate cybersecurity measures and breach response protocols. For instance, the Payment Card Industry Data Security Standard (PCI DSS) requires organizations handling payment card data to adhere to stringent security standards and report breaches promptly. The Health Information Portability and Accountability Act (HIPAA) in the healthcare sector mandates specific breach notification requirements for protected health information. Compliance with these industry-specific regulations is integral to maintaining the trust of stakeholders and avoiding regulatory sanctions.

International considerations also come into play, especially for organizations operating across borders. Cross-border data transfer regulations, such as those outlined in GDPR, require organizations to assess the impact of a breach on the personal data of individuals residing in different countries. Compliance with international data protection laws necessitates a global perspective on breach response, ensuring that organizations navigate the intricate landscape of varying legal requirements and cultural considerations.

In addition to legal and regulatory requirements, industry-specific standards and contractual obligations contribute to the complex compliance landscape following a data breach. Adherence to cybersecurity frameworks, such as the National Institute of Standards and Technology (NIST) Cybersecurity Framework or the ISO/IEC

27001 standard, provides organizations with a structured approach to managing the aftermath of a breach. Contractual obligations with partners, vendors, and third-party service providers may include specific provisions related to breach notification, incident response, and cybersecurity measures. Failure to meet these contractual obligations can have legal ramifications and impact the organization's standing in the business ecosystem.

Timely and accurate communication is a fundamental aspect of compliance following a data breach. Organizations must navigate the delicate balance between providing sufficient information to affected individuals and stakeholders while avoiding unnecessary panic or confusion. Clear and transparent communication about the breach, its scope, and the steps being taken to remediate the incident is essential. Compliance requirements often mandate specific content to be included in breach notifications, such as a description of the incident, the types of data affected, and the measures individuals can take to protect themselves. Crafting effective communications that align with legal and regulatory requirements is crucial for maintaining trust and meeting compliance standards.

A comprehensive incident response plan is a cornerstone of compliance requirements following a data breach. Regulatory authorities often expect organizations to have documented and tested incident response plans that outline the steps to be taken when a breach occurs. This includes the identification and isolation of affected systems, the preservation of digital evidence for forensic analysis, and the development of a communication strategy for notifying regulatory bodies, affected individuals, and other stakeholders. Regular testing and updating of incident response plans ensure that organizations remain agile and well-prepared to meet compliance requirements in the dynamic landscape of cybersecurity threats.

Privacy by design and data protection impact assessments are increasingly becoming integral to compliance requirements following a data breach. Organizations are expected to embed privacy considerations into their systems and processes from the outset, ensuring that data protection measures are an inherent part of their operations. Conducting impact assessments helps organizations identify and mitigate privacy risks associated with their data processing activities. In the aftermath of a breach, being able to demonstrate a commitment to privacy by design principles and having conducted thorough impact assessments can positively influence the organization's standing with regulatory authorities.

Post-breach audits and assessments are essential for compliance and provide organizations with insights into the effectiveness of their security measures. Regulatory authorities may require organizations to conduct post-incident reviews to evaluate the breach response, identify areas for improvement, and implement corrective actions. These audits contribute to a continuous improvement cycle, allowing organizations to enhance their cybersecurity posture, address vulnerabilities, and demonstrate a commitment to ongoing compliance with legal and regulatory standards.

Legal considerations also extend to potential litigation following a data breach. Organizations may face lawsuits from affected individuals seeking damages for the exposure of their personal information. Compliance with legal requirements, such as providing timely and accurate breach notifications, can influence the outcome of legal proceedings. Having a legal strategy in place, including engagement with legal counsel and the establishment of attorney-client privilege, is essential for navigating potential legal challenges and meeting compliance obligations in the context of litigation.

Collaboration with regulatory authorities is a key aspect of compliance following a data breach. Many jurisdictions require organizations to engage with supervisory bodies, such as data protection authorities, to report the breach, provide details of the incident, and cooperate in investigations. Open and transparent communication with regulatory authorities is crucial for demonstrating a commitment to compliance and avoiding potential sanctions. Engaging in constructive dialogue with regulators can also provide organizations with valuable insights and guidance on meeting compliance requirements in the aftermath of a breach.

While compliance requirements focus on meeting legal and regulatory obligations, organizations must also consider the broader ethical implications of a data breach. Ethical considerations involve more than just legal compliance; they encompass the organization's responsibility to its stakeholders, including affected individuals, customers, employees, and the broader community. Demonstrating ethical behavior involves going beyond the minimum legal requirements and actively seeking to minimize harm, protect individuals' rights, and contribute to the overall well-being of those impacted by the breach.

In conclusion, compliance requirements following a data breach constitute a multifaceted and evolving landscape that encompasses legal, regulatory, industry-specific, contractual, and ethical considerations. Organizations must navigate this complex terrain with a comprehensive understanding of the specific requirements applicable to their industry and geographic location. Timely and transparent communication, robust incident response plans, adherence to privacy by design principles, and collaboration with regulatory authorities are essential components of meeting compliance obligations in the aftermath of a data breach. A proactive and ethical approach not only helps organizations avoid legal and regulatory consequences but also fosters trust with stakeholders and contributes to a resilient cybersecurity posture in the face of evolving cyber threats.

Potential legal consequences for organizations.

The potential legal consequences for organizations in the wake of a data breach are far-reaching and can have significant implications across various jurisdictions, industries, and legal frameworks.

One of the primary legal consequences is the risk of facing regulatory fines and penalties, particularly in regions with robust data protection laws. The European Union's General Data Protection Regulation (GDPR), for example, empowers supervisory authorities to impose fines of up to 4% of a company's global annual revenue for serious violations, such as failure to promptly report a data breach or insufficient data protection measures. Similar regulatory consequences exist in various countries, reinforcing the importance of organizations aligning their practices with data protection regulations to mitigate legal risks.

Legal action from affected individuals represents another potential consequence for organizations following a data breach. Individuals whose personal information is compromised may pursue legal remedies, including class-action lawsuits seeking damages for financial losses, identity theft, or emotional distress. Courts may award compensation to affected parties, and organizations could face financial liabilities and reputational damage resulting from these legal actions. Crafting a robust legal strategy, engaging with affected individuals transparently, and demonstrating diligent efforts to address the breach are essential components of mitigating the legal consequences associated with private legal actions.

In the United States, state-level data breach notification laws add complexity to the legal landscape, exposing organizations to legal consequences for non-compliance. Failure to adhere to notification requirements or other provisions specified in state laws can result in legal actions brought by state attorneys general, with potential fines and injunctions. The multi-jurisdictional nature of these laws requires organizations to navigate a patchwork of legal requirements, adding layers of complexity to their compliance efforts and legal risk management.

Class-action lawsuits, often initiated by affected individuals or groups of individuals, are a common legal consequence for organizations experiencing a data breach. Plaintiffs may allege negligence, breach of contract, or violations of consumer protection laws, seeking compensation for damages resulting from the breach. The scale and financial impact of class-action lawsuits can be substantial, underscoring the importance of organizations implementing comprehensive cybersecurity measures and incident response plans to reduce the risk of legal consequences stemming from litigation.

Securities litigation is an emerging legal consequence for organizations in the aftermath of a data breach, particularly when the incident has a material impact on the company's financial standing. Shareholders may file lawsuits alleging that the organization failed to adequately disclose cybersecurity risks, leading to financial losses. The evolving landscape of securities laws and regulations requires organizations to consider the potential legal consequences in the context of their disclosure obligations and the impact of a data breach on their financial performance.

Government enforcement actions represent another layer of potential legal consequences for organizations, especially when regulatory authorities deem the breach as a violation of specific laws or regulations. Regulatory agencies, such as the Federal Trade Commission (FTC) in the United States or the Information Commissioner's Office (ICO) in the United Kingdom, may investigate the circumstances surrounding a data breach and take enforcement actions against organizations found to be in violation of privacy and security regulations. These actions can include fines, consent decrees, and ongoing oversight, adding a layer of regulatory scrutiny and potential legal consequences for organizations.

International legal consequences may arise for organizations operating in multiple jurisdictions, particularly if they fail to comply with the data protection laws of the countries where they conduct business. Cross-border data transfer regulations, such as those outlined in GDPR, require organizations to assess the impact of a breach on the personal data of individuals residing in different countries. This introduces the potential for legal consequences from regulatory authorities in multiple jurisdictions, each with its own set of legal standards and enforcement mechanisms.

The contractual repercussions of a data breach are a significant legal consideration for organizations, especially when contracts with partners, vendors, or customers include specific provisions related to data protection and cybersecurity. Breaching these contractual obligations can lead to legal consequences, including financial liabilities, termination of contracts, and reputational damage. Contractual disputes may arise if organizations fail to meet their obligations under service level agreements or other contractual arrangements, resulting in legal actions and potential financial settlements.

Intellectual property concerns can amplify legal consequences following a data breach, especially when proprietary information or trade secrets are compromised. Organizations may face legal actions from competitors or former employees alleging intellectual property theft, unfair competition, or violations of non-disclosure agreements. The legal consequences in such cases may include damages, injunctive relief, and the potential erosion of competitive advantage, emphasizing the need for organizations to safeguard intellectual property and trade secrets as part of their cybersecurity efforts.

Criminal investigations and legal consequences can unfold if a data breach involves criminal activities, such as hacking, fraud, or the theft of sensitive information for illicit purposes. Law enforcement agencies may initiate investigations, leading to legal consequences for individuals or entities involved in the cybercriminal activities. Organizations may become embroiled in legal proceedings as witnesses, victims, or, in some cases, as entities facing charges related to insufficient cybersecurity measures or failure to report the breach promptly.

The potential for legal consequences extends to the realm of consumer protection laws, where organizations may face legal actions and regulatory scrutiny for deceptive practices or inadequate protection of consumer data. Federal and state consumer protection laws empower regulatory authorities to take legal actions against organizations that engage in unfair or deceptive practices related to data security. This includes misrepresentations about the level of security measures in place or failure to fulfill promises made in privacy policies.

Cybersecurity-related legal consequences can manifest in the form of consent decrees, settlement agreements, or other regulatory mandates imposed by supervisory authorities. These legal instruments may require organizations to implement specific remedial measures, undergo regular cybersecurity assessments, or adhere to stringent data protection standards. Non-compliance with these legal requirements can lead to further legal consequences, including additional fines, penalties, or ongoing regulatory oversight.

Reputational damage is a consequential legal consideration for organizations following a data breach, as it can have profound and lasting effects on the business. The erosion of trust among customers, partners, and stakeholders may result in reduced market share, diminished customer loyalty, and negative impacts on the organization's bottom line. Legal consequences stemming from reputational damage may include the costs associated with public relations efforts, marketing campaigns to rebuild trust, and potential financial compensation for affected parties.

In conclusion, the potential legal consequences for organizations following a data breach are diverse, complex, and interconnected. From regulatory fines and private lawsuits to government enforcement actions and reputational damage, the legal landscape is multifaceted and evolving. Organizations must proactively address cybersecurity risks, implement robust data protection measures, and have comprehensive incident response plans in place to minimize the potential legal consequences. Legal compliance, ethical considerations, and a commitment to transparency are essential components of a strategic approach to navigating the legal aftermath of a data breach in an increasingly interconnected and regulated business environment.

Crafting effective communication strategies during and after a data breach.

Crafting effective communication strategies during and after a data breach is a critical aspect of mitigating the impact on an organization's reputation, fostering transparency, and maintaining trust with stakeholders. In the immediate aftermath of a data breach, communication must be prompt, clear, and targeted. Timely notification to affected parties, including customers, employees, and relevant regulatory authorities, is essential. The initial communication should provide a concise overview of the incident, detailing the nature of the breach, the types of data affected, and the organization's response plan. Transparency is paramount, as stakeholders appreciate forthrightness and openness during times of crisis. This early communication sets the tone for the organization's commitment to addressing the breach responsibly.

A well-crafted communication strategy must go beyond the initial notification to encompass ongoing updates and information dissemination throughout the incident response process. Regular updates, even if there are no significant developments, demonstrate the organization's continued commitment to transparency and keeping stakeholders informed. Providing insights into the steps being taken to remediate the breach, enhance cybersecurity measures, and prevent future incidents reassures stakeholders about the organization's dedication to addressing the root causes of the breach. These updates should be tailored to different stakeholder groups, acknowledging their specific concerns and expectations.

Acknowledging responsibility and accountability is a crucial component of effective communication during and after a data breach. Organizations should avoid deflecting blame or downplaying the severity of the incident. Accepting responsibility demonstrates integrity and a commitment to addressing the consequences of the breach. Communicating a clear plan of action, including steps to prevent similar incidents in the future, reinforces the organization's accountability. Legal considerations should be taken into account, and communications should be carefully crafted to balance transparency with the organization's legal obligations and potential litigation risks.

Communication strategies should extend beyond external stakeholders to encompass internal audiences, including employees, executives, and other staff members. Keeping internal stakeholders informed is vital for maintaining a cohesive response to the breach and ensuring that employees are aligned with the organization's communication strategy. Internal communications should provide guidance on how employees should respond to inquiries from external parties, emphasize the importance of data security measures, and foster a sense of unity in addressing the breach. Employees who feel informed and supported can become valuable advocates for the organization during a crisis.

Consideration of the emotional impact on affected parties is a nuanced element of effective communication strategies. Recognizing the potential distress caused by a data breach, especially one involving personal or sensitive information, is essential. Communication should convey empathy, acknowledging the concerns and emotions of those affected. Offering resources and support, such as credit monitoring services or assistance in managing the potential consequences of identity theft, demonstrates the organization's commitment to mitigating the impact on affected individuals. This human-centric approach contributes to rebuilding trust and mitigating reputational damage.

Coordination with external partners, including law enforcement, regulatory authorities, and public relations professionals, is a critical aspect of an effective communication strategy. Collaborating with law enforcement agencies may be necessary for investigations, while engagement with regulatory bodies is often required by data protection laws. Public relations professionals can provide expertise in managing the external perception of the breach and crafting communications that resonate with the media and the public. Coordinated efforts ensure a consistent and well-informed approach to external communications, reducing the risk of conflicting messages or misinterpretations.

Social media plays a prominent role in communication strategies during and after a data breach. Organizations must be proactive in managing their online presence, responding to inquiries, and disseminating accurate information through social media channels. Rapid response to social media conversations, both positive and negative, helps shape the narrative surrounding the breach. Transparent and authentic communication on social media platforms contributes to maintaining credibility and trust with a broad audience. Organizations should also be prepared for potential social media crises and have strategies in place to address misinformation and manage the narrative effectively.

Preparing spokespeople and key representatives for media interactions is a fundamental element of communication strategies during a data breach. Designated spokespeople should undergo media training to ensure they can effectively convey the organization's key messages, respond to challenging questions, and project a calm and composed demeanor. Consistency in messaging across different communication channels and spokespersons is crucial for building credibility. Organizations should anticipate the types of questions likely to arise from the media and have well-prepared responses that align with the broader communication strategy.

Legal considerations are integral to communication strategies during and after a data breach. Organizations must strike a balance between transparency and legal obligations, considering the potential impact on ongoing investigations, litigation risks, and regulatory compliance. Legal counsel should be involved in shaping communication strategies to ensure that statements do not inadvertently compromise the organization's legal position. Confidentiality and privilege should be maintained where appropriate, and communications should be aligned with any legal constraints imposed by data protection laws or other relevant regulations.

Post-incident communication is a vital component of a comprehensive communication strategy, focusing on rebuilding trust, providing updates on remediation efforts, and reinforcing the organization's commitment to cybersecurity. Organizations should communicate the lessons learned from the incident, the measures implemented to enhance security, and the steps taken to prevent a recurrence. Transparent reporting on the outcomes of any internal investigations or audits contributes to rebuilding confidence among stakeholders. Continuous engagement with affected parties and other stakeholders through follow-up communications reinforces the organization's dedication to accountability and ongoing improvement.

Long-term communication strategies should extend beyond the immediate aftermath of a data breach to encompass efforts to rebuild the organization's reputation and strengthen relationships with stakeholders. Organizations should consider proactive communication initiatives, such as cybersecurity awareness campaigns, demonstrating their commitment to data protection, and showcasing the implementation of enhanced security measures. Building a narrative around the organization's resilience, lessons learned, and commitment to continuous improvement contributes to the long-term success of communication strategies in the aftermath of a data breach.

In conclusion, crafting effective communication strategies during and after a data breach is a multifaceted and dynamic process that requires a combination of transparency, accountability, and empathy. Timely and targeted communication, both internally and externally, contributes to maintaining trust, mitigating reputational damage, and fostering a positive perception of the organization's response to the breach. Collaboration with internal and external partners, careful consideration of legal implications, and ongoing engagement with affected parties are essential components of a communication strategy that aligns with the organization's values and contributes to its resilience in the face of cybersecurity challenges.

Managing public relations and reputation damage.

Managing public relations and reputation damage is a complex and nuanced process, especially in the aftermath of events like a data breach, crisis, or other adverse situations that can significantly impact an organization's standing in the eyes of the public. Effective reputation management involves a combination of strategic communication, transparency, proactive engagement, and a commitment to rebuilding trust.

When faced with a crisis that has the potential to harm an organization's reputation, the first step in managing public relations is to establish a crisis communication plan. This plan should outline key messaging, designate spokespersons, and provide guidance on communication channels. A rapid and well-coordinated response is crucial to mitigate the initial impact of the crisis and to demonstrate to the public that the organization is taking the situation seriously.

Transparency is a cornerstone of effective reputation management. In the context of a data breach or other crisis, being transparent about the incident, its causes, and the steps being taken to address it is essential. Hiding information or downplaying the severity of the situation can erode trust further. Acknowledging mistakes, taking responsibility, and providing a clear plan for remediation are critical elements of transparent communication.

Engaging with the media is a key aspect of managing public relations during a crisis. Establishing open lines of communication with journalists and being proactive in sharing information can help shape the narrative surrounding the incident. Organizations should aim to control the messaging by providing accurate and timely information, addressing concerns, and emphasizing the steps being taken to prevent a recurrence.

Selecting the right spokesperson is crucial in managing public relations effectively. The spokesperson should be someone with credibility, authority, and the ability to convey empathy and assurance. Media training is essential to ensure that the spokesperson can navigate challenging questions, stay on message, and project a calm and composed demeanor, especially during high-pressure situations.

Social media has become a powerful tool in public relations, and its role is even more pronounced during a crisis. Organizations must actively manage their social media presence, respond to inquiries promptly, and use these platforms to disseminate accurate information. Monitoring social media conversations allows organizations to gauge public sentiment, identify concerns, and address issues in real-time.

In addition to external communication, internal communication is equally important in managing public relations. Employees are often considered ambassadors of an organization, and their understanding of the situation, alignment with key messages, and morale can impact external perceptions. Keeping employees informed, addressing their concerns, and fostering a sense of unity can contribute positively to an organization's public image.

Reputation repair requires not only addressing the immediate crisis but also implementing long-term strategies to rebuild trust.

This involves demonstrating sustained commitment to corrective actions, improvements, and ethical practices. Communicating these efforts transparently helps stakeholders understand that the organization is taking concrete steps to prevent future issues.

Seeking external expertise, such as public relations consultants or crisis management professionals, can provide valuable insights and guidance in managing reputation damage. These professionals bring experience, objectivity, and a strategic perspective to the table, helping organizations navigate the complexities of public relations during and after a crisis. Collaboration with external experts can enhance the effectiveness of communication strategies and reputation management efforts.

Proactive engagement with stakeholders is a critical component of reputation management. Organizations should not wait for a crisis to engage with their audience. Building positive relationships with customers, partners, and the community beforehand creates a reservoir of goodwill that can be crucial during challenging times. Regularly communicating the organization's values, commitment to ethical practices, and community engagement initiatives contributes to a positive public perception.

Monitoring and analyzing media coverage and public sentiment is an ongoing process in reputation management. Organizations should use tools and metrics to assess the impact of their communication efforts, identify areas that require attention, and adjust their strategies accordingly. Regularly evaluating the effectiveness of communication initiatives helps organizations stay agile and responsive in managing reputation damage.

Crisis simulations and scenario planning are valuable exercises in preparing for reputation management challenges. By simulating potential crises and practicing communication responses, organizations can identify gaps, refine their strategies, and ensure that key stakeholders are prepared to respond effectively during an actual crisis. These simulations contribute to organizational readiness and resilience in the face of unexpected events.

Legal considerations are integral to reputation management, particularly in sensitive situations such as a data breach. Organizations must work closely with legal counsel to ensure that their communication strategies align with legal requirements, protect against potential liabilities, and adhere to regulations. Balancing transparency with legal constraints requires a nuanced approach to communication during a crisis.

Rebuilding trust is a gradual process that requires consistency and sustained effort. Organizations must demonstrate over time that they have learned from the crisis, implemented meaningful changes, and are committed to ethical practices. This may involve ongoing communication about the progress of remediation efforts, transparency about challenges faced, and a genuine commitment to continuous improvement.

In some cases, organizations may choose to offer reparations or restitution as part of their reputation management strategy. This could involve compensating affected parties, implementing enhanced security measures, or taking other tangible steps to address the impact of the crisis. Offering reparations can be a proactive way to demonstrate accountability and a commitment to making amends.

Stakeholder engagement should extend beyond communication during a crisis to involve ongoing efforts to understand and address the concerns of various stakeholders. This could include conducting surveys, holding focus groups, and actively seeking feedback. Incorporating stakeholder perspectives into decision-making processes demonstrates a commitment to inclusivity and responsiveness.

Media monitoring tools and sentiment analysis can provide valuable insights into public perception and help organizations gauge the effectiveness of their reputation management efforts. By monitoring

media coverage, social media conversations, and other online channels, organizations can identify trends, sentiment shifts, and areas
that may require additional attention. These insights inform adaptive
strategies for reputation management.

In conclusion, managing public relations and reputation damage
is a multifaceted and ongoing process that requires a combination
of strategic communication, transparency, and a commitment to rebuilding trust. From the initial response to a crisis to the long-term
efforts of reputation repair, organizations must navigate a complex
landscape that includes media engagement, internal communication,
legal considerations, and proactive stakeholder engagement. By
adopting a comprehensive and proactive approach, organizations
can not only weather crises effectively but also emerge stronger and
more resilient in the eyes of the public.

Chapter 5: The Human Factor: Psychology in Cybersecurity

The role of human behavior in cybersecurity.

The role of human behavior in cybersecurity is a multifaceted and critical aspect of the broader landscape of digital security. Understanding how individuals interact with technology, make decisions, and respond to various cyber threats is fundamental to developing effective cybersecurity strategies. Human behavior can be both an asset and a vulnerability, influencing the success or failure of cybersecurity measures.

At the core of human behavior in cybersecurity is the concept of the "human factor." Individuals, whether employees in an organization or end-users accessing digital systems, play a central role in shaping the security posture of an environment. One prominent aspect is the psychology of cybersecurity, delving into cognitive processes, decision-making mechanisms, and the psychological factors that influence how people perceive and respond to security risks.

Human susceptibility to social engineering attacks is a significant manifestation of the human factor in cybersecurity. Social engineering exploits psychological vulnerabilities to manipulate individuals into divulging sensitive information, clicking on malicious links, or taking actions that compromise security. Techniques such as phishing, where attackers impersonate trustworthy entities to deceive individuals, leverage psychological triggers like urgency or fear to exploit human behavior.

The interplay between human behavior and technology is evident in the realm of password security. Despite the prevalence of cybersecurity awareness programs, individuals often exhibit poor password practices due to factors such as the difficulty of remembering complex passwords or a tendency to reuse passwords across multiple accounts. Understanding the challenges individuals face in managing and securing their credentials is essential for developing user-friendly yet robust authentication mechanisms.

The workplace environment introduces another dimension to the role of human behavior in cybersecurity. Employees are both assets and potential liabilities to an organization's security posture. Insider threats, whether intentional or unintentional, can arise from employees' actions, highlighting the importance of fostering a security-aware culture within organizations. Human-centric security training programs, emphasizing the risks and best practices, aim to equip employees with the knowledge and skills to make security-conscious decisions.

The concept of the "weakest link" underscores the impact of individual behavior on overall cybersecurity. A single individual falling victim to a phishing attack or engaging in risky online behavior can create a breach point that adversaries exploit. Organizations recognize the need to strengthen this link through continuous education, awareness campaigns, and measures that empower individuals to act as vigilant defenders against cyber threats.

The rise of remote work has introduced new dynamics to the role of human behavior in cybersecurity. Individuals accessing corporate networks and sensitive data from diverse locations and devices present additional challenges. Balancing the flexibility of remote work with the need for robust security requires addressing human factors such as awareness of potential threats in different environments, securing home networks, and adapting cybersecurity policies to the evolving work landscape.

Behavioral economics provides insights into the decision-making processes related to cybersecurity. Individuals may exhibit irrational behaviors, such as neglecting security measures due to a perceived inconvenience or underestimating the severity of potential risks. Behavioral economics principles, including nudges and incentives, can be leveraged to guide individuals toward more secure practices by aligning security measures with perceived benefits and addressing cognitive biases.

The concept of the "security paradox" reflects the tension between the desire for convenience and the necessity of security. Human behavior often seeks the path of least resistance, favoring convenience over stringent security measures. Striking a balance between usability and security is a persistent challenge, requiring innovative solutions that align with human behavior while maintaining robust cybersecurity protocols.

The proliferation of personal devices in the digital age amplifies the impact of individual behavior on cybersecurity. Bring Your Own Device (BYOD) policies introduce complexities, as personal devices may lack the same security controls as corporate assets. The challenge lies in harmonizing individual preferences for device flexibility with organizational security requirements, recognizing that human behavior influences the use and security of personal devices.

Cybersecurity fatigue is a phenomenon wherein individuals, bombarded by constant security warnings and measures, become desensitized and less motivated to adhere to security practices. Understanding the factors contributing to cybersecurity fatigue, such as information overload and the perceived inconvenience of security measures, is essential for designing interventions that maintain individuals' engagement with security protocols.

The intersection of human behavior and emerging technologies, such as artificial intelligence (AI) and the Internet of Things (IoT), introduces new dimensions to cybersecurity challenges. AI-driven attacks that exploit human vulnerabilities, as well as the potential for IoT devices to be manipulated by adversaries, underscore the evolving nature of the human factor in the cybersecurity landscape. Addressing these challenges requires a holistic approach that considers both technological advancements and the intricacies of human behavior.

Cultural aspects also play a role in shaping human behavior in cybersecurity. Different cultures may have distinct attitudes toward privacy, information sharing, and perceptions of security risks. Recognizing cultural nuances is vital for developing global cybersecurity strategies that resonate with diverse populations and foster a collective commitment to security practices.

Behavioral analytics, a branch of cybersecurity that leverages machine learning to analyze patterns of human behavior, has emerged as a proactive defense mechanism. By understanding normal user behavior, organizations can detect anomalies that may indicate malicious activities. Behavioral analytics complement traditional security measures by providing insights into deviations from established patterns, enabling early detection and response to potential threats.

The role of leadership in shaping organizational culture and influencing human behavior in cybersecurity cannot be overstated. Leadership commitment to cybersecurity, the establishment of clear policies, and the promotion of a security-first mindset contribute to creating a culture where individuals prioritize cybersecurity in their daily activities. Leadership-driven initiatives, coupled with ongoing education, reinforce the organization's resilience against evolving cyber threats.

Ethical considerations also come into play when examining the role of human behavior in cybersecurity. Individuals may face ethical dilemmas related to the use of cybersecurity tools, reporting vulnerabilities, or engaging in practices that impact privacy. Cultivating an ethical framework within organizations encourages responsible behavior and aligns individual actions with broader ethical standards in the cybersecurity domain.

In conclusion, the role of human behavior in cybersecurity is a dynamic and pervasive element that significantly influences the effectiveness of security measures. Recognizing the intricacies of human decision-making, cognitive biases, and the impact of cultural and organizational factors is essential for designing cybersecurity strategies that align with, rather than contradict, human behavior. By fostering a security-aware culture, leveraging behavioral insights, and integrating human-centric approaches, organizations can enhance their cybersecurity resilience and empower individuals to play an active role in safeguarding digital assets against evolving cyber threats.

Cognitive biases and decision-making in the context of cyber threats.

Cognitive biases and decision-making play a pivotal role in the context of cyber threats, shaping how individuals perceive, assess, and respond to security risks in the digital realm. Understanding the intricate interplay between cognitive biases and decision-making processes is crucial for developing effective cybersecurity strategies that account for the human factor.

Anchoring bias, a cognitive bias where individuals rely too heavily on the first piece of information encountered (the "anchor") when making decisions, can influence cybersecurity perceptions. In the context of cyber threats, if an individual's initial exposure is to a seemingly benign email, they may anchor their perception of subsequent emails, potentially overlooking indicators of phishing or malicious intent. Anchoring biases can lead to a false sense of security, emphasizing the importance of cybersecurity education to help individuals recognize and reassess their anchors in the digital landscape.

Overconfidence bias poses a significant challenge in cybersecurity decision-making, as individuals tend to overestimate their ability to discern and respond to cyber threats accurately. This bias can manifest in various contexts, such as employees believing they are immune to falling for phishing attacks or individuals underestimating the complexity of password security. Addressing overconfidence requires a combination of awareness training, realistic threat simulations, and continuous reinforcement of the dynamic nature of cyber threats.

Confirmation bias, the tendency to interpret information in a way that confirms preexisting beliefs, is particularly relevant in the context of cybersecurity. Individuals may overlook warning signs or dismiss cybersecurity alerts that contradict their existing perceptions of digital security. Recognizing and mitigating confirmation bias involves fostering a culture of open-mindedness, where individuals are encouraged to critically evaluate information and consider alternative perspectives in the realm of cyber threats.

Availability bias, wherein individuals rely on readily available information rather than seeking out comprehensive and accurate data, can impact cybersecurity decision-making. If an individual has encountered a recent cyber threat, they may disproportionately weigh the likelihood of similar threats occurring again. Addressing availability bias involves promoting a broader understanding of the cyber threat landscape, emphasizing the diversity of potential threats, and encouraging individuals to seek out updated and comprehensive information.

The optimism bias, characterized by individuals underestimating their susceptibility to negative events, is a pertinent cognitive bias in cybersecurity. Users may believe that cyber threats are unlikely to target them specifically, leading to lax security practices. Mitigating the optimism bias involves highlighting real-world examples of cyber threats affecting individuals similar to the target audience, fostering a sense of relatability and a more accurate perception of personal risk.

The bandwagon effect, where individuals align their beliefs or behaviors with those of a larger group, can impact cybersecurity decision-making in organizational settings. If employees perceive a lack of concern or adherence to security practices among their peers, they may be more inclined to follow suit, leading to a collective vulnerability. Combatting the bandwagon effect involves establishing a cybersecurity culture that prioritizes shared responsibility, emphasizing the collective impact of individual actions on overall security.

Loss aversion, the tendency to prefer avoiding losses rather than acquiring equivalent gains, can influence decision-making regarding cybersecurity measures. Individuals may resist adopting new security protocols or technologies if they perceive potential inconvenience or loss of convenience. Overcoming loss aversion involves framing cybersecurity practices as a gain in protection rather than a loss of convenience, coupled with clear communication about the potential risks of not adopting secure practices.

The framing effect, where the presentation of information influences decision-making, is pertinent in cybersecurity communication. How security risks are framed—whether as potential losses or gains—can impact how individuals perceive and respond to threats. Effective communication strategies involve framing cybersecurity messages in a way that resonates with the audience, emphasizing the positive outcomes of secure behavior and the potential consequences of neglecting security measures.

Trust biases, including authority bias and familiarity bias, can significantly influence individuals' decisions in the context of cyber threats. Authority bias leads individuals to trust information or requests from perceived authoritative figures, making them susceptible to impersonation attacks. Familiarity bias can result in individuals trusting seemingly familiar entities without proper verification. Addressing trust biases involves enhancing digital literacy, teaching individuals to verify the authenticity of communication, and instilling a healthy skepticism toward unsolicited requests.

Time discounting, the tendency to undervalue future rewards or penalties in favor of immediate gratification, poses challenges in maintaining long-term cybersecurity practices. Individuals may prioritize convenience in the present over the potential risks of compromised security in the future. Strategies to mitigate time discounting involve emphasizing the long-term benefits of sustained cybersecurity practices, including protection against evolving threats and potential financial and reputational consequences.

Decision fatigue, the deteriorating quality of decisions after a prolonged period of decision-making, can impact cybersecurity in the context of repeated security-related choices. Users may become fatigued with constant security prompts, leading to hasty or negligent decisions. To counter decision fatigue, cybersecurity measures should prioritize simplicity, automation, and the reduction of unnecessary decision points, allowing individuals to focus on critical choices without succumbing to fatigue.

The Dunning-Kruger effect, a cognitive bias wherein individuals with low ability at a task overestimate their ability, can influence cybersecurity decision-making. Individuals with limited cybersecurity knowledge may overestimate their proficiency, leading to potentially risky behaviors. Addressing the Dunning-Kruger effect requires tailored education programs, self-assessment tools, and ongoing training to help individuals accurately gauge their cybersecurity knowledge and skills.

Social conformity, the tendency to conform to social norms or group expectations, is a relevant factor in organizational cybersecurity culture. Employees may adopt security practices or behaviors prevalent in their social or professional circles, impacting the overall security posture. Fostering a positive cybersecurity culture involves promoting best practices, encouraging shared responsibility, and highlighting the benefits of adherence to security norms.

Cognitive biases in decision-making extend to the realm of password security, where individuals may exhibit behaviors influenced by biases such as the familiarity bias, overconfidence bias, or optimism bias. Users may choose easily guessable passwords, reuse passwords across multiple accounts, or underestimate the likelihood of their credentials being compromised. Password security strategies should consider these biases, incorporating user-friendly yet robust authentication mechanisms and emphasizing the importance of secure password practices.

In conclusion, cognitive biases and decision-making significantly influence how individuals navigate the complex landscape of cyber threats. Addressing these biases requires a multifaceted approach that combines cybersecurity education, behavioral insights, and the integration of human-centric strategies into cybersecurity measures. By recognizing the impact of cognitive biases, organizations can develop more effective and tailored approaches to cybersecurity, empowering individuals to make informed decisions and contribute to a more resilient digital environment.

Definition and examples of social engineering attacks.

Social engineering attacks constitute a sophisticated category of cyber threats that exploit human psychology rather than technological vulnerabilities. These attacks manipulate individuals into divulging sensitive information, performing actions that compromise security, or granting unauthorized access. Understanding the definition and various examples of social engineering attacks is crucial for developing effective cybersecurity strategies.

One prevalent form of social engineering attack is phishing, where attackers employ deceptive emails, messages, or websites to trick individuals into disclosing confidential information such as usernames, passwords, or financial details. Phishing often involves impersonating trustworthy entities, such as banks or reputable organizations, and creating a sense of urgency or fear to prompt immediate action. The success of phishing attacks hinges on exploiting human curiosity, trust, and the willingness to comply with seemingly legitimate requests.

Pretexting is another form of social engineering that involves creating a fabricated scenario to elicit specific information or actions from individuals. Attackers assume a false identity or pretext, such as a co-worker, IT support, or a service provider, and use this guise to manipulate individuals into sharing sensitive information or performing tasks that facilitate unauthorized access. Pretexting relies on social engineering techniques such as building rapport, creating a sense of urgency, or exploiting a perceived authority figure.

Baiting leverages individuals' curiosity or desire for gain by offering something enticing, such as a free download, software, or a physical device like a USB drive. Unsuspecting individuals who take the bait unknowingly introduce malware into their systems, compromising security. Baiting exploits human tendencies to seek rewards or succumb to curiosity, highlighting the psychological aspect of social engineering attacks.

Quid pro quo attacks involve the exchange of something valuable in return for information or actions from the target. For instance, an attacker posing as technical support may offer assistance or a service in exchange for login credentials or access to sensitive data. Quid pro quo attacks exploit individuals' willingness to reciprocate favors or accept assistance, ultimately compromising security in the process.

Impersonation, or identity deception, is a social engineering tactic where attackers pose as someone the target knows and trusts. This can involve impersonating a colleague, supervisor, friend, or family member to manipulate the target into revealing sensitive information or performing actions that compromise security. Impersonation relies on exploiting familiarity and trust to create a false sense of security.

Tailgating, also known as piggybacking, involves an attacker physically following an authorized person into a secured area without proper authentication. By blending in with legitimate personnel, the attacker gains unauthorized access to restricted locations. Tailgating exploits the human inclination to be courteous or helpful, allowing attackers to bypass security measures by appearing as if they belong.

Similarly, shoulder surfing is a social engineering technique where attackers observe or capture sensitive information, such as passwords or PINs, by directly looking over the shoulder of an individual entering the information. This type of attack preys on the lack of privacy in public spaces, relying on the vulnerability of individuals who may not shield their input or take precautions against visual eavesdropping.

Pharming is a social engineering attack that involves redirecting website traffic from a legitimate site to a fraudulent one without the user's knowledge. Attackers manipulate the Domain Name System (DNS) or use malware to alter the website's IP address, leading users to believe they are interacting with a legitimate site when, in reality, they are providing sensitive information to malicious actors. Pharming exploits trust in familiar online interfaces and the assumption that website URLs accurately represent their intended destinations.

A more sophisticated form of social engineering is known as spear phishing, which targets specific individuals or organizations. Spear phishing involves customizing deceptive communications to appear highly personalized and relevant to the target, increasing the likelihood of success. Attackers often research their targets extensively to craft convincing messages, combining elements of familiarity and urgency to manipulate recipients into taking specific actions or divulging sensitive information.

Vishing, or voice phishing, is a social engineering attack conducted over the phone. Attackers use voice communication to impersonate legitimate entities, such as banks or government agencies, and manipulate individuals into providing sensitive information or performing actions that compromise security. Vishing relies on the persuasive power of spoken communication and the trust associated with official-sounding voices.

A related technique is smishing, which involves using SMS (Short Message Service) or text messages to deceive individuals. Attackers send fraudulent messages containing links or instructions, often posing as reputable organizations or trusted contacts. Individuals who interact with these messages may unknowingly download malware onto their devices or provide sensitive information. Smishing exploits the immediacy and perceived informality of text messaging.

Watering hole attacks are social engineering tactics that involve compromising websites frequented by a specific target audience. Attackers identify websites regularly visited by their targets and inject them with malware or malicious code. When individuals from the target audience access these compromised sites, they unknowingly download malware onto their devices. Watering hole attacks exploit the trust associated with familiar online environments.

The human element in social engineering attacks is evident in the manipulation of emotions, particularly fear and urgency. Threat actors often capitalize on individuals' fears or anxieties, creating scenarios that induce panic and compel immediate action. This emotional manipulation is a powerful tool in social engineering, as individuals may overlook typical cautionary measures when driven by fear or a sense of urgency.

Social engineering attacks can also exploit the dynamics of authority and hierarchy within organizations. Attackers may pose as executives, IT personnel, or other figures of authority to manipulate employees into providing sensitive information or taking actions that compromise security. The implicit trust placed in authority figures can be leveraged to bypass security protocols and gain unauthorized access.

In conclusion, social engineering attacks represent a sophisticated category of cyber threats that manipulate human psychology to achieve malicious objectives. From phishing and pretexting to baiting and impersonation, these attacks exploit various cognitive biases, emotions, and social dynamics to compromise security. Understanding the diverse forms of social engineering is essential for individuals and organizations to implement effective cybersecurity measures, including awareness training, robust authentication processes, and a culture of vigilance against deceptive tactics.

Recognizing and mitigating the impact of social engineering.

Recognizing and mitigating the impact of social engineering attacks is paramount in the ongoing battle against cyber threats that exploit human vulnerabilities. The first line of defense involves cultivating a culture of cybersecurity awareness within organizations and among individuals. Recognizing the signs of social engineering requires education on the various tactics employed by attackers, such as phishing, pretexting, and impersonation. By fostering a vigilant mindset, individuals become more adept at identifying suspicious communications, requests, or unexpected scenarios that may indicate a social engineering attempt.

Mitigating the impact of social engineering begins with robust cybersecurity training programs that empower individuals to make informed decisions and recognize potential threats. Training should encompass real-world examples, simulations, and practical guidance on how to verify the legitimacy of requests or communications. Regular, ongoing training ensures that individuals remain vigilant in the face of evolving social engineering tactics and reinforces a culture of collective responsibility for cybersecurity.

Email security plays a pivotal role in recognizing and mitigating the impact of social engineering, as phishing remains one of the most prevalent tactics. Implementing advanced email filtering systems that analyze sender behavior, content, and links helps detect and filter out malicious emails. Additionally, organizations should encourage the use of email authentication protocols like DMARC (Domain-based Message Authentication, Reporting, and Conformance) to prevent email spoofing and enhance the trustworthiness of incoming messages.

Multi-factor authentication (MFA) is a powerful tool in mitigating the impact of social engineering by adding an extra layer of verification beyond passwords. Even if attackers manage to obtain login credentials through social engineering tactics, MFA acts as a barrier, requiring additional authentication steps. This significantly reduces the risk of unauthorized access even in the event of successful phishing or credential theft attempts.

Implementing a comprehensive and adaptive cybersecurity policy is essential for mitigating the impact of social engineering. This includes regular security audits, risk assessments, and the establishment of clear guidelines for handling sensitive information. Policies should cover secure communication practices, data handling procedures, and the reporting mechanisms for suspected social engineering incidents. Creating a security-centric environment reinforces the importance of adhering to established protocols and raises the overall cybersecurity posture.

Endpoint security solutions play a critical role in recognizing and mitigating the impact of social engineering attacks that target individual devices. Endpoint protection should include robust antivirus software, intrusion detection/prevention systems, and behavioral analysis tools. These solutions can identify and block malicious activities, such as the installation of malware or the exfiltration of sensitive data, even when initiated through deceptive social engineering tactics.

Regularly updating and patching software and systems is a fundamental practice for mitigating the impact of social engineering. Attackers often exploit vulnerabilities in outdated software to deliver malware or gain unauthorized access. By maintaining up-to-date systems, organizations reduce the attack surface and enhance their resilience against social engineering attempts that leverage known vulnerabilities.

User awareness and education programs are central to recognizing and mitigating the impact of social engineering. Beyond initial training, organizations should conduct simulated phishing exercises to test and reinforce users' ability to discern phishing attempts. These simulations provide valuable insights into the organization's susceptibility to social engineering and help identify areas for improvement in user awareness and response.

Establishing a robust incident response plan is crucial for mitigating the impact of successful social engineering attacks. A well-defined plan outlines the steps to be taken in the event of a security incident, including the identification, containment, eradication, recovery, and lessons learned. Timely and coordinated responses can minimize the damage caused by social engineering attacks and facilitate the restoration of normal operations.

Collaboration and information sharing within the cybersecurity community contribute to recognizing and mitigating the impact of social engineering. Sharing threat intelligence, indicators of compromise, and lessons learned from social engineering incidents helps organizations stay ahead of emerging tactics and adapt their defenses accordingly. Participating in industry-specific information-sharing platforms and leveraging threat intelligence feeds enhance the collective ability to recognize and respond to social engineering threats.

Security awareness should extend beyond employees to include customers, partners, and other stakeholders. Organizations can play a proactive role in educating their user base about potential social engineering risks, providing guidance on secure practices, and fostering a collective commitment to cybersecurity. This broader approach strengthens the overall resilience of the ecosystem in which an organization operates.

Advanced security technologies, such as artificial intelligence (AI) and machine learning (ML), can significantly contribute to recognizing and mitigating the impact of social engineering. These technologies can analyze vast amounts of data to detect patterns, anomalies, and suspicious behaviors indicative of social engineering attempts. AI-driven solutions enhance the speed and accuracy of threat detection, enabling organizations to respond swiftly to emerging social engineering threats.

Regularly conducting security assessments, including penetration testing and vulnerability scanning, helps organizations identify and address potential weaknesses that could be exploited through social engineering. These assessments simulate real-world attack scenarios, allowing organizations to evaluate their defenses, identify gaps, and implement corrective measures to mitigate the impact of social engineering attacks.

Employee empowerment through reporting mechanisms is crucial for recognizing and mitigating the impact of social engineering. Establishing clear channels for reporting suspicious activities or potential social engineering attempts encourages a proactive approach to cybersecurity. Organizations should create a non-punitive reporting culture, ensuring that individuals feel comfortable reporting incidents without fear of reprisal.

In-depth analysis of social engineering incidents, including post-incident forensics, provides valuable insights into the tactics, techniques, and procedures employed by attackers. Understanding the specifics of how social engineering attacks unfold enables organizations to refine their defenses, update policies, and enhance training programs to address the evolving nature of these threats.

Legal and regulatory compliance measures contribute to recognizing and mitigating the impact of social engineering. Compliance frameworks often include requirements for safeguarding sensitive information, implementing security controls, and reporting security incidents. By aligning with applicable regulations, organizations establish a baseline for cybersecurity practices and demonstrate a commitment to protecting sensitive data from social engineering threats.

Continuous monitoring of network and user activities is essential for recognizing and mitigating the impact of social engineering attacks in real time. Anomalies, unusual patterns of behavior, or unauthorized access attempts may indicate ongoing social engineering campaigns. Implementing security information and event management (SIEM) solutions, along with behavior analytics, enhances the ability to detect and respond to social engineering incidents promptly.

Establishing partnerships with cybersecurity experts and consulting firms can provide organizations with specialized knowledge and resources for recognizing and mitigating the impact of social engineering. Collaborating with external experts allows organizations to benefit from industry best practices, receive tailored guidance, and access cutting-edge solutions to bolster their defenses against social engineering threats.

In conclusion, recognizing and mitigating the impact of social engineering require a multifaceted and proactive approach that encompasses technology, education, policies, and collaboration. By fostering a culture of cybersecurity awareness, implementing robust technical defenses, and staying informed about emerging threats, organizations can significantly enhance their resilience against social engineering attacks. Continuous adaptation, education, and collaboration form the foundation for a comprehensive defense strategy that effectively mitigates the impact of social engineering in an ever-evolving cybersecurity landscape.

Examining the tactics used in phishing and spear phishing attacks.

Examining the tactics used in phishing and spear phishing attacks unveils a sophisticated landscape of deceptive strategies employed by cybercriminals to exploit human vulnerabilities. Phishing, a broad term encompassing a range of deceptive techniques, typically involves the use of fraudulent communication to trick individuals into divulging sensitive information, clicking on malicious links, or taking actions that compromise security. One prevalent tactic in phishing attacks is email spoofing, where attackers manipulate the sender's information to make an email appear as though it originates from a trustworthy source. By impersonating reputable entities, such as banks or government agencies, attackers aim to deceive recipients into trusting the authenticity of the communication.

Moreover, phishing attacks often leverage social engineering tactics to manipulate emotions and induce a sense of urgency or fear. Attackers craft messages that convey a critical situation, such as a compromised account or an impending financial loss, prompting recipients to act hastily without verifying the legitimacy of the communication. This psychological manipulation plays on individuals' instincts to respond promptly to perceived threats, making them more susceptible to phishing attempts.

Another common tactic in phishing attacks is the use of malicious attachments or links. Attackers embed malware in attachments or provide links to compromised websites that, when clicked, lead to the download and execution of malicious payloads. These payloads may include ransomware, keyloggers, or other types of malware designed to compromise the security of the victim's device. Phishing emails often employ enticing language or urgent calls to action to encourage recipients to open attachments or click on links without proper scrutiny.

Spear phishing, a more targeted and personalized form of phishing, involves tailoring deceptive communications to a specific individual, organization, or group. Attackers invest time in researching their targets to create messages that appear highly relevant and convincing. One tactic employed in spear phishing is reconnaissance, where attackers gather information about the target, such as their role in the organization, relationships, and recent activities. This information is then used to craft personalized messages that exploit the target's context, making the phishing attempt more convincing.

Another tactic in spear phishing involves the use of pretexting, where attackers create a fabricated scenario to establish credibility and manipulate the target into divulging sensitive information. This could involve posing as a colleague, supervisor, or trusted entity to request information or initiate actions that compromise security. By leveraging context-specific details and a pretext that aligns with the target's expectations, attackers increase the likelihood of success in spear phishing attacks.

Spear phishing attacks often exploit trusted relationships within an organization. Attackers may compromise the email account of a trusted colleague or executive and use it to send seemingly legitimate messages to other employees. This tactic leverages the inherent trust individuals place in familiar contacts, making them more likely to follow through with requests or provide sensitive information without suspicion.

Impersonation is a key tactic in both phishing and spear phishing attacks. Attackers may impersonate executives, IT personnel, or other authoritative figures to manipulate individuals into complying with requests or divulging confidential information. By exploiting the perceived authority of these figures, attackers enhance the credibility of their messages and increase the chances of successful phishing attempts.

URL manipulation is a prevalent tactic in both types of phishing attacks. Attackers often create deceptive URLs that closely resemble legitimate websites, tricking individuals into entering sensitive information. This tactic, known as domain spoofing, involves using slight variations in the URL or employing subdomains to mimic authentic sites. In spear phishing, attackers may tailor the deceptive URLs to match the target's expectations, such as posing as a corporate intranet or a commonly used login portal.

Credential harvesting is a primary goal in phishing and spear phishing attacks. Attackers design deceptive login pages or forms that mimic legitimate ones, tricking individuals into entering their usernames and passwords. These harvested credentials can be used for various malicious purposes, including unauthorized access to accounts, identity theft, or further exploitation within an organization's network. Phishing attacks may cast a wide net to collect a large volume of credentials, while spear phishing focuses on obtaining specific individuals' login information.

Clone phishing is a tactic in which attackers create replicas of legitimate emails, making subtle modifications to deceive recipients. The modified emails often contain malicious links or attachments, and attackers leverage the trust associated with the original communication to increase the likelihood of success. Clone phishing is particularly effective in spear phishing, as attackers can tailor the cloned content to align with the target's previous interactions, making it harder to detect the deception.

In both phishing and spear phishing attacks, attackers frequently exploit the human tendency to trust and comply with seemingly legitimate requests. By creating a sense of urgency, fear, or trust, attackers manipulate individuals into bypassing normal security precautions. Additionally, the use of psychological triggers, such as curiosity or the promise of rewards, is a common tactic to entice recipients into engaging with malicious content.

In conclusion, examining the tactics used in phishing and spear phishing attacks reveals a complex and evolving landscape of deception. From email spoofing and social engineering to personalized reconnaissance and URL manipulation, attackers employ a diverse set of tactics to exploit human vulnerabilities. Recognizing these tactics is crucial for individuals and organizations to implement effective cybersecurity measures, including continuous education, robust email filtering, multi-factor authentication, and a vigilant approach to scrutinizing incoming communications. As phishing and spear phishing attacks continue to evolve, a proactive and informed defense strategy remains essential to mitigate the risks posed by these pervasive and deceptive cyber threats.

Strategies for educating users and reducing susceptibility.

Implementing effective strategies for educating users and reducing susceptibility to cybersecurity threats is paramount in fortifying the human element of defense against evolving cyber risks. A comprehensive approach to user education involves cultivating a culture of cybersecurity awareness within organizations and among individuals. One fundamental strategy is the development and implementation of regular, targeted training programs that equip users with the knowledge and skills to recognize and respond to various cyber threats. These programs should cover a wide range of topics, including phishing, social engineering, password security, and safe online practices.

To enhance the effectiveness of user education, organizations can employ interactive and engaging training modules that simulate real-world scenarios. Incorporating simulated phishing exercises allows users to experience firsthand the tactics employed by cybercriminals and reinforces their ability to discern phishing attempts. These exercises provide valuable insights into user vulnerabilities and offer opportunities for targeted education and improvement.

Tailoring educational content to the specific needs and roles of users is essential for relevance and impact. Different departments and job functions may face distinct cybersecurity challenges, and customized training ensures that users receive information that directly applies to their responsibilities. For example, finance personnel may focus on recognizing financial scams, while IT staff may receive training on identifying and mitigating technical threats.

Fostering a continuous learning environment is crucial for staying ahead of evolving cyber threats. Organizations should provide ongoing training opportunities, updates, and resources to keep users informed about the latest cybersecurity trends and best practices. Cyber threats are dynamic, and a proactive approach to education ensures that users remain vigilant and adaptable to emerging risks.

Utilizing a variety of educational formats, such as video tutorials, webinars, and interactive workshops, caters to diverse learning preferences and enhances the overall effectiveness of user education. Additionally, organizations can leverage gamification elements to make training more engaging and enjoyable, turning cybersecurity education into a collaborative and interactive experience.

Establishing a clear and accessible communication channel for cybersecurity-related information is vital for keeping users informed and engaged. Regularly disseminating newsletters, security alerts, or informative articles helps reinforce key concepts and provides users with practical tips for enhancing their cybersecurity posture. Open communication channels also encourage users to report suspicious activities promptly, fostering a collaborative approach to security.

Incorporating real-world examples and case studies into educational materials adds a practical dimension to user training. Analyzing actual incidents, whether within the organization or from external sources, helps users understand the potential consequences of security lapses and reinforces the importance of adhering to cybersecurity best practices. Case studies create a relatable context that resonates with users, increasing the likelihood of behavior change.

Promoting a sense of shared responsibility is a foundational strategy for reducing susceptibility to cyber threats. Users should understand that cybersecurity is a collective effort, and their actions directly contribute to the overall security posture of the organization. Emphasizing the impact of individual behaviors on the broader security landscape fosters a culture where users feel accountable for maintaining a secure digital environment.

Implementing role-based access controls and least privilege principles enhances security by restricting user access to only the resources and information necessary for their specific roles. This strategy minimizes the potential damage caused by compromised accounts and reinforces the principle of granting access based on job requirements. User education should highlight the importance of adhering to access control policies and the potential risks associated with unnecessary privileges.

Multi-factor authentication (MFA) is a powerful tool for reducing susceptibility to unauthorized access. Educating users about the benefits of MFA and guiding them through the setup process enhances security by adding an additional layer of verification beyond passwords. Clear and user-friendly instructions, coupled with an understanding of the rationale behind MFA, contribute to user acceptance and compliance.

Regularly updating and patching software and systems is a fundamental strategy for reducing susceptibility to cyber threats. Users should be educated about the importance of applying software updates promptly to address vulnerabilities and enhance security. Automated update mechanisms and user-friendly interfaces can simplify the update process, making it more likely for users to adhere to best practices.

Creating a secure password culture is integral to reducing susceptibility to unauthorized access. User education should emphasize the importance of strong, unique passwords and discourage the reuse of passwords across multiple accounts. Providing guidance on creating complex passwords, using password managers, and regularly updating passwords contributes to a robust defense against credential-based attacks.

Simulated phishing exercises, mentioned earlier as a training tool, can also serve as an ongoing strategy for assessing and improving user susceptibility. By regularly conducting simulated phishing campaigns, organizations can track user progress, identify areas for improvement, and tailor education efforts based on evolving user behaviors. This iterative approach reinforces the learning process and ensures that users consistently apply cybersecurity principles.

Integrating cybersecurity awareness into the onboarding process for new employees establishes a strong foundation for secure practices from the outset. New hires should receive comprehensive training on cybersecurity policies, procedures, and best practices as part of their orientation. This early education sets expectations for security-conscious behavior and establishes a baseline understanding of cybersecurity principles.

Promoting a positive cybersecurity culture involves recognizing and rewarding secure behaviors. Acknowledging and celebrating individuals or departments that demonstrate exemplary cybersecurity practices reinforces the importance of security-conscious actions. Positive reinforcement can include recognition in newsletters, awards, or other forms of acknowledgment, fostering a sense of pride and motivation among users to prioritize cybersecurity.

Collaboration with external partners, industry groups, and cybersecurity experts can provide valuable resources for user education. Organizations can leverage webinars, conferences, or workshops conducted by experts to supplement internal training efforts. External partnerships also offer insights into industry-specific threats and best practices, enriching the scope and depth of user education initiatives.

Conducting periodic security awareness campaigns focused on specific themes or topics ensures that users remain engaged and attentive to evolving cybersecurity challenges. Campaigns can include posters, email reminders, and interactive activities that align with the chosen theme. These campaigns create a sense of novelty and excitement around cybersecurity education, making it more likely for users to actively participate and retain key information.

Measuring the effectiveness of user education is essential for refining strategies and addressing specific areas of improvement. Organizations can utilize metrics such as click-through rates in simulated phishing exercises, completion rates for training modules, and the frequency of reported security incidents. Analyzing these metrics provides valuable insights into the impact of user education initiatives and informs continuous improvement efforts.

In conclusion, implementing comprehensive strategies for educating users and reducing susceptibility to cybersecurity threats requires a multifaceted and proactive approach. By combining regular training programs, interactive learning formats, continuous communication, and a sense of shared responsibility, organizations can empower users to recognize and respond effectively to evolving cyber risks. As technology and threat landscapes evolve, an ongoing commitment to user education remains pivotal in creating a resilient defense against a wide array of cyber threats.

Psychological factors contributing to insider threats.

Psychological factors play a significant role in understanding and mitigating insider threats, which involve individuals within an organization exploiting their access and privileges to compromise security. One contributing factor is disgruntlement or dissatisfaction with the organization. Employees who harbor resentment due to perceived unfair treatment, workplace conflicts, or dissatisfaction with their role may be more susceptible to insider threats. Feelings of being undervalued or overlooked can create a sense of betrayal, motivating individuals to engage in malicious activities as a form of retaliation or to vent their frustrations.

Moreover, personal financial pressures can contribute to insider threats. Employees facing financial difficulties, such as debt, personal crises, or unexpected expenses, may be susceptible to bribery or coercion by external entities seeking to exploit their vulnerabilities. Financial stressors can compromise an individual's ethical stance, making them more susceptible to engaging in insider activities for personal gain, either willingly or under duress.

Psychological factors related to job-related stress and burnout can also contribute to insider threats. Employees overwhelmed by excessive workload, tight deadlines, or unrealistic expectations may experience heightened stress levels. In such situations, individuals might rationalize engaging in insider threats as a way to cope with job-related pressures or gain a sense of control in a challenging work environment.

The sense of entitlement or a perceived superiority complex can be another psychological factor leading to insider threats. Employees who believe they deserve more recognition, higher positions, or greater rewards may feel justified in exploiting their access to sensitive information or systems as a way of asserting their perceived entitlement. This sense of superiority can contribute to an individual's willingness to engage in malicious activities to fulfill perceived unmet needs or desires.

Insider threats are also influenced by an individual's loyalty or allegiance to external entities. Employees with dual loyalties, such as holding allegiance to a competitor or having affiliations with external groups, may be swayed to compromise their organization's security for the benefit of those external entities. This dual loyalty can be driven by personal beliefs, ideological alignments, or financial incentives offered by external actors seeking insider information.

Psychological factors related to the desire for recognition and notoriety can contribute to insider threats, especially in cases of employees seeking acknowledgment or attention. Individuals driven by a desire for recognition may engage in malicious activities to showcase their skills or to draw attention to perceived organizational vulnerabilities. This desire for notoriety can manifest in various forms, including data breaches, sabotage, or unauthorized disclosure of sensitive information.

Individuals with low levels of job satisfaction and a lack of organizational commitment may also pose a higher risk of insider threats. Employees who do not feel a sense of loyalty or connection to their organization may be more inclined to engage in malicious activities, as they perceive fewer consequences for betraying the trust of the organization. A lack of commitment to the organization's values and goals can erode the ethical foundation that would otherwise deter insider threats.

Psychological factors related to an individual's susceptibility to manipulation or coercion can be exploited in insider threat scenarios. Employees who are easily influenced or manipulated, either due to naivety, social engineering tactics, or personal vulnerabilities, may unwittingly become insider threats. Threat actors can leverage psychological tactics to coerce individuals into divulging sensitive information or facilitating unauthorized access.

Additionally, the perception of being overlooked or undervalued within the organization can contribute to feelings of resentment and a desire for revenge, leading to insider threats. Employees who perceive that their contributions are not adequately recognized or rewarded may harbor a sense of injustice, potentially motivating them to take malicious actions to settle perceived scores or seek retribution against the organization.

Psychological factors associated with an individual's moral or ethical compass can influence their susceptibility to insider threats. Employees who possess a lower moral threshold or a willingness to rationalize unethical behavior may be more prone to engaging in insider activities. This moral flexibility can be exacerbated by a lack of awareness about the consequences of their actions, as individuals may downplay the impact of insider threats on the organization and its stakeholders.

The level of trust within an organization can also impact insider threats. In environments where trust is eroded due to poor communication, lack of transparency, or perceived unfair treatment, employees may be more inclined to exploit their insider access. Trust is a fundamental psychological factor that, when compromised, can contribute to an environment conducive to insider threats.

Psychological factors related to an individual's perception of organizational injustices or inequities can be a driving force behind insider threats. Employees who perceive bias, favoritism, or discriminatory practices within the organization may feel a sense of injustice. This perception of injustice can motivate individuals to engage in insider threats as a way of rectifying what they perceive to be organizational wrongdoing.

Moreover, the influence of social dynamics within the workplace can contribute to insider threats. Individuals who feel excluded, isolated, or marginalized within their teams may be more susceptible to engaging in malicious activities as a means of seeking recognition or retribution. The social environment plays a crucial role in shaping an individual's psychological state and can significantly impact their likelihood of becoming an insider threat.

In conclusion, the landscape of insider threats is deeply intertwined with various psychological factors that influence an individual's motivations, behaviors, and susceptibility. Disgruntlement, financial pressures, job-related stress, a sense of entitlement, dual loyalties, a desire for recognition, low job satisfaction, susceptibility to manipulation, feelings of revenge, moral flexibility, trust issues, perceptions of organizational injustices, and social dynamics all contribute to the complex psychology behind insider threats. Understanding these factors is critical for organizations to implement effective preventive measures, foster a positive and inclusive workplace culture, and develop robust strategies to mitigate the risks posed by insiders.

Building awareness and resilience against insider attacks.

Building awareness and resilience against insider attacks is a multifaceted and critical endeavor that requires a comprehensive approach encompassing education, technology, and organizational culture. The first pillar of this strategy involves cultivating a heightened awareness among employees about the risks and consequences of insider threats. Organizations should invest in robust cybersecurity awareness training programs that educate employees about the various forms of insider attacks, ranging from unintentional errors to malicious actions. These programs should cover the red flags indicative of insider threat behavior, emphasizing the importance of reporting suspicious activities promptly. By fostering a culture of vigilance and shared responsibility, employees become the first line of defense against potential insider threats.

Simulated exercises and drills are effective tools for building awareness and testing the organization's resilience against insider attacks. Conducting realistic scenarios that mimic potential insider threat situations allows employees to apply their knowledge in a practical setting. These exercises can include simulated phishing campaigns, social engineering tests, and scenarios involving unauthorized access attempts. Regularly engaging in such simulations not only reinforces awareness but also helps organizations identify areas for improvement in their response mechanisms and employee readiness.

Technological solutions play a crucial role in building resilience against insider attacks. Implementing advanced user activity monitoring tools allows organizations to track and analyze employee actions within the network. These tools can detect unusual patterns of behavior, deviations from normal activity, or access to sensitive information that may indicate insider threats. By leveraging artificial intelligence and machine learning, organizations can enhance their ability to identify anomalous behavior, enabling a proactive response to potential insider threats before significant damage occurs.

Access controls and privilege management are fundamental components of building resilience against insider attacks. Implementing the principle of least privilege ensures that employees only have access to the resources necessary for their specific roles. This limits the potential impact of insider threats by minimizing the scope of unauthorized access. Regularly reviewing and updating access privileges in alignment with job roles and responsibilities enhances security and reduces the risk of insider attacks, especially those involving misuse of privileged accounts.

Building a strong cybersecurity culture within the organization is essential for resilience against insider threats. Organizations should establish clear policies and procedures that outline acceptable use of systems, data handling practices, and consequences for policy violations. Communicating these policies effectively and ensuring that employees understand the reasons behind them fosters a sense of accountability. Transparent communication also helps employees recognize the significance of their role in maintaining the organization's security and encourages a collective commitment to preventing insider threats.

Establishing a robust incident response plan specifically tailored to address insider threats is crucial for building resilience. The plan should outline clear steps for identifying, containing, and mitigating the impact of insider attacks. It should also include communication protocols, legal considerations, and procedures for conducting internal investigations. Regularly testing and updating the incident response plan ensures that the organization is well-prepared to handle insider threats effectively and minimize the potential damage.

Continuous monitoring of user behavior, network activities, and data access is a proactive measure for building resilience against insider attacks. Security information and event management (SIEM) solutions, coupled with behavior analytics, enable organizations to detect subtle indicators of insider threats. Real-time monitoring allows for swift responses to suspicious activities, reducing the dwell time of potential insider attacks and mitigating their impact. By staying vigilant and proactive, organizations enhance their ability to identify and address insider threats before they escalate.

Collaboration between cybersecurity teams, human resources, and other relevant departments is essential for building resilience against insider attacks. Sharing insights and information across departments enables a holistic understanding of employee behaviors and potential risks. Human resources can play a crucial role in identifying and addressing workplace issues that may contribute to insider threats, such as conflicts, job dissatisfaction, or personal challenges. This collaborative approach strengthens the organization's overall resilience by addressing both technical and human factors associated with insider threats.

Implementing user behavior analytics (UBA) tools enhances an organization's ability to detect subtle changes in user behavior that may indicate insider threats. These tools analyze patterns of activity, login times, data access, and other behavioral indicators to identify deviations from normal behavior. By establishing baseline behavior profiles for each user, UBA tools can detect anomalies that may signal insider threats, allowing organizations to intervene promptly and minimize the potential damage.

Education and awareness programs should extend beyond initial training to include ongoing reinforcement and updates. As the threat landscape evolves, organizations should adapt their training materials to address emerging risks and tactics associated with insider attacks. Regularly communicating about the evolving nature of insider threats, sharing real-world examples, and providing guidance on recognizing and reporting suspicious activities contribute to a continuously educated and vigilant workforce.

Creating a culture of trust and open communication is integral to building resilience against insider attacks. Employees should feel comfortable reporting concerns or potential insider threat indicators without fear of reprisal. Establishing anonymous reporting mechanisms, such as hotlines or confidential channels, encourages employees to share information about their own observations or suspicions related to insider threats. Trust between employees and the organization is a cornerstone for early detection and prevention of insider attacks.

Implementing a robust employee onboarding and offboarding process contributes to building resilience against insider threats. During onboarding, employees should receive comprehensive training on cybersecurity policies, acceptable use of systems, and the organization's expectations regarding information security. Offboarding processes should include the prompt revocation of access privileges and thorough exit interviews to understand potential reasons for departing employees to become insider threats.

Technology-enforced data loss prevention (DLP) solutions can assist in building resilience against insider threats by preventing unauthorized access, sharing, or exfiltration of sensitive data. These solutions can monitor and control the flow of data within the organization, ensuring that data is handled in accordance with established policies. By implementing granular controls and real-time monitoring, DLP solutions contribute to mitigating the risk of insider threats compromising sensitive information.Regularly conducting security awareness campaigns focused specifically on insider threats helps reinforce the importance of vigilance among employees. These campaigns can include newsletters, posters, workshops, and other communication channels that highlight the consequences of insider attacks and provide practical tips for recognizing and reporting potential threats. By keeping insider threats at the forefront of employees' minds, organizations foster a security-conscious culture that contributes to overall resilience.

In conclusion, building awareness and resilience against insider attacks requires a holistic and dynamic approach that combines education, technology, and organizational practices. From cultivating a culture of cybersecurity awareness to implementing advanced monitoring solutions, organizations can strengthen their defenses against insider threats. By addressing both the human and technical aspects associated with insider attacks, organizations can create a resilient cybersecurity posture that effectively mitigates the risks posed by insiders.

Designing effective security training programs for employees.

Designing effective security training programs for employees is a critical endeavor in fortifying an organization's defense against evolving cyber threats. The foundation of these programs lies in cultivating a comprehensive understanding of cybersecurity principles among employees, ensuring they are equipped to recognize and respond to potential risks. The training should commence with a clear articulation of the organization's cybersecurity policies, emphasizing the importance of information security and the role each employee plays in safeguarding sensitive data. This initial phase sets the tone for the training, establishing a baseline understanding of the significance of cybersecurity in the organizational context.

One pivotal aspect of effective security training is tailoring the content to the specific needs and roles of different employees. Recognizing that various departments and job functions may encounter distinct cybersecurity challenges, customization ensures that training is relevant and directly applicable to employees' responsibilities. For instance, finance personnel may require focused training on financial scams, while IT staff may need in-depth knowledge about technical threats and vulnerabilities. Tailoring the content enhances engagement and resonates more profoundly with employees, as they can directly relate the training to their day-to-day tasks and potential risks within their respective roles.

Engaging and interactive learning formats contribute significantly to the effectiveness of security training programs. Rather than relying solely on traditional lectures or static presentations, incorporating elements of interactivity, such as simulations, scenario-based exercises, and hands-on workshops, promotes active participation and knowledge retention. Simulated phishing exercises, where employees experience and learn to identify phishing attempts in a controlled environment, are particularly impactful. Interactive elements not only make the training more engaging but also provide employees with practical skills they can apply in real-world situations, enhancing their preparedness to counter cybersecurity threats.

Maintaining relevance in the face of rapidly evolving cyber threats is a perpetual challenge for security training programs. To address this, training content should be dynamic and regularly updated to reflect the latest cybersecurity trends, tactics, and vulnerabilities. Continuous learning modules, supplemented by periodic refreshers and updates, keep employees informed about emerging risks and best practices. Regular communication channels, such as newsletters or alerts, can provide ongoing insights into current cybersecurity threats, fostering a culture of awareness and adaptability among employees.

Fostering a culture of cybersecurity awareness is a fundamental objective of effective training programs. Beyond disseminating information, these programs aim to instill a mindset of vigilance and shared responsibility among employees. Training should emphasize that every employee plays a crucial role in maintaining the organization's security posture. Encouraging employees to view cybersecurity as a collective effort fosters a sense of accountability and empowerment, where individuals understand the impact of their actions on the overall security of the organization.

Phishing awareness is a key component of security training programs, considering the prevalence of phishing attacks as a gateway for various cyber threats. Employees should be educated about the tactics used in phishing attempts, the red flags to look for, and the potential consequences of falling victim to phishing. Simulated phishing exercises, as mentioned earlier, provide practical experience in identifying and avoiding phishing attacks. Furthermore, training programs should educate employees about the importance of verifying the legitimacy of emails, avoiding clicking on suspicious links, and reporting potential phishing attempts promptly.

Incorporating real-world examples and case studies into security training programs enhances their impact by providing tangible contexts for understanding cybersecurity principles. Analyzing actual incidents, whether within the organization or from external sources, helps employees grasp the real-world consequences of security lapses. Case studies create relatable scenarios that resonate with employees, illustrating the potential risks and consequences of cybersecurity threats. Learning from past incidents fosters a deeper understanding of the importance of adhering to cybersecurity best practices and reinforces the relevance of the training content.

Establishing a clear and accessible communication channel for cybersecurity-related information is vital for building an informed and aware workforce. In addition to formal training sessions, organizations should regularly disseminate newsletters, security alerts, or informative articles to keep employees updated on cybersecurity matters. Open communication channels not only provide valuable information but also encourage employees to stay vigilant and report any suspicious activities promptly. Creating an ongoing dialogue about cybersecurity reinforces its importance and keeps the topic at the forefront of employees' minds.

Promoting a positive cybersecurity culture involves recognizing and rewarding secure behaviors. Acknowledging and celebrating individuals or departments that demonstrate exemplary cybersecurity practices reinforces the importance of security-conscious actions. Positive reinforcement can take various forms, such as recognition in newsletters, awards, or other forms of acknowledgment. By highlighting and celebrating instances of security awareness and adherence to best practices, organizations create a positive feedback loop that motivates employees to prioritize cybersecurity in their daily activities.

Conducting periodic security awareness campaigns focused on specific themes or topics is an effective strategy for reinforcing training and keeping cybersecurity in the spotlight. These campaigns can include posters, email reminders, and interactive activities that align with the chosen theme. Campaigns create a sense of novelty and excitement around cybersecurity education, making it more likely for employees to actively participate and retain key information. The periodic nature of campaigns ensures that cybersecurity remains a continuous and evolving focus within the organization.

Implementing role-based security training ensures that employees receive education relevant to their specific roles and responsibilities. Different job functions may face distinct cybersecurity challenges, and tailoring training content to address these specific needs enhances its effectiveness. For example, administrative staff may require training on secure data handling and access control, while customer service representatives may focus on social engineering awareness. Role-based training not only provides targeted information but also makes the content more relatable and applicable to employees' daily tasks.

Creating a secure password culture is an integral aspect of security training programs. Employees should be educated about the importance of strong, unique passwords and the risks associated with password reuse. Training should include guidance on creating complex passwords, using password managers, and the significance of regularly updating passwords. Emphasizing the role of strong passwords in protecting sensitive information reinforces a foundational element of cybersecurity hygiene and contributes to a more resilient defense against unauthorized access.

Multi-factor authentication (MFA) is a powerful tool in enhancing security, and training programs should educate employees about its benefits and importance. Guidance on setting up and using MFA, coupled with clear explanations of the added security it provides, contributes to user acceptance and compliance. MFA significantly reduces the risk of unauthorized access even in the event of compromised credentials, and employees should understand its role as an additional layer of protection for their accounts and sensitive information.

Regularly updating and patching software and systems is a fundamental aspect of cybersecurity, and training programs should underscore its importance. Employees should be educated about the significance of applying software updates promptly to address vulnerabilities and enhance security. Training should emphasize that regular updates contribute to protecting not only individual devices but also the overall security of the organization. Automated update mechanisms and user-friendly interfaces can simplify the update process, making it more likely for employees to adhere to best practices.

Providing guidance on the secure use of mobile devices is essential in the contemporary work environment. As mobile devices become ubiquitous, employees should be educated on best practices for securing their smartphones and tablets. Training programs should cover topics such as device passcodes, encryption, secure Wi-Fi usage, and the risks associated with downloading apps from untrusted sources. Given the increasing prevalence of mobile threats, ensuring that employees are well-informed about mobile security contributes to a holistic cybersecurity strategy.

Establishing a clear protocol for reporting security incidents is a crucial aspect of security training programs. Employees should be educated about the steps to take if they suspect a security incident, encounter a phishing attempt, or observe any unusual activities. Training programs should provide guidance on whom to contact, what information to include in incident reports, and the importance of timely reporting. Encouraging a culture where employees feel empowered to report potential security incidents without fear of reprisal contributes to early detection and mitigation of cybersecurity threats.

Social engineering awareness is a cornerstone of effective security training programs. Employees should be educated about the tactics used in social engineering attacks, such as manipulation, deception, and impersonation. Training programs should cover common social engineering scenarios, including phishing emails, phone calls, and in-person interactions. By providing employees with knowledge about these tactics and teaching them to recognize red flags, organizations empower their workforce to resist manipulation and avoid falling victim to social engineering attacks.

Creating a secure remote work environment is a pertinent aspect of modern security training programs. With the increasing prevalence of remote work, employees should be educated on best practices for securing their home offices, using virtual private networks (VPNs), and safeguarding sensitive information in non-traditional work settings. Training programs should address the unique cybersecurity challenges associated with remote work, emphasizing the importance of maintaining the same security standards as in the office environment.

Regularly conducting cybersecurity drills and exercises enhances the practical application of knowledge gained through training programs. Simulated scenarios, such as responding to a data breach, handling a phishing attack, or mitigating a ransomware incident, allow employees to apply their training in a controlled environment. These exercises not only reinforce the skills acquired during training but also identify areas for improvement in incident response and coordination. By regularly practicing responses to various cybersecurity incidents, organizations build resilience and preparedness among employees.

Ensuring that security training programs are accessible and inclusive is crucial for their effectiveness. Organizations should consider the diverse learning preferences and needs of their workforce, providing training materials in various formats, such as video tutorials, written guides, and interactive modules. Moreover, accommodating different learning styles, languages, and accessibility requirements ensures that all employees can actively engage with and benefit from the training content. Creating a culture of inclusivity in cybersecurity education contributes to a more informed and empowered workforce.

In conclusion, designing effective security training programs for employees is a multifaceted undertaking that requires careful consideration of content, delivery methods, and ongoing adaptability. From tailoring content to specific roles and incorporating interactive elements to promoting a culture of cybersecurity awareness, organizations can build resilient defenses against a wide array of cyber threats. By addressing both the human and technical aspects of cybersecurity, these programs empower employees to actively contribute to the organization's overall security posture and navigate the evolving landscape of cyber risks.

Measuring the success of awareness initiatives.

Measuring the success of awareness initiatives is a multifaceted endeavor that requires a comprehensive approach to evaluate the impact and effectiveness of campaigns aimed at increasing public consciousness on specific issues or causes. The evaluation process encompasses various dimensions, starting with the establishment of clear objectives and key performance indicators (KPIs) that align with the overarching goals of the awareness initiative. These objectives serve as a roadmap for gauging the initiative's success by providing a structured framework for assessment.

Quantitative metrics play a pivotal role in the evaluation process, offering tangible and numerical insights into the reach and engagement levels of the awareness initiative. Metrics such as website traffic, social media impressions, and click-through rates provide valuable data on the extent to which the campaign has penetrated the target audience and generated interest or interaction. Analyzing these quantitative indicators allows for a quantitative assessment of the initiative's reach, helping stakeholders understand the scale of impact and identify areas for improvement.

In tandem with quantitative metrics, qualitative assessments are equally crucial in capturing the nuanced aspects of awareness initiatives. Qualitative data, derived from surveys, interviews, and focus groups, allows for a deeper understanding of the initiative's impact on individual perceptions, attitudes, and behaviors. Qualitative insights offer a more nuanced perspective, shedding light on the qualitative shifts in awareness and knowledge levels among the target audience. This qualitative lens is essential for comprehending the initiative's influence on attitudes, beliefs, and the overall mindset of the audience.

A robust evaluation of awareness initiatives also entails measuring the effectiveness of communication strategies deployed throughout the campaign. Analyzing the clarity, resonance, and relevance of messaging helps gauge how well the intended information was conveyed and received by the audience. Assessing the alignment between the chosen communication channels and the preferences of the target demographic is vital in optimizing the dissemination of information and ensuring that the initiative resonates with the intended audience.

Furthermore, tracking changes in behavioral indicators is integral to assessing the tangible impact of awareness initiatives. Whether it involves increased participation in related events, adoption of recommended practices, or a surge in support for associated causes, observing behavioral shifts provides concrete evidence of the initiative's success in motivating action. These behavioral changes serve as a key indicator of the initiative's transformative power, indicating not only increased awareness but also a tangible shift in the audience's engagement with the advocated cause or issue.

Long-term sustainability is a crucial aspect of measuring the success of awareness initiatives. Examining the enduring impact beyond the immediate campaign period involves assessing whether the initiative has triggered lasting changes in awareness, behavior, or societal norms. Monitoring sustained interest, ongoing engagement, and the perpetuation of positive outcomes over time contribute to understanding the initiative's enduring influence on the target audience and the broader community.

Social impact measurement frameworks, such as the Social Return on Investment (SROI) and the Theory of Change, provide valuable tools for a holistic evaluation of awareness initiatives. These frameworks guide the systematic assessment of the initiative's inputs, activities, outputs, outcomes, and impacts, offering a structured approach to understanding the interconnected elements that contribute to success. By mapping the causal pathways and identifying key drivers of impact, these frameworks enable stakeholders to make informed decisions, refine strategies, and enhance the overall effectiveness of awareness initiatives.

In conclusion, measuring the success of awareness initiatives demands a comprehensive and integrative approach that considers both quantitative and qualitative dimensions. From setting clear objectives and KPIs to assessing communication strategies, behavioral changes, and long-term sustainability, the evaluation process must be multifaceted to capture the multifaceted nature of awareness impact. Utilizing a combination of quantitative metrics, qualitative insights, and social impact measurement frameworks provides a nuanced understanding of an initiative's success, empowering stakeholders to refine strategies and maximize the positive influence of awareness campaigns on individuals and society as a whole.

Chapter 6: Emerging Technologies and Cybersecurity: A Symbiotic Evolution

Definition and scope of emerging technologies in the digital landscape.

Emerging technologies in the digital landscape encompass a dynamic and expansive realm defined by the continuous evolution and integration of innovative tools and methodologies that redefine the way we interact with information, conduct business, and navigate daily life. At its core, the term "emerging technologies" refers to those advancements that are in the early stages of development, adoption, and application, often representing cutting-edge solutions with the potential to disrupt and transform established norms. The scope of these technologies is vast, spanning a multitude of sectors, including but not limited to information technology, healthcare, finance, manufacturing, and communication.

Within the digital landscape, artificial intelligence (AI) stands out as a central pillar of emerging technologies, encompassing machine learning, natural language processing, and computer vision. AI's transformative potential lies in its capacity to simulate human intelligence, enabling machines to analyze data, recognize patterns, and make informed decisions, thereby enhancing automation and efficiency across various industries. Blockchain technology, another key player, has revolutionized the landscape of secure and transparent digital transactions. Operating on decentralized and distributed ledgers, blockchain ensures the integrity and traceability of data, particularly in financial transactions and supply chain management.

The Internet of Things (IoT) is a foundational element in the digital transformation, connecting devices and systems to facilitate data exchange and communication. This interconnected network of devices, ranging from smart home appliances to industrial sensors, enables real-time monitoring, analysis, and control, fostering a more responsive and efficient environment. Augmented reality (AR) and virtual reality (VR) technologies, on the other hand, introduce immersive and interactive experiences, revolutionizing industries like gaming, education, and healthcare by blending the digital and physical realms.

The scope of emerging technologies also extends to include 5G technology, which represents the next generation of mobile communication. Renowned for its high-speed data transmission, low latency, and increased connectivity, 5G lays the groundwork for enhanced mobile experiences, advanced robotics, and the widespread adoption of the IoT. Quantum computing, though still in its infancy, promises unparalleled computational power by leveraging the principles of quantum mechanics, potentially revolutionizing fields such as cryptography, optimization, and materials science.

In the healthcare sector, emerging technologies contribute to the development of personalized medicine, leveraging genomics, data analytics, and AI to tailor medical treatments to individual genetic profiles. Telemedicine, facilitated by digital technologies, enables remote healthcare services, transforming the patient-doctor relationship and increasing accessibility to medical expertise. Furthermore, wearable devices and health apps empower individuals to actively monitor and manage their health, fostering a shift towards preventive and personalized healthcare.

The scope of emerging technologies in the digital landscape is not confined to individual sectors; it extends to the overarching concept of smart cities. Smart city initiatives leverage technology to enhance urban living through efficient infrastructure, sustainable practices, and improved citizen services. Sensors, data analytics, and interconnected systems work collaboratively to optimize energy usage, transportation networks, and public services, creating cities that are not only technologically advanced but also environmentally sustainable and citizen-centric.

While the potential benefits of emerging technologies are immense, their rapid evolution also presents challenges related to ethical considerations, security, and societal impact. Ethical concerns arise in areas such as AI, where issues of bias, accountability, and transparency demand careful consideration. The increasing interconnectedness of devices in the IoT raises cybersecurity concerns, necessitating robust measures to safeguard sensitive data and privacy. Additionally, the impact of automation on employment and the potential for exacerbating existing societal divides require thoughtful examination and proactive measures.

In conclusion, the realm of emerging technologies in the digital landscape is characterized by a dynamic interplay of innovations that redefine the way we live, work, and interact. From artificial intelligence and blockchain to the Internet of Things and quantum computing, these technologies collectively shape the trajectory of digital transformation across various sectors. Their scope extends beyond individual applications to encompass broader concepts such as smart cities, personalized healthcare, and the evolution of communication networks. While unlocking unprecedented opportunities, the responsible development and deployment of emerging technologies demand careful consideration of ethical, security, and societal implications to ensure a future where technology enhances human well-being and fosters inclusive progress.

The rapid evolution of technological innovations.

The rapid evolution of technological innovations represents a hallmark of the contemporary era, ushering in transformative changes across diverse facets of human existence. This relentless pace of advancement, fueled by a confluence of scientific breakthroughs, computational power, and an interconnected global landscape, has redefined the boundaries of what is possible. At the heart of this evolution is the digital revolution, a phenomenon that has catalyzed unprecedented progress across various sectors, from communication and healthcare to manufacturing and entertainment.

One of the primary drivers of this technological surge is the exponential growth of computing power, exemplified by Moore's Law, which posits that the number of transistors on a microchip doubles approximately every two years. This unyielding march toward increased computational capacity has propelled innovations such as artificial intelligence (AI) and machine learning (ML) to the forefront of technological discourse. AI, in particular, stands as a testament to the synergistic relationship between algorithmic sophistication and the abundance of data, enabling machines to emulate human cognitive functions and undertake complex tasks, from natural language processing to image recognition.

The digital transformation is further propelled by the proliferation of connectivity and the advent of the Internet of Things (IoT). With billions of devices now interlinked in a vast network, the IoT engenders a seamless exchange of data, creating an environment where everyday objects, from household appliances to industrial machinery, are imbued with the capacity to communicate and collaborate. This interconnectedness not only enhances efficiency and convenience but also lays the groundwork for smart cities, where data-driven insights optimize urban infrastructure and services.

Parallelly, the rise of big data analytics has emerged as a linchpin in harnessing the immense volumes of information generated daily. The ability to glean actionable insights from massive datasets has revolutionized decision-making processes across industries. Businesses leverage data analytics to refine marketing strategies, predict consumer behavior, and streamline operations, while healthcare practitioners utilize it for personalized treatment plans and epidemiological surveillance. The omnipresence of data, combined with advanced analytics, underpins the agility required in navigating the complexities of the modern world.

In the realm of communication, the evolution of technology has transcended traditional boundaries, reshaping how individuals connect and share information. The advent of 5G technology represents a quantum leap in telecommunications, offering unprecedented data speeds and low latency. This not only facilitates enhanced mobile experiences but also serves as a catalyst for innovations in areas such as augmented reality (AR) and virtual reality (VR), redefining how we perceive and interact with the digital realm.

Technological evolution is not confined to the virtual space; it permeates the physical world through advancements in materials science and manufacturing. 3D printing, for instance, has revolutionized prototyping and small-scale production, offering a nimble and cost-effective alternative to traditional manufacturing methods. The convergence of digital design and additive manufacturing techniques empowers industries to create intricate and customized products with remarkable efficiency.

Furthermore, the rapid evolution of biotechnology and genomics is reshaping the landscape of healthcare and personalized medicine. Breakthroughs in gene editing technologies, such as CRISPR-Cas9, herald a new era of precision medicine, enabling targeted interventions at the genetic level. This holds the promise of treating previously incurable genetic disorders and tailoring therapeutic approaches to individual genetic profiles, ushering in a paradigm shift from reactive to proactive healthcare.

However, this relentless pace of technological evolution is not without its challenges and ethical considerations. The deployment of AI raises concerns about job displacement, bias in algorithms, and the ethical implications of autonomous systems. Cybersecurity vulnerabilities emerge as a pressing issue, given the increasing interconnectedness of devices and the escalating sophistication of cyber threats. Additionally, the ethical implications of biotechnological advancements, particularly in areas like cloning and genetic engineering, necessitate careful scrutiny to ensure responsible and equitable use.

In conclusion, the rapid evolution of technological innovations is a defining characteristic of the contemporary era, permeating every facet of human existence. From the transformative power of AI and the interconnectivity of the IoT to the precision of 5G and the revolution in biotechnology, these innovations collectively shape the trajectory of societal progress. As we navigate this dynamic landscape, it is imperative to address the challenges posed by ethical considerations, cybersecurity risks, and societal implications to ensure that technological evolution aligns with the principles of inclusivity, responsibility, and human well-being. The unfolding narrative of technological progress underscores the need for a thoughtful and collaborative approach to harness the potential of innovation for the betterment of humanity.

Applications of AI and ML in threat detection and analysis.

The integration of Artificial Intelligence (AI) and Machine Learning (ML) in threat detection and analysis represents a paradigm shift in cybersecurity, fortifying the defense against an ever-evolving landscape of cyber threats. AI, as a broad field of computer science, encompasses the development of systems that can perform tasks that typically require human intelligence. In the realm of threat detection, AI algorithms exhibit a capacity to analyze massive datasets, identify patterns, and discern anomalies that might elude traditional security measures. Machine Learning, a subset of AI, facilitates the creation of models that improve their performance over time through iterative learning from data, enabling a proactive and adaptive approach to cybersecurity.

One pivotal application of AI and ML in threat detection is in the realm of anomaly detection. Traditional signature-based approaches are effective against known threats but falter when confronted with novel or sophisticated attacks. Anomaly detection, powered by machine learning, enables systems to establish a baseline of normal behavior and flag any deviations from this norm as potential threats. This dynamic approach allows for the identification of previously unseen attack patterns, providing a crucial layer of defense against emerging cyber threats.

Moreover, AI and ML play a crucial role in the analysis of vast and complex datasets generated by network activities. Security Information and Event Management (SIEM) systems, bolstered by machine learning algorithms, can sift through enormous volumes of log data, network traffic, and system events to discern meaningful patterns indicative of malicious activities. This level of automated analysis is indispensable in handling the scale and speed of modern cyber threats, reducing the reliance on manual intervention and enabling rapid response to potential security incidents.

Intrusion detection systems (IDS) benefit significantly from the capabilities of AI and ML, particularly in distinguishing between benign and malicious network activities. By training on historical data and continuously learning from new information, these systems can identify anomalous behaviors that may signify an ongoing or imminent cyber attack. The ability to adapt and evolve based on the changing threat landscape enhances the accuracy of intrusion detection, reducing false positives and negatives and providing security teams with more reliable alerts.

AI-driven threat intelligence is another critical facet of modern cybersecurity. Machine learning algorithms analyze vast amounts of data from diverse sources, including open-source intelligence, dark web forums, and incident reports, to discern emerging threats and trends. This proactive approach enables organizations to anticipate potential risks, update their defenses accordingly, and stay ahead of the rapidly evolving threat landscape. By automating the collection and analysis of threat intelligence, AI and ML empower cybersecurity professionals to make informed decisions and respond promptly to emerging threats.

Furthermore, the deployment of AI in behavioral analysis enhances the ability to detect subtle indicators of malicious intent. By examining user behavior, system interactions, and network activities, AI models can establish normal patterns for entities within a network. Deviations from these patterns, such as unusual login times or abnormal file access, can trigger alerts for potential security incidents. Behavioral analysis, powered by machine learning, goes beyond static rule-based approaches, offering a more nuanced and adaptive means of identifying threats that may otherwise go unnoticed.

The application of AI and ML extends into the realm of malware detection and analysis. Traditional signature-based methods struggle to keep pace with the rapid evolution of malware variants. In contrast, machine learning models can learn from the characteristics of known malware and identify novel threats based on shared attributes. Behavioral analysis, combined with feature extraction techniques, allows these models to recognize malicious patterns, enabling real-time identification and containment of malware before it can wreak havoc on systems.

Moreover, AI and ML contribute significantly to the automation of incident response processes. The ability to analyze and prioritize alerts, correlate information from multiple sources, and recommend appropriate remediation measures enhances the efficiency of security teams. Automated incident response powered by AI can orchestrate complex workflows, isolate compromised systems, and even initiate countermeasures in real time. This rapid and coordinated response is essential in minimizing the impact of cyber attacks and preventing their escalation.

The fusion of AI and ML with User and Entity Behavior Analytics (UEBA) further enhances threat detection capabilities. By scrutinizing patterns of user behavior, these systems can identify potential insider threats or compromised accounts. Machine learning models can discern anomalies in user activities, such as unauthorized access or abnormal data transfers, prompting timely intervention and mitigating the risks associated with insider threats.

Additionally, AI and ML contribute to the evolution of predictive analytics in cybersecurity. By leveraging historical data, these technologies can forecast potential security threats and vulnerabilities. Predictive modeling enables organizations to prioritize their security efforts, focusing resources on areas most likely to be targeted or exploited. This forward-looking approach empowers organizations to implement preemptive measures, reducing the likelihood and impact of cyber attacks.

In conclusion, the application of AI and ML in threat detection and analysis represents a transformative leap in cybersecurity capabilities. From anomaly detection and behavioral analysis to threat intelligence and automated incident response, these technologies empower organizations to confront the dynamic and sophisticated nature of modern cyber threats. The ability to adapt, learn, and evolve in real time enhances the efficacy of security measures, providing a proactive defense against a diverse range of cyber attacks. As the cybersecurity landscape continues to evolve, the integration of AI and ML stands as a linchpin in fortifying digital defenses and ensuring the resilience of organizations in the face of an ever-changing threat landscape.

Challenges and ethical considerations in AI-driven cybersecurity.

The intersection of Artificial Intelligence (AI) and cybersecurity brings forth a myriad of challenges and ethical considerations, underscoring the complexities inherent in deploying advanced technologies to safeguard digital assets. One of the foremost challenges lies in the inherent vulnerability of AI systems to adversarial attacks. These attacks involve manipulating the input data in a way that can deceive AI algorithms, leading to misclassifications or other unintended outcomes. As AI-driven cybersecurity solutions heavily rely on the accuracy of models trained on historical data, the susceptibility to adversarial attacks raises concerns about the reliability and robustness of these systems in the face of sophisticated adversaries. Mitigating this challenge requires ongoing research into adversarial machine learning, the development of resilient models, and the implementation of proactive defenses to thwart potential attacks on AI-driven cybersecurity.

Moreover, the ethical considerations surrounding the use of AI in cybersecurity extend to issues of transparency and explainability. As AI algorithms become more intricate and operate as black-box systems, it becomes challenging to comprehend how decisions are made, leading to a lack of transparency in the decision-making process. The opacity of AI models raises concerns about accountability, making it difficult for cybersecurity professionals and end-users to understand, interpret, and trust the outcomes generated by these systems. Ethical AI practices necessitate a balance between the complexity of models and the imperative for transparency, fostering a better understanding of how AI-driven cybersecurity decisions are reached and allowing for meaningful oversight.

Bias in AI models poses yet another formidable challenge, particularly in the context of cybersecurity. The datasets used to train AI systems may inadvertently incorporate biases, leading to skewed outcomes that disproportionately impact certain groups or neglect specific types of threats. In cybersecurity, where the consequences of false positives or negatives can be severe, biased models can result in discriminatory outcomes, leaving certain vulnerabilities unaddressed or wrongly targeting specific user groups. Addressing bias requires diligent efforts in data curation, algorithmic fairness, and ongoing monitoring to ensure that AI-driven cybersecurity systems provide equitable protection across diverse user profiles and threat scenarios.

The scarcity of skilled professionals capable of understanding and managing AI-driven cybersecurity systems contributes to the overarching challenge of a cybersecurity talent gap. Organizations often struggle to recruit and retain experts who possess the inter-disciplinary knowledge required to navigate the complex interface between AI and cybersecurity. The shortage of skilled professionals hampers the effective deployment and management of AI-driven se-curity solutions, creating a potential bottleneck in the efforts to har-ness the full potential of these technologies. Addressing this chal-lenge demands strategic investments in education, training pro-grams, and initiatives to foster a robust workforce capable of bridg-ing the gap between AI expertise and cybersecurity proficiency.

Furthermore, the dynamic nature of the cyber threat landscape introduces challenges related to the adaptability and agility of AI-driven cybersecurity systems. Cyber threats evolve rapidly, and ad-versaries continually innovate to bypass existing defenses. AI systems must exhibit a comparable level of adaptability to effectively counter emerging threats. However, the pace of evolution in AI models and algorithms must be carefully balanced with the need for rigorous testing, validation, and assurance of reliability. Striking this balance is a delicate challenge, requiring organizations to implement mecha-nisms that foster agility without compromising the security and sta-bility of AI-driven cybersecurity solutions.

Ethical considerations in AI-driven cybersecurity extend beyond the technical realm to encompass issues related to privacy and sur-veillance. The collection and analysis of vast amounts of data to train AI models can encroach upon individual privacy rights. The use of surveillance technologies powered by AI raises concerns about the scope and extent of data collection, as well as the potential for misuse or unauthorized access. Striking a balance between enhancing cyber-security measures and respecting privacy rights requires robust data governance frameworks, transparency in data practices, and adher-ence to privacy regulations to ensure responsible and ethical use of AI-driven cybersecurity technologies.

The ethical implications of AI in cybersecurity also manifest in the context of autonomous decision-making and response. As AI sys-tems increasingly operate in real-time environments, making split-second decisions to counteract threats, questions arise about the eth-ical dimensions of delegating such authority to machines. The po-tential for unintended consequences, the lack of human oversight, and the accountability for AI-driven decisions pose ethical dilemmas that demand careful consideration. Balancing the autonomy of AI systems with the need for human intervention and ethical oversight remains a critical challenge in the ethical deployment of AI-driven cybersecurity solutions.

Additionally, the global nature of cyber threats introduces eth-ical considerations related to international collaboration, informa-tion sharing, and the potential weaponization of AI for offensive purposes. The deployment of AI in offensive cyber operations raises questions about responsible conduct in the digital realm, the poten-tial for cyber escalation, and the need for international norms and agreements to govern the ethical use of AI in cyberspace. Ethical considerations extend to the responsible disclosure of vulnerabilities, the sharing of threat intelligence, and the avoidance of actions that may disproportionately harm civilian infrastructure or violate inter-national law.

In conclusion, the integration of AI into cybersecurity intro-duces a host of challenges and ethical considerations that require careful navigation to ensure the responsible and effective deploy-ment of these advanced technologies. Addressing adversarial attacks, mitigating bias, enhancing transparency, closing the talent gap, fostering adaptability, and navigating the ethical dimensions of autonomous decision-making represent pressing challenges in the evolving landscape of AI-driven cybersecurity. As organizations strive to harness the benefits of AI in fortifying digital defenses, it is imperative to approach these challenges with a commitment to ethical practices, transparency, and a holistic understanding of the societal implications of AI in the realm of cybersecurity. Responsible innovation, ongoing research, and collaborative efforts are essential to building a secure and ethically sound future in the dynamic intersection of AI and cybersecurity.

How blockchain enhances security in digital transactions.

Blockchain technology, renowned for its decentralized and tamper-resistant nature, stands as a groundbreaking innovation that fundamentally enhances security in digital transactions across various industries. At its core, a blockchain is a distributed ledger that records transactions in a secure, transparent, and immutable manner. The decentralized architecture of blockchain eliminates the need for a central authority or intermediary, mitigating the vulnerabilities associated with single points of failure. One of the primary ways in which blockchain enhances security is through cryptographic techniques. Transactions on a blockchain are secured using cryptographic hashes, ensuring the integrity and immutability of the data. Each block in the chain contains a unique hash, generated based on the information in the block and the hash of the previous block. This interconnection of blocks creates a chain of trust, making it computationally infeasible to alter any block without modifying all subsequent blocks, providing a robust defense against tampering and fraud.

The transparency inherent in blockchain technology also contributes significantly to the security of digital transactions. In a blockchain network, all participants have access to a synchronized and immutable record of transactions. This transparency ensures that any discrepancies or malicious activities are quickly identified, as participants can independently verify the entire transaction history. The visibility into the transactional flow fosters a level of accountability that is absent in traditional centralized systems, where transaction details are often obscured from the view of end-users. Blockchain's transparent and auditable nature instills trust in the digital transaction process, reducing the likelihood of fraudulent activities and enhancing the overall security posture.

Smart contracts, self-executing contracts with the terms of the agreement directly written into code, represent another facet of blockchain technology that elevates security in digital transactions. By automating the execution of contractual clauses, smart contracts minimize the reliance on intermediaries and reduce the potential for human error or manipulation. The code governing smart contracts is deployed on the blockchain, ensuring transparency and immutability. Once conditions specified in the contract are met, the smart contract is executed automatically, providing a secure and tamper-resistant mechanism for enforcing agreements. This automation not only streamlines transaction processes but also eliminates the need for intermediaries, reducing the attack surface and enhancing overall security.

The decentralization of blockchain networks also plays a pivotal role in fortifying the security of digital transactions. Traditional centralized systems are vulnerable to single points of failure, where compromising a central authority could lead to widespread security breaches. In contrast, blockchain operates on a distributed network of nodes, with each node holding a copy of the entire ledger. For a malicious actor to compromise the system, they would need to gain control of a majority of the network, a feat that becomes increasingly impractical as the network size grows. The decentralized nature of blockchain thus enhances the resilience and security of digital transactions by dispersing control and minimizing the risk of unauthorized manipulation.

Furthermore, the implementation of consensus mechanisms in blockchain networks contributes to the security of digital transactions. Consensus mechanisms, such as Proof of Work (PoW) or Proof of Stake (PoS), ensure agreement among network participants on the validity of transactions before they are added to the blockchain. These mechanisms prevent malicious actors from introducing fraudulent transactions or attempting to rewrite transaction history. PoW, for example, requires participants (miners) to solve complex mathematical puzzles to validate transactions, making it computationally expensive to launch attacks. PoS, on the other hand, leverages participants' ownership stakes in the cryptocurrency to determine their ability to validate transactions. These consensus mechanisms add a layer of security by requiring broad agreement within the network before transactions are confirmed and added to the blockchain.

The secure handling of identities is another dimension in which blockchain enhances security in digital transactions. Traditional identity management systems are susceptible to data breaches and identity theft due to centralized storage of sensitive information. Blockchain-based identity solutions, often referred to as self-sovereign identities, enable users to control their own identity information. Users can selectively share only the necessary details, reducing the exposure of sensitive information. The decentralized and encrypted nature of blockchain ensures that identity data is stored securely, and individuals have greater control over who can access their information. This not only enhances privacy but also mitigates the risks associated with centralized identity management, contributing to a more secure digital transaction environment.

In the realm of financial transactions, blockchain's impact is particularly significant. Cross-border transactions, characterized by complex and time-consuming processes in traditional banking systems, benefit from the efficiency and security offered by blockchain.

The decentralized and borderless nature of blockchain facilitates faster and more cost-effective international transactions. The elimination of intermediary banks reduces the risk of errors, delays, and potential points of failure. Moreover, the transparency of blockchain transactions allows participants to track the movement of funds in real time, reducing the likelihood of fraud and enhancing the overall security of cross-border financial transactions.

The integration of blockchain in supply chain management also augments security in digital transactions. The transparency and traceability provided by blockchain ensure that every step of the supply chain is recorded and can be audited. This transparency mitigates the risk of counterfeit products entering the supply chain, as stakeholders can verify the authenticity of products by tracing their origins on the blockchain. Additionally, smart contracts can automate various aspects of the supply chain, such as payment processing and quality assurance, reducing the reliance on manual processes and minimizing the potential for errors or fraudulent activities.

However, despite the myriad benefits, the adoption of blockchain technology also introduces its own set of challenges and ethical considerations. The energy consumption associated with certain consensus mechanisms, particularly PoW, has raised concerns about the environmental impact of blockchain networks. As the demand for blockchain transactions grows, addressing these environmental concerns becomes imperative to ensure the ethical and sustainable deployment of blockchain technology.

Moreover, the regulatory landscape surrounding blockchain and cryptocurrencies remains dynamic and varies across jurisdictions. Navigating regulatory compliance poses challenges for businesses and individuals engaging in digital transactions using blockchain technology. Striking a balance between the decentralized, privacy-focused nature of blockchain and the need for regulatory oversight is an ongoing challenge that requires collaborative efforts between the technology sector, regulators, and policymakers.

In conclusion, blockchain technology emerges as a cornerstone in enhancing the security of digital transactions by offering decentralized, transparent, and tamper-resistant mechanisms. Through cryptographic techniques, transparency, smart contracts, decentralized networks, consensus mechanisms, and secure identity management, blockchain addresses vulnerabilities present in traditional centralized systems. Its impact spans across various sectors, from finance and supply chain to identity management and beyond. However, the challenges related to energy consumption, regulatory compliance, and ongoing technological evolution underscore the importance of responsible deployment and continued innovation in harnessing the full potential of blockchain for secure digital transactions. As the landscape evolves, the ethical considerations surrounding blockchain technology will necessitate a thoughtful and collaborative approach to ensure its integration aligns with principles of sustainability, security, and ethical use.

Potential applications of blockchain in cybersecurity.

Blockchain technology holds significant promise in enhancing cybersecurity across various domains. One prominent application is in securing identity management systems. Traditional identity verification methods are often susceptible to breaches, as centralized databases become lucrative targets for hackers. By implementing blockchain, a decentralized and tamper-resistant ledger, identity information can be securely stored, reducing the risk of unauthorized access and identity theft. Smart contracts, self-executing code on the blockchain, further enhance identity management by automating authentication processes, ensuring greater accuracy and efficiency.

Another critical area where blockchain can fortify cybersecurity is in securing data integrity. The immutable nature of blockchain ensures that once data is recorded, it cannot be altered or deleted without consensus from the network. This feature makes it invaluable in safeguarding sensitive information, such as financial records, medical data, or intellectual property. Enterprises can use blockchain to create transparent and auditable trails of data, enabling real-time verification of its integrity and origin, thus mitigating the risk of data manipulation or tampering.

Supply chain security is a domain where blockchain's decentralized ledger can play a transformative role. The supply chain is vulnerable to various threats, including counterfeit products, fraud, and theft. Blockchain facilitates end-to-end visibility by recording every transaction and movement of goods on an immutable ledger. This transparency ensures the authenticity of products, prevents counterfeiting, and enhances traceability, enabling swift identification of any compromised components within the supply chain.

Blockchain technology also introduces a paradigm shift in securing communications through decentralized and encrypted messaging systems. Traditional centralized communication platforms are susceptible to single points of failure and are vulnerable to hacking. Decentralized messaging platforms built on blockchain ensure that messages are securely transmitted and stored across a distributed network, making it significantly more challenging for malicious actors to compromise the confidentiality and integrity of communications.

In the realm of access control and authorization, blockchain's decentralized architecture provides a robust framework for enhancing security. Traditional access control systems often rely on centralized authorities, making them susceptible to attacks. Blockchain-based identity solutions enable users to control their digital identities and permissions securely. Users can manage access to their data and resources through cryptographic keys, reducing the risk of unauthorized access and minimizing the impact of potential security breaches.

Moreover, the application of blockchain in cybersecurity extends to the realm of threat intelligence sharing. Timely and accurate exchange of threat intelligence is crucial in combating cyber threats. Blockchain provides a secure and transparent platform for sharing threat intelligence among trusted parties while maintaining the confidentiality of sensitive information. This decentralized approach fosters collaboration and enables organizations to collectively defend against emerging cyber threats.

Blockchain's impact on securing Internet of Things (IoT) devices is noteworthy. The proliferation of connected devices has increased the attack surface for cyber threats. Blockchain can be employed to create a decentralized and secure framework for managing IoT devices, ensuring that only authorized devices can communicate with each other. This enhances the overall integrity and security of IoT ecosystems, safeguarding against unauthorized access, data manipulation, and device compromise.

Financial transactions and cybersecurity are inherently linked, and blockchain technology has the potential to revolutionize the financial sector's security landscape. Cryptocurrencies, built on blockchain, offer a secure and decentralized alternative to traditional financial systems. The use of blockchain in financial transactions ensures transparency, reduces the risk of fraud, and provides a tamper-resistant record of all transactions. Smart contracts on blockchain further automate and secure financial processes, reducing the reliance on intermediaries and minimizing the risk of financial fraud.

In the healthcare sector, where the confidentiality and integrity of patient data are paramount, blockchain can serve as a robust solution. Patient records stored on a blockchain are secure, transparent, and accessible only to authorized individuals. This decentralized approach reduces the risk of data breaches and unauthorized access to sensitive medical information, ensuring patient privacy and compliance with regulatory standards.

In conclusion, the potential applications of blockchain in cybersecurity are vast and diverse. From identity management and data integrity to supply chain security, communications, access control, threat intelligence sharing, IoT device security, financial transactions, and healthcare data management, blockchain technology offers innovative solutions to address the evolving challenges of the digital landscape. The decentralized, transparent, and tamper-resistant nature of blockchain holds the promise of significantly enhancing cybersecurity across various industries, paving the way for a more secure and resilient digital future.

Security risks associated with the proliferation of IoT devices.

The proliferation of Internet of Things (IoT) devices in our interconnected world brings unprecedented convenience and efficiency, but it also introduces a myriad of security risks that demand careful consideration. One major concern revolves around the inherent diversity in the design, manufacturing, and deployment of IoT devices, leading to a lack of standardized security protocols. Many devices enter the market with inadequate security measures, such as default passwords or weak authentication mechanisms, making them susceptible to exploitation by malicious actors.

A significant security risk associated with the widespread adoption of IoT devices is the vulnerability of these devices to remote exploitation and unauthorized access. As these devices often collect and transmit sensitive data, from personal information to critical infrastructure data, their compromise poses serious privacy and security threats. Attackers can exploit vulnerabilities in the device's software or firmware, gaining unauthorized access to sensitive information or even using compromised devices to launch larger-scale attacks on networks and systems.

The sheer volume of IoT devices and the vast attack surface they create present a considerable challenge for cybersecurity. Traditional security measures may struggle to keep pace with the rapid growth of IoT ecosystems, leaving many devices inadequately protected. Moreover, the interconnected nature of these devices means that a compromise in one device can potentially lead to a domino effect, enabling attackers to move laterally within a network and compromise other devices or systems.

Another critical security risk associated with IoT devices is the insufficient attention given to data encryption during transmission and storage. Many devices transmit data in clear text, making it susceptible to interception and eavesdropping by malicious actors. Additionally, inadequate encryption measures for stored data on these devices can lead to unauthorized access and data breaches. As IoT devices often handle sensitive information, such as health data in medical devices or personal preferences in smart home devices, the compromise of this data can have severe consequences for individuals and organizations.

The issue of insecure firmware and software updates poses a significant challenge in maintaining the security of IoT devices. Many devices lack a robust mechanism for receiving and applying updates, leaving them exposed to known vulnerabilities. Additionally, manufacturers may not prioritize or provide timely updates, leaving devices unsupported and vulnerable to exploits. This lack of a standardized and streamlined approach to firmware and software updates undermines the long-term security of IoT ecosystems, as devices become outdated and increasingly susceptible to attacks over time.

Compounding these challenges is the often-overlooked issue of physical security for IoT devices. Many devices are deployed in uncontrolled environments, making them susceptible to physical tampering or theft. Attackers can exploit physical vulnerabilities to gain direct access to the device, compromise its integrity, or extract sensitive information. In scenarios where the physical security of IoT devices is not adequately addressed, the overall security posture of the

IoT ecosystem is compromised, and the potential for unauthorized access and data breaches escalates.

The interconnectivity of IoT devices introduces a unique challenge related to the potential for cascading failures. A compromise in one device could lead to a chain reaction, impacting the functionality and security of other interconnected devices or systems. This interconnectedness amplifies the consequences of security breaches, as a single vulnerability can be leveraged to compromise an entire network or ecosystem. Mitigating this risk requires a holistic approach to security that considers the entire IoT ecosystem and its dependencies.

The lack of a standardized approach to IoT device authentication and authorization is another significant security concern. Many devices rely on default or weak credentials, making them susceptible to brute-force attacks. Additionally, the absence of robust identity management mechanisms can result in unauthorized access to devices, leading to data breaches or the compromise of critical systems. Strengthening authentication and authorization practices across the IoT landscape is essential to mitigate the risk of unauthorized access and protect the integrity of IoT ecosystems.

Furthermore, the increasing use of IoT devices in critical infrastructure, such as energy grids, transportation systems, and healthcare facilities, raises the stakes for security breaches. A successful attack on IoT devices in critical infrastructure can have severe consequences, including service disruptions, financial losses, and, in extreme cases, threats to public safety. The potential for widespread impact underscores the need for robust security measures, continuous monitoring, and proactive risk management in the deployment of IoT devices in critical sectors.

The evolving nature of IoT-related threats poses an ongoing challenge for cybersecurity professionals. As attackers adapt and develop new methods to exploit vulnerabilities in IoT devices, security measures must evolve in tandem. The lack of standardized security practices across the IoT landscape complicates efforts to address emerging threats effectively. Collaborative initiatives, industry standards, and regulatory frameworks are essential to establishing a baseline of security practices that can be universally applied to mitigate the evolving risks associated with IoT devices.

In conclusion, the proliferation of IoT devices introduces a complex landscape of security risks that demand immediate attention and comprehensive solutions. From inadequate device security measures to the challenges of managing updates, encryption, and physical security, the security risks associated with IoT devices are diverse and multifaceted. As the number of connected devices continues to grow, addressing these challenges requires a concerted effort from manufacturers, policymakers, and cybersecurity professionals to establish and enforce robust security practices, standards, and regulations that can safeguard the integrity and privacy of IoT ecosystems in our increasingly interconnected world.

Strategies for securing IoT networks and devices.

Securing Internet of Things (IoT) networks and devices is a complex task that demands a multifaceted approach encompassing various strategies to address the diverse challenges posed by the proliferation of connected devices. One fundamental strategy is to prioritize robust device authentication and authorization mechanisms. Implementing strong authentication protocols, such as two-factor authentication or biometric verification, ensures that only authorized users and devices gain access to the IoT network, mitigating the risk of unauthorized access and potential security breaches.

Encryption plays a pivotal role in securing IoT communications, both during transmission and storage. Employing end-to-end encryption for data in transit prevents eavesdropping and unauthorized access. Additionally, encrypting stored data on IoT devices safeguards sensitive information even if a device is compromised. Adopting industry-standard encryption algorithms and practices strengthens the overall security posture of IoT networks and contributes to the protection of user data and privacy.

To address the challenge of insecure firmware and software updates, a proactive strategy involves establishing a robust and streamlined update process. Device manufacturers must prioritize timely and regular updates to patch known vulnerabilities and enhance security. Implementing over-the-air (OTA) updates facilitates the seamless delivery of patches and updates, ensuring that devices remain resilient against evolving threats. Moreover, manufacturers should provide clear instructions to users on how to apply updates, promoting a security-conscious user base.

An essential component of securing IoT devices is implementing stringent access control policies. Role-based access control (RBAC) can be employed to define and manage user and device permissions within the IoT ecosystem. By assigning specific roles and access levels based on the principle of least privilege, organizations can minimize the potential impact of a security breach and enhance overall access management. Regularly reviewing and updating access control policies is crucial to adapt to changing circumstances and user roles.

Given the diverse nature of IoT devices, establishing a comprehensive inventory and asset management system is imperative. Organizations should maintain an up-to-date record of all connected devices, including their specifications, firmware versions, and locations. This inventory enables efficient monitoring, vulnerability assessments, and the prompt identification of unauthorized or compromised devices. Implementing device tracking solutions can further enhance visibility and aid in rapid response to security incidents.

Physical security measures are integral to safeguarding IoT devices, especially in scenarios where devices are deployed in uncontrolled environments. Physical tampering or theft can compromise the integrity of devices and pose a significant security risk. Employing tamper-evident packaging, secure enclosures, and location-based security protocols can deter physical attacks and enhance the overall resilience of IoT deployments.

Network segmentation is a critical strategy to contain potential security breaches and limit the lateral movement of attackers within an IoT ecosystem. By dividing the network into isolated segments, organizations can restrict unauthorized access to sensitive areas and mitigate the impact of a compromised device. Implementing firewalls, intrusion detection systems, and virtual LANs (VLANs) further strengthens network segmentation, providing an additional layer of defense against unauthorized access and potential attacks.

Continuous monitoring and threat detection are essential components of an effective IoT security strategy. Utilizing intrusion detection systems and security information and event management (SIEM) solutions enables real-time monitoring of network activity, anomalous behavior detection, and prompt response to security incidents. Machine learning and artificial intelligence algorithms can enhance the ability to identify patterns indicative of potential threats, allowing for proactive mitigation measures.

Collaboration and information sharing within the cybersecurity community are critical strategies for staying ahead of emerging threats and vulnerabilities. Participating in threat intelligence sharing platforms and industry alliances facilitates the exchange of information about new attack vectors, vulnerabilities, and mitigation strategies. By fostering a collaborative approach, organizations can collectively strengthen their defenses and contribute to a more resilient global IoT security landscape.

Regulatory compliance and adherence to industry standards are integral aspects of a comprehensive IoT security strategy. Compliance with established frameworks, such as the IoT Cybersecurity Improvement Act, ensures that organizations follow best practices and meet minimum security requirements. Additionally, industry-specific standards and certifications provide a benchmark for evaluating and enhancing the security of IoT devices. Adhering to these standards not only safeguards organizations from legal implications but also promotes a culture of security consciousness.

Educating users and stakeholders about cybersecurity best practices is a proactive strategy to mitigate human-centric risks. Establishing training programs that raise awareness about potential threats, phishing attacks, and secure device usage fosters a security-conscious culture. Users should be informed about the importance of updating passwords, recognizing social engineering attempts, and reporting suspicious activities. A well-informed user base contributes significantly to the overall resilience of IoT networks and devices.

In conclusion, securing IoT networks and devices necessitates a holistic and adaptive approach that addresses the diverse challenges posed by the interconnected nature of these devices. From robust authentication and encryption practices to proactive firmware updates, access control, physical security measures, and continuous monitoring, organizations must employ a combination of strategies to fortify their IoT ecosystems. Collaboration, compliance with standards, and user education further contribute to building a secure foundation in the dynamic and evolving landscape of IoT security.

The impact of quantum computing on traditional cryptographic methods.

Quantum computing, with its unparalleled ability to process vast amounts of information exponentially faster than classical computers, poses a significant threat to traditional cryptographic methods that have long been the cornerstone of secure communication and data protection. One of the most prominent impacts of quantum computing on cryptography is its potential to render widely used asymmetric encryption algorithms, such as RSA and ECC (Elliptic Curve Cryptography), vulnerable to efficient factorization.

Quantum computers leverage Shor's algorithm, a quantum algorithm specifically designed for factoring large numbers exponentially faster than the best-known classical algorithms. This threatens the security of public-key cryptography, as the time complexity of factoring large numbers is drastically reduced, compromising the confidentiality of encrypted communications.

Furthermore, quantum computers have the potential to undermine the security of digital signatures, which rely on the difficulty of solving certain mathematical problems. The widely adopted Digital Signature Algorithm (DSA) and the Elliptic Curve Digital Signature Algorithm (ECDSA) could be broken using quantum algorithms, such as Grover's algorithm, which searches unsorted databases quadratically faster than classical algorithms. As a result, the integrity and authenticity of digital signatures may be compromised, undermining the trustworthiness of signed documents and transactions. This has profound implications for the security of digital communication and the verification of the origin and authenticity of digital messages.

Hash functions, essential components of cryptographic protocols that ensure data integrity and provide a fixed-size representation of variable-size data, are also susceptible to the potential threats posed by quantum computing. Grover's algorithm, in this case, can be employed to find collisions in hash functions exponentially faster than classical algorithms. This means that the security provided by hash functions, such as SHA-256, is weakened, as an adversary with a sufficiently powerful quantum computer could more efficiently find two different inputs producing the same hash value, compromising the integrity of digital data.

The advent of quantum computing also challenges the security of symmetric key encryption algorithms, which are widely used for securing the confidentiality of data during transmission. While symmetric key algorithms like AES (Advanced Encryption Standard) are generally considered to be more resilient against quantum attacks compared to their asymmetric counterparts, the risk emerges with the potential development of quantum algorithms, like Grover's, that could search the key space exponentially faster than classical algorithms. Consequently, the effective key length of symmetric encryption schemes may need to be increased to maintain their security in the quantum era.

Post-quantum cryptography, an emerging field dedicated to developing cryptographic algorithms resistant to quantum attacks, is gaining traction as a strategic response to the vulnerabilities introduced by quantum computing. Researchers are actively exploring alternative cryptographic approaches that leverage mathematical problems believed to be hard for both classical and quantum computers. Lattice-based cryptography, hash-based cryptography, code-based cryptography, and multivariate polynomial cryptography are among the candidates for post-quantum cryptographic solutions. These approaches aim to provide security against quantum attacks and ensure the continued confidentiality, integrity, and authenticity of digital communications in the post-quantum era.

The transition to post-quantum cryptography, however, presents numerous challenges and complexities. Existing cryptographic infrastructure, protocols, and standards are deeply embedded in the fabric of digital systems, and migrating to new algorithms requires careful planning and coordination. The backward compatibility of post-quantum cryptographic solutions with legacy systems must be addressed to ensure a smooth transition without compromising the security of existing infrastructure.

Quantum key distribution (QKD) emerges as a promising solution to the quantum threat, providing a secure method for distributing cryptographic keys based on the principles of quantum mechanics. QKD leverages the quantum properties of particles to enable the detection of eavesdropping attempts during the key exchange process. Even with the advent of quantum computers, QKD remains theoretically secure, offering a means to establish cryptographic keys with a level of assurance that is not achievable using classical key distribution methods. However, practical challenges such as the limited range of QKD systems and the vulnerability of certain implementations to side-channel attacks must be addressed for widespread adoption.

The impact of quantum computing on cryptographic methods extends beyond the realms of confidentiality and integrity to encompass the realm of post-quantum digital resilience. Quantum-resistant cryptographic algorithms and protocols are not only essential for securing current communication channels but are also crucial for protecting sensitive information stored in archives that may be subject to decryption attempts in the future. The long-term security implications of quantum computing necessitate a proactive and collaborative effort from the cryptographic community, industry stakeholders, and policymakers to develop and implement quantum-resistant cryptographic standards.

In conclusion, the advent of quantum computing introduces unprecedented challenges to traditional cryptographic methods that have long been the bedrock of secure digital communication. The potential vulnerabilities of widely used cryptographic algorithms to quantum attacks necessitate a paradigm shift towards post-quantum cryptography. As researchers strive to develop quantum-resistant cryptographic solutions, the transition to a quantum-safe cryptographic infrastructure requires careful consideration of compatibility, scalability, and the evolving threat landscape. The future of secure communication hinges on the ability of the cryptographic community to adapt and innovate in the face of quantum advancements, ensuring the continued confidentiality, integrity, and authenticity of digital information in the quantum era.

Post-quantum cryptography as a countermeasure.

Post-quantum cryptography emerges as a vital countermeasure in the face of the transformative potential of quantum computing, which poses a significant threat to traditional cryptographic methods. The urgency to develop post-quantum cryptographic solutions stems from the fact that widely adopted cryptographic algorithms, particularly those based on integer factorization and discrete logarithm problems, face imminent vulnerability to quantum algorithms like Shor's algorithm. Recognizing this vulnerability, the cryptographic community is actively engaged in the exploration and development of alternative cryptographic approaches that can withstand the computational power of quantum computers.

One promising avenue within post-quantum cryptography lies in lattice-based cryptography. Lattices, mathematical structures defined in terms of vectors and matrices, form the foundation for cryptographic problems believed to be resistant to quantum attacks. Lattice-based cryptographic algorithms rely on the hardness of lattice problems, such as the Learning With Errors (LWE) problem, for their security. These problems involve finding a short vector in a lattice, and their complexity remains formidable even for quantum computers. The exploration of lattice-based cryptography represents a proactive response to the quantum threat, providing a foundation for cryptographic systems that can resist the potential quantum onslaught on classical algorithms.

Hash-based cryptography is another post-quantum approach that leverages the one-way nature of hash functions to secure digital communications. Hash-based signatures and Merkle tree structures are explored as potential alternatives to traditional digital signatures and public-key infrastructures vulnerable to quantum attacks. The simplicity and theoretical resilience of hash-based cryptographic schemes make them attractive candidates for a quantum-resistant cryptographic toolbox. While practical implementation challenges, such as the size of signatures and key management, need to be addressed, hash-based cryptography offers a promising avenue for post-quantum cryptographic resilience.

Code-based cryptography, rooted in error-correcting codes, presents another avenue for post-quantum security. The hardness of decoding certain linear codes forms the basis for cryptographic primitives that resist quantum attacks. The McEliece and Niederreiter cryptosystems are notable examples within code-based cryptography. These schemes rely on the difficulty of decoding random linear codes and offer a level of security that withstands quantum algorithms, providing a potential alternative for secure communication in a quantum-powered landscape.

Multivariate polynomial cryptography explores the complexity of solving systems of multivariate polynomial equations as the foundation for cryptographic primitives. The security of these systems hinges on the inherent difficulty of solving polynomial equations, even for quantum computers. Multivariate polynomial cryptography includes schemes like the Unbalanced Oil and Vinegar (UOV) scheme and the Rainbow scheme, both of which exhibit resistance to quantum attacks. While implementation challenges and the need for efficient key sizes remain considerations, multivariate polynomial cryptography contributes to the diverse arsenal of post-quantum cryptographic tools.

Navigating the transition to post-quantum cryptography requires careful consideration of standardization efforts to ensure interoperability, security, and a smooth migration process. Recognizing this need, organizations such as the National Institute of Standards and Technology (NIST) have embarked on initiatives to solicit, evaluate, and standardize post-quantum cryptographic algorithms. The NIST Post-Quantum Cryptography Standardization project aims to identify cryptographic algorithms that can serve as secure alternatives to current standards, promoting the development and adoption of quantum-resistant cryptographic solutions.

Quantum-resistant key exchange mechanisms, such as those based on lattices or code-based cryptography, play a pivotal role in post-quantum cryptographic ecosystems. Quantum Key Distribution (QKD) is another key exchange method that leverages the principles of quantum mechanics to secure key exchange. QKD relies on the fundamental properties of quantum states, such as the non-cloning theorem, to detect eavesdropping attempts and ensure secure key exchange. Although QKD has demonstrated theoretical security, practical challenges such as limited range and vulnerability to certain attacks require further research and development to make it a practical and scalable solution.

The integration of post-quantum cryptographic algorithms into existing communication protocols and infrastructure poses a significant challenge. Legacy systems and protocols that rely on traditional cryptographic methods may need to undergo substantial updates or even complete overhauls to accommodate the new era of quantum-resistant cryptography. This necessitates a careful transition strategy, including hybrid cryptographic schemes that combine classical and post-quantum algorithms during the migration phase. Hybrid schemes provide a transitional bridge, allowing organizations to adapt to post-quantum cryptography without immediately abandoning existing cryptographic protocols.

One notable aspect of post-quantum cryptographic research is the emphasis on not just resisting quantum attacks but also providing practical and efficient solutions for real-world deployment. The computational and memory requirements of cryptographic algorithms play a crucial role in their feasibility for widespread use. Cryptographers strive to strike a balance between security and efficiency, ensuring that post-quantum cryptographic solutions can be implemented on a broad scale without introducing impractical computational overhead.

The quantum threat has prompted industry stakeholders, government agencies, and cryptographic researchers to collaborate in addressing the challenges posed by quantum computing. Open-source initiatives, research conferences, and collaborative projects facilitate the exchange of knowledge and ideas within the cryptographic community. This collaborative approach fosters the development of robust and standardized post-quantum cryptographic algorithms that can withstand scrutiny and contribute to a secure digital future.

In addition to the technical challenges, the human factor in the adoption of post-quantum cryptography cannot be overlooked. Educating stakeholders, including developers, administrators, and end-users, about the implications of quantum computing for traditional cryptography and the importance of transitioning to quantum-resistant solutions is crucial. As organizations plan for the post-quantum era, a comprehensive awareness and training program can contribute to a smoother adoption process and foster a proactive mindset towards quantum-resistant cryptographic practices.

In conclusion, post-quantum cryptography represents a crucial countermeasure against the potential threats posed by quantum computing to traditional cryptographic methods. The exploration of alternative mathematical problems, such as lattice-based cryptography, hash-based cryptography, code-based cryptography, and multivariate polynomial cryptography, offers a diverse range of solutions that can withstand quantum attacks. Standardization efforts, quantum-resistant key exchange mechanisms, and the integration of post-quantum cryptography into existing infrastructure are essential components of a comprehensive strategy to navigate the quantum revolution. The collaborative efforts of the cryptographic community, industry stakeholders, and policymakers are paramount in ensuring the development and deployment of robust post-quantum cryptographic solutions that safeguard the confidentiality, integrity, and authenticity of digital communication in the quantum era and beyond.

Chapter 7: Global Cybersecurity Challenges: A Cross-Border Perspective

The interconnected nature of cybersecurity challenges on a global scale.

The contemporary landscape of cybersecurity is characterized by an intricate web of interconnected challenges that transcend geographic boundaries, permeating the fabric of the global digital ecosystem. In an era where technology underpins virtually every aspect of modern life, the vulnerabilities of interconnected systems have become increasingly apparent, giving rise to a complex array of threats that demand a multifaceted and collaborative approach to mitigation. The rapid proliferation of interconnected devices, fueled by the advent of the Internet of Things (IoT), has created a vast attack surface, rendering traditional security measures insufficient in the face of sophisticated cyber adversaries. As the digital realm transcends national borders, the repercussions of cyber incidents reverberate across the globe, transcending geopolitical boundaries and challenging the traditional frameworks of national sovereignty. The interconnected nature of the global economy further amplifies the impact of cyber threats, with disruptions in one region cascading through supply chains and financial systems, underscoring the systemic risks inherent in our hyperconnected world.

The evolution of cyber threats from isolated incidents to orchestrated campaigns orchestrated by state and non-state actors has heightened the urgency for a coordinated international response. Nation-states, once primarily engaged in conventional warfare, now wield cyber capabilities as potent tools for espionage, influence operations, and sabotage. The blurring of lines between state-sponsored and cybercriminal activities has created a murky landscape, where attribution becomes a formidable challenge, complicating efforts to enforce accountability and establish norms of responsible behavior in cyberspace. This geopolitical dimension of cybersecurity extends beyond mere technical considerations, encompassing diplomatic, legal, and ethical dimensions that necessitate a collaborative and inclusive approach.

Moreover, the interconnectedness of critical infrastructure systems, such as energy grids, transportation networks, and healthcare systems, exposes societies to cascading failures with far-reaching consequences. A successful cyber attack on a single node within this interconnected web can have a domino effect, triggering systemic disruptions that compromise the safety, security, and well-being of populations. The ransomware epidemic, exemplified by high-profile incidents affecting healthcare institutions and municipal services, highlights the transnational nature of cyber threats, with criminal actors exploiting vulnerabilities for financial gain across borders, often with impunity.

The globalization of cyber threats is further compounded by the diffusion of offensive cyber capabilities beyond traditional state actors to include non-state entities, hacktivists, and even individuals with malicious intent. The democratization of cyber tools and techniques through the dark web facilitates a landscape where threat actors with varying motivations and skill levels can engage in cyber warfare, creating a dynamic and adaptive ecosystem that challenges the static nature of traditional defense mechanisms. This diffusion of capabilities introduces a plethora of actors with distinct objectives, ranging from ideological motivations to economic interests, thereby diversifying the threat landscape and complicating efforts to establish a unified defense posture.

The challenge of cybersecurity on a global scale also extends to the realm of information warfare and the manipulation of public perception. Cyber-enabled disinformation campaigns leverage the interconnectedness of social media platforms to spread false narratives, sow discord, and influence political processes on a global scale. The weaponization of information poses a unique threat, as the boundaries between physical and digital realms blur, and the manipulation of information becomes a potent tool for achieving strategic objectives. The interconnected nature of the information ecosystem allows for the rapid dissemination of narratives that can shape public opinion, erode trust in institutions, and destabilize democracies, transcending borders and challenging the foundations of open societies.

In addressing these multifaceted challenges, the imperative for international cooperation becomes evident. The interconnected nature of cyber threats necessitates collaborative efforts in information sharing, threat intelligence, and the development of shared norms and principles that govern behavior in cyberspace. Initiatives such as the Budapest Convention on Cybercrime and the Paris Call for Trust and Security in Cyberspace reflect the global recognition of the need for a collective response to cyber threats, transcending national interests in favor of a more resilient and secure digital environment.

However, the path to effective global cybersecurity governance is fraught with challenges, ranging from differing national priorities and legal frameworks to concerns over sovereignty and the potential militarization of cyberspace. Striking a balance between preserving the openness of the internet and safeguarding national security interests requires a delicate diplomatic dance, where states, international organizations, and the private sector must collaborate to foster a common understanding of the norms that should govern state behavior in cyberspace. The lack of a universally accepted framework for attributing cyber attacks, coupled with the absence of enforceable mechanisms for holding malicious actors accountable, hampers the development of a robust international legal regime for cybersecurity.

In conclusion, the interconnected nature of cybersecurity challenges on a global scale underscores the imperative for a holistic and collaborative approach to safeguarding the digital realm. The rapid evolution of technology, the diffusion of cyber capabilities, and the transnational nature of cyber threats necessitate a paradigm shift in how we conceptualize and address cybersecurity. The interconnectedness of our digital ecosystem requires a collective effort to establish norms, enhance resilience, and foster international cooperation to navigate the complex and dynamic landscape of cyberspace. Only through a united front that transcends geopolitical boundaries can we hope to effectively mitigate the evolving threats that imperil the foundations of our interconnected world.

The need for international cooperation in addressing cyber threats.

The imperatives of our digital age demand a profound recognition of the critical necessity for international cooperation in addressing the escalating and complex landscape of cyber threats. In an era where borders are blurred by the interconnected fabric of the internet, traditional notions of sovereignty and national security are increasingly inadequate to confront the transnational challenges posed by malicious actors in cyberspace. The very nature of cyber threats, with their ability to transcend geographic boundaries and impact diverse sectors simultaneously, underscores the futility of unilateral efforts in ensuring the security and resilience of digital ecosystems. As nation-states grapple with the multifaceted dimensions of cyber warfare, it becomes abundantly clear that a collaborative, coordinated, and inclusive approach is not merely desirable but an existential imperative for the global community.

The interconnectedness of our world, facilitated by the proliferation of digital technologies, has ushered in unprecedented levels of interdependence. Critical infrastructure, such as energy grids, financial systems, and healthcare networks, relies on a web of interconnected technologies, rendering them susceptible to cascading failures triggered by a single cyber incident. The recent spate of ransomware attacks on vital institutions serves as a stark reminder that the consequences of such incidents are not confined to the immediate targets but radiate across borders, impacting individuals, economies, and societies on a global scale. The interwoven nature of our digital infrastructure necessitates collaborative efforts to fortify defenses, share threat intelligence, and establish common protocols that enhance the overall cybersecurity posture.

Moreover, the evolving landscape of cyber threats extends beyond traditional state-based actors to include non-state entities, hacktivists, and criminal organizations operating with global reach. The democratization of cyber capabilities, evidenced by the accessibility of sophisticated tools on the dark web, underscores the need for collective action to curb the proliferation of malicious activities. International collaboration becomes imperative in addressing the root causes of cybercrime, disrupting criminal networks, and establishing a unified front against those who exploit the interconnectedness of our digital world for nefarious purposes. The sheer diversity of threat actors and their motivations demands a shared understanding and a coordinated response that transcends individual jurisdictions.

In the realm of state-sponsored cyber activities, the need for international norms and rules of engagement becomes increasingly apparent. The absence of universally accepted standards for attributing cyber attacks, coupled with the challenges of distinguishing between state and non-state actors, hampers efforts to establish accountability and discourage malicious behavior. The development of international agreements, such as the Tallinn Manual and the Paris Call for Trust and Security in Cyberspace, signifies a recognition of the imperative to define rules and norms governing state behavior in cyberspace. However, the path to a comprehensive and universally accepted framework is fraught with diplomatic challenges, requiring sustained international dialogue and cooperation.

The economic dimension of cybersecurity further underscores the need for collaboration. As economies become more digitally intertwined, disruptions in one region can have ripple effects globally. The theft of intellectual property, economic espionage, and cyber-enabled financial crimes transcend national borders, necessitating collaborative efforts to investigate, prosecute, and deter such activities. The interconnected nature of the global economy demands a collective response to safeguard economic stability, protect intellectual property rights, and foster a secure environment for digital commerce.

The ongoing challenge of cyber-enabled disinformation campaigns and influence operations further emphasizes the imperative for international cooperation. The manipulation of information, facilitated by the interconnectedness of social media platforms, poses a threat to the foundations of democracies worldwide. Coordinated efforts to share insights, best practices, and technological solutions can help mitigate the impact of disinformation campaigns and protect the integrity of democratic processes. International collaboration in this domain is not just a matter of national interest but a shared responsibility to uphold the principles of open societies and democratic governance.

While the need for international cooperation in addressing cyber threats is evident, the practicalities of achieving such collaboration are complex and multifaceted. Divergent national priorities, legal frameworks, and concerns over sovereignty create barriers to the development of a cohesive and effective global cybersecurity strategy. Moreover, the inherently dynamic and adaptive nature of cyber threats requires mechanisms that can evolve in real-time, necessitating a level of agility and responsiveness that traditional diplomatic processes may struggle to achieve. Bridging these gaps requires a commitment to sustained dialogue, the development of shared norms and principles, and the cultivation of mutual trust among nations.

Efforts to foster international cooperation in cybersecurity must extend beyond the realm of states to include collaboration with the private sector, academia, and civil society. The expertise and resources of private entities, which often own and operate critical infrastructure, are indispensable in fortifying defenses and responding to cyber incidents. Public-private partnerships can facilitate the exchange of information, the development of best practices, and the creation of joint initiatives that strengthen the overall cybersecurity ecosystem. Inclusion of non-governmental stakeholders ensures a more comprehensive and holistic approach to addressing cyber threats, acknowledging that the interconnected nature of cyberspace implicates a diverse array of actors.

In conclusion, the imperative for international cooperation in addressing cyber threats is a defining feature of the digital age. The interconnected nature of our world, the evolving landscape of cyber threats, and the transnational reach of malicious actors necessitate a collaborative and inclusive approach. The development of shared norms, the establishment of international agreements, and the forging of partnerships among states, private entities, and civil society are essential components of a resilient global cybersecurity strategy. As the challenges in cyberspace continue to evolve, the collective response of the international community must also adapt, recognizing that the security and stability of our interconnected world depend on collaborative efforts to navigate the complexities of the digital frontier.

Examples of cyber threats that transcend national borders.

The realm of cyberspace is fraught with a myriad of threats that transcend national borders, reflecting the interconnected and borderless nature of the digital landscape. One notable example is the proliferation of sophisticated state-sponsored cyber attacks that extend far beyond the territories of their origin. Nation-states leverage advanced cyber capabilities to conduct espionage, disrupt critical infrastructure, and engage in cyber warfare, with the potential for widespread repercussions across the globe. The notorious Stuxnet malware, discovered in 2010, exemplifies the transnational impact of state-sponsored cyber operations. Attributed to joint efforts by the United States and Israel, Stuxnet targeted Iran's nuclear facilities, illustrating how a cyber weapon developed in one country can have international consequences by disrupting critical infrastructure and influencing geopolitical dynamics.

Ransomware attacks represent another glaring example of cyber threats with global ramifications. The interconnected nature of our digital infrastructure allows ransomware to propagate rapidly across borders, impacting organizations and individuals worldwide. The WannaCry ransomware attack in 2017 is a prime illustration of the transnational reach of such threats. Exploiting vulnerabilities in Microsoft Windows, WannaCry infected hundreds of thousands of computers in over 150 countries, disrupting healthcare systems, financial institutions, and critical infrastructure. The attack underscored how a single piece of malicious code, once unleashed, can traverse national boundaries, causing widespread chaos and financial losses on a global scale.

The phenomenon of nation-state-backed cyber espionage further exemplifies the transboundary nature of cyber threats. Advanced persistent threat (APT) groups, often linked to nation-states, conduct long-term, targeted campaigns to infiltrate foreign governments, businesses, and organizations. One notable example is the Chinese-sponsored APT known as APT41, which has been implicated in cyber espionage activities targeting entities in multiple countries. The group's tactics, techniques, and procedures extend across borders, highlighting the challenge of attributing cyber attacks to specific nations and the need for international collaboration to counter such threats effectively.

Financial cybercrime represents yet another category of threats that extends its impact globally. Cybercriminal organizations, often operating across borders, deploy tactics such as banking trojans, phishing campaigns, and ransomware to target financial institutions and individuals. The Carbanak and FIN7 cybercrime groups provide a compelling example of the international reach of financial cyber threats. These groups orchestrated large-scale, transnational campaigns that resulted in substantial financial losses for banks and corporations across the United States, Europe, and beyond. The interconnected nature of the global financial system makes it susceptible to such attacks, emphasizing the need for coordinated international efforts to combat cybercriminal networks.

State-sponsored disinformation campaigns and influence operations present another dimension of cyber threats that transcend national borders. In the digital age, the manipulation of information has become a potent tool for shaping narratives and influencing public opinion on a global scale. Russia's interference in the 2016 U.S. presidential election serves as a prominent example of how state-backed actors can exploit the interconnectedness of social media to disseminate disinformation and sow discord in foreign nations. The impact of such campaigns reverberates beyond individual countries, affecting the stability of democratic processes and international relations, necessitating collaborative efforts to counteract the spread of misinformation and protect the integrity of democratic systems worldwide.

The interconnectedness of supply chains adds an additional layer of complexity to the transnational dimension of cyber threats. Cyber attacks targeting one node in a global supply chain can have cascading effects, disrupting the production and distribution of goods and services across borders. The SolarWinds supply chain attack, discovered in 2020, exemplifies this form of threat. A sophisticated supply chain compromise, attributed to Russian state-sponsored actors, resulted in the infiltration of numerous U.S. government agencies and private sector organizations. The incident underscored the vulnerability of interconnected supply chains to transnational cyber threats, emphasizing the necessity of international collaboration to fortify the resilience of critical infrastructure.

The vulnerability of the healthcare sector to cyber threats with cross-border consequences has become increasingly evident, especially in the wake of the COVID-19 pandemic. Cyber attacks on healthcare organizations, ranging from ransomware incidents to data breaches, can have immediate and far-reaching impacts on public health. The 2020 cyber attack on the World Health Organization (WHO), amid the global health crisis, exemplifies the audacious nature of such threats. The incident highlighted how malicious actors, unbounded by borders, exploit the critical nature of healthcare infrastructure for financial gain and geopolitical leverage, emphasizing the need for international cooperation to protect global health institutions and the sensitive data they steward.

The emerging threat landscape of the Internet of Things (IoT) further accentuates the transboundary nature of cyber risks. As smart devices permeate homes, cities, and industries globally, vulnerabilities in IoT devices can be exploited by malicious actors to launch large-scale attacks with international repercussions. The Mirai botnet attack in 2016 serves as a pertinent example. Exploiting insecure IoT devices, the Mirai botnet orchestrated distributed denial-of-service (DDoS) attacks that disrupted internet services for millions of users across the United States and Europe. The incident demonstrated how vulnerabilities in connected devices can be leveraged to create a global threat, necessitating collaborative efforts to establish security standards and mitigate risks associated with the proliferation of IoT.

In conclusion, the examples of cyber threats that transcend national borders underscore the intricate and interconnected nature of the digital realm. State-sponsored cyber operations, ransomware attacks, financial cybercrime, disinformation campaigns, supply chain compromises, healthcare sector vulnerabilities, and IoT-related threats exemplify the diversity and complexity of challenges that extend beyond individual countries. The transnational impact of these threats necessitates a collective and coordinated response, emphasizing the imperative for international cooperation to fortify cybersecurity measures, share threat intelligence, and develop common strategies to address the evolving landscape of cyber risks on a global scale.

Challenges in attributing and responding to cross-border attacks.

The challenges inherent in attributing and responding to cross-border cyber attacks represent a complex and multifaceted landscape, marked by technological intricacies, diplomatic considerations, and the evolving nature of cyber threats. Attribution, the process of identifying the responsible party behind a cyber attack, poses a formidable challenge due to the anonymity and obfuscation techniques employed by sophisticated threat actors. The use of proxy servers, false flag operations, and the strategic deployment of malware by nation-states and cybercriminal organizations alike complicates the task of definitively linking an attack to a specific entity. The lack of universally accepted standards and norms for attributing cyber incidents further exacerbates the difficulty, leading to a situation where conclusive evidence is often elusive, and attributions remain contested.

The blurred boundaries between state-sponsored and non-state cyber activities add a layer of complexity to the attribution challenge. Nation-states, engaging in cyber operations for espionage, influence campaigns, or sabotage, often deploy techniques that mirror those used by independent cybercriminals. This deliberate blending of tactics makes it difficult to distinguish between state-sponsored and non-state actors, hampering efforts to accurately attribute attacks. The emergence of hybrid threats, where state-sponsored actors collaborate with or sponsor criminal groups for cyber operations, further muddles the attribution landscape, highlighting the need for nuanced analysis and intelligence sharing among nations to unravel the layers of complexity.

Moreover, the international diplomatic implications of attribution add a dimension of sensitivity to the process. Accusing a foreign government or entity of cyber aggression requires careful consideration of geopolitical relations, potential retaliation, and the overall stability of international affairs. The lack of established norms for responding to cyber attacks, especially in the absence of clear attribution, creates a situation where states may be reluctant to publicly attribute attacks for fear of escalation or diplomatic fallout. The diplomatic challenges are further compounded by the absence of a universally agreed-upon definition of what constitutes an act of war in cyberspace, leaving a legal and strategic void that hampers effective response mechanisms.

The dynamic and rapid evolution of cyber threats exacerbates the difficulties in timely and accurate attribution. The agility of threat actors to change tactics, infrastructure, and tools in real-time presents a moving target for investigators. Advanced persistent threats (APTs), characterized by their long-term, covert nature, often involve sophisticated and patient adversaries who carefully cover their tracks, making it challenging to detect and attribute their activities. The ephemeral nature of the digital evidence, coupled with the continuous adaptation of cybercriminal techniques, requires an equally dynamic and agile response capability that many traditional law enforcement and intelligence agencies struggle to maintain.

In addition to the technical and diplomatic challenges, the private sector's role further complicates the attribution and response landscape. Private entities, often the primary targets of cyber attacks, possess valuable insights and data crucial for attribution efforts. However, concerns over the protection of proprietary information, reputational damage, and the potential for legal repercussions may hinder their willingness to collaborate with governments in attribution processes. Striking the right balance between public and private collaboration requires the establishment of trust and the development of frameworks that address the concerns of both sectors, fostering a collaborative environment that enhances collective cybersecurity efforts.

The lack of a unified international legal framework for cyber attribution and response poses a significant impediment to effective cross-border cooperation. While there have been efforts to establish norms and guidelines, such as the Tallinn Manual and the Paris Call for Trust and Security in Cyberspace, the absence of legally binding agreements hampers the enforcement of norms and the establishment of clear rules for responding to cyber incidents. The absence of consequences for violating established norms weakens the deterrent effect and undermines efforts to create a stable and secure cyberspace. The challenges in reaching consensus on legal frameworks reflect the broader complexities of international relations and the divergent interests of states in the evolving digital landscape.

The strategic dilemma of proportionate and effective responses to cyber attacks further complicates the landscape. The absence of a clear threshold for determining the severity of a cyber incident that warrants a robust response creates ambiguity and inhibits decisive action. Striking the right balance between deterring malicious actors and avoiding undue escalation requires a nuanced understanding of the strategic implications of cyber responses. The interconnected nature of cyberspace means that responses, whether defensive or offensive, have the potential to reverberate across borders, necessitating careful consideration of the broader implications and unintended consequences.

Cross-border attacks often exploit the jurisdictional challenges inherent in cyberspace. The digital landscape allows threat actors to operate from jurisdictions with lax cybersecurity regulations or limited law enforcement capabilities, providing a safe haven for their activities. The lack of harmonized international legal mechanisms for extradition, prosecution, and cooperation in cybercrime investigations further impedes the ability to hold perpetrators accountable. The challenge of extraditing individuals involved in cyber attacks becomes particularly acute when the actions are attributed to state-sponsored actors, raising questions about the accountability of nation-states for the actions of entities operating within their borders.

The proliferation of non-state actors engaged in cyber attacks introduces an additional layer of complexity. Hacktivist groups, cyber mercenaries, and criminal organizations operate with varying motivations and objectives, challenging traditional paradigms of state responsibility. The attribution and response mechanisms designed for state-sponsored activities may not be readily applicable to these diverse threat actors. The absence of a comprehensive framework that encompasses the full spectrum of cyber threats, irrespective of the actor's identity, underscores the need for a more inclusive and adaptable approach to attribution and response.

In conclusion, the challenges in attributing and responding to cross-border cyber attacks epitomize the intricate and evolving nature of the cybersecurity landscape. The technical complexities of attribution, the diplomatic sensitivities, the private sector's role, the absence of a unified legal framework, the strategic dilemmas, and the jurisdictional challenges collectively form a web of intricacies that demand international cooperation and collaboration. Addressing these challenges requires a concerted effort to establish norms, share threat intelligence, build trust among nations and private entities, and develop agile response mechanisms that can navigate the complexities of the digital frontier. Only through collective action can the international community hope to effectively address the persistent and evolving threats that transcend national borders in the dynamic and interconnected world of cyberspace.

Overview of existing international laws and treaties related to cybersecurity.

The landscape of international laws and treaties related to cybersecurity is characterized by a complex tapestry of agreements, conventions, and frameworks that have evolved to address the challenges posed by cyber threats. At the core of this legal framework is the recognition that cyberspace is a domain that transcends national borders, requiring collaborative efforts to establish norms, deter malicious activities, and promote responsible behavior in the digital realm. The United Nations (UN) has played a central role in shaping the international legal discourse on cybersecurity, with various entities and initiatives contributing to the development of norms and principles governing state behavior in cyberspace. The most notable of these is the Group of Governmental Experts (GGE) on Developments in the Field of Information and Telecommunications in the Context of International Security, which has produced several reports outlining voluntary norms and confidence-building measures in cyberspace.

The Tallinn Manual, though not a binding legal document, represents a significant contribution to the understanding of how existing international law applies to cyber operations. Drafted by a group of legal experts, the manual addresses issues such as sovereignty, the law of armed conflict, and the prohibition of the use of force in the context of cyber activities. It serves as a reference point for states in interpreting and applying existing international law to cyber operations, offering valuable insights into the legal aspects of state conduct in cyberspace. Additionally, the Tallinn Manual 2.0, published in 2017, delves deeper into the application of international law to cyber operations occurring during peacetime.

The UN has also seen efforts to develop a binding treaty on cybersecurity. However, progress in this regard has been slow, primarily due to divergent views among member states on issues such as the definition of cyber threats, the scope of applicability, and the balance between national security interests and individual privacy rights. The absence of a comprehensive treaty specifically addressing cybersecurity reflects the challenges of achieving consensus in the international community, given the rapidly evolving nature of technology and the diverse interests of states.

Within the European Union (EU), the General Data Protection Regulation (GDPR) stands as a key legal instrument addressing cybersecurity concerns. While not exclusively focused on cybersecurity, the GDPR includes provisions related to the protection of personal data, imposing strict requirements on organizations handling such data. The regulation has extraterritorial applicability, affecting entities outside the EU that process the personal data of EU residents. The GDPR serves as an example of regional efforts to enhance cybersecurity and protect individual privacy, showcasing the EU's commitment to shaping digital policies that extend beyond national borders.

The Budapest Convention on Cybercrime, also known as the Council of Europe Convention on Cybercrime, is a pioneering international treaty specifically addressing cybercrime. Adopted in 2001, the convention establishes a framework for the harmonization of national laws, the enhancement of law enforcement cooperation, and the facilitation of extradition in cases related to cybercrime. Its broad scope covers offenses such as unauthorized access, data interference, and content-related crimes. The Budapest Convention exemplifies international efforts to combat cybercrime by fostering cooperation and mutual legal assistance among signatory states, recognizing the transnational nature of cyber threats.

On the regional front, the Organization of American States (OAS) has played a role in developing norms and principles related to cybersecurity through the Inter-American Committee against Terrorism (CICTE). The OAS has hosted discussions and workshops to promote cooperation among its member states in addressing cybersecurity challenges. Similarly, the ASEAN Regional Forum (ARF) has explored avenues for regional cooperation on cybersecurity within the Asia-Pacific region. While these initiatives may not result in legally binding treaties, they contribute to the development of regional norms and cooperation mechanisms to address common cybersecurity concerns.

In the realm of arms control and disarmament, discussions around cybersecurity have gained traction. The UN Group of Governmental Experts on Disarmament has explored the potential for norms and rules to prevent the militarization of cyberspace. The challenges lie in defining what constitutes an act of war in cyberspace and establishing mechanisms for verifying compliance with any potential agreements. The dual-use nature of many cyber capabilities, which can be employed for both offensive and defensive purposes, further complicates efforts to formulate effective arms control measures.

The norms of responsible state behavior in cyberspace have gained prominence through various initiatives. The Paris Call for Trust and Security in Cyberspace, launched in 2018, is a non-binding political declaration that outlines principles for ensuring a secure and open cyberspace. It encourages signatories, including states, private sector entities, and civil society, to commit to the protection of individuals and infrastructure from cyber threats. Similarly, the Charter of Trust, initiated by a group of global companies in collaboration with the Munich Security Conference, focuses on enhancing the security of critical infrastructure and promoting trust in the digital ecosystem.

While these international laws, treaties, and initiatives contribute to the evolving legal framework for cybersecurity, challenges persist. The absence of a comprehensive, universally accepted treaty leaves gaps in addressing the full spectrum of cyber threats. Differing interpretations of existing international law and norms, coupled with the rapid pace of technological change, contribute to uncertainties in the application of legal principles to emerging cyber challenges. The persistent issue of attribution, as highlighted by numerous high-profile cyber incidents, remains a significant obstacle in responding effectively to cross-border attacks.

In conclusion, the landscape of international laws and treaties related to cybersecurity reflects ongoing efforts to adapt legal frameworks to the challenges posed by an interconnected and rapidly evolving digital world. While existing instruments provide valuable guidance on issues such as state behavior, cybercrime, and data protection, the absence of a comprehensive and universally accepted treaty underscores the complexities of achieving consensus among states with diverse interests. As cyberspace continues to shape global affairs, the development of a robust and adaptive legal framework remains a dynamic process, requiring ongoing dialogue, cooperation, and shared commitment among the international community.

Gaps and challenges in the current legal framework.

The current legal framework governing cybersecurity, while evolving, faces significant gaps and challenges that reflect the complexity and rapid evolution of the digital landscape. One of the fundamental challenges lies in the absence of a comprehensive, universally accepted treaty specifically addressing cybersecurity. The lack of a binding international agreement leaves considerable gaps in establishing clear norms and rules governing state behavior in cyberspace. Divergent interpretations of existing international law, varying national interests, and the challenge of balancing security concerns with individual privacy rights contribute to the difficulty in achieving consensus on a global scale. The slow progress in reaching a comprehensive treaty underscores the intricate nature of international relations and the difficulty in crafting a framework that accommodates the diverse interests of states in the realm of cyberspace.

Attribution remains a persistent challenge within the current legal framework. The ability to accurately attribute cyber attacks to specific actors is hampered by the use of sophisticated techniques, such as the deliberate use of false flags, the employment of proxy servers, and the involvement of non-state actors. The lack of universally accepted standards for attributing cyber incidents complicates efforts to hold malicious actors accountable for their actions. States may be hesitant to publicly attribute attacks due to the potential for diplomatic fallout or the risk of miscalculation that could lead to escalation. The ambiguity surrounding attribution hinders the development of effective response mechanisms and contributes to a sense of impunity for those engaging in malicious cyber activities.

The dual-use nature of many cyber capabilities poses challenges in the context of arms control and disarmament. The difficulty in distinguishing between offensive and defensive cyber capabilities makes it challenging to formulate clear rules and norms to prevent the militarization of cyberspace. The lack of consensus on what constitutes an act of war in cyberspace further complicates efforts to develop effective arms control measures. The absence of agreed-upon mechanisms for verifying compliance with any potential agreements hampers progress in establishing rules to govern the development and use of cyber weapons. As a result, the potential for an arms race in cyberspace looms, with states enhancing their capabilities without clear constraints.

The jurisdictional challenges inherent in cyberspace contribute to the difficulties in enforcing international laws related to cybersecurity. The borderless nature of the internet allows threat actors to operate from jurisdictions with lax cybersecurity regulations or limited law enforcement capabilities, providing a safe haven for their activities. The absence of a harmonized international legal framework for extradition, prosecution, and cooperation in cybercrime investigations allows malicious actors to evade accountability. The challenges in holding perpetrators accountable are particularly pronounced when the actions are attributed to state-sponsored actors, raising questions about the accountability of nation-states for entities operating within their borders.

The legal framework's adaptability and responsiveness to emerging cyber threats represent another significant challenge. The rapid evolution of technology and the dynamic nature of cyber threats outpace the ability of legal frameworks to keep pace. Traditional legal processes may be slow and cumbersome in addressing the swift and agile nature of cyber attacks. The lack of mechanisms for international cooperation and coordination in real-time further impedes the ability to respond effectively to cyber incidents. As a result, the legal framework may struggle to provide timely and relevant solutions to emerging challenges, leaving a gap in the ability to address the constantly evolving nature of cyber threats.

The issue of state-sponsored cyber activities, which often blur the lines between traditional espionage, cybercrime, and acts of war, poses a unique challenge. The current legal framework lacks clear distinctions and mechanisms for addressing the complex interplay between state and non-state actors in cyberspace. State-sponsored attacks, conducted with varying motivations and objectives, challenge traditional paradigms of state responsibility and accountability. The absence of agreed-upon consequences for violating established norms weakens the deterrent effect and undermines efforts to establish a stable and secure cyberspace. Navigating the legal complexities of state-sponsored cyber activities requires a nuanced understanding of the dynamic and evolving nature of the digital realm.

The tension between national security interests and individual privacy rights represents an ongoing challenge within the legal framework. As states enhance their capabilities for cyber surveillance in the name of national security, concerns over the erosion of privacy rights and civil liberties mount. The lack of a harmonized approach to balancing security imperatives with the protection of individual rights contributes to a fragmented legal landscape. The extraterritorial reach of some national laws, such as the General Data Protection Regulation (GDPR) in the European Union, raises questions about the harmonization of legal standards and the potential for conflicting jurisdictional claims. Bridging the gap between security and privacy in the digital age remains a persistent challenge that demands international cooperation and consensus.

The prevalence of non-state actors, including hacktivist groups, cyber mercenaries, and criminal organizations, introduces additional complexities. The current legal framework, primarily designed to address state behavior, may struggle to adapt to the diverse motivations and activities of non-state actors in cyberspace. The absence of a comprehensive framework that encompasses the full spectrum of cyber threats, irrespective of the actor's identity, underscores the need for a more inclusive and adaptable approach. Crafting legal mechanisms that can effectively address the actions of non-state actors while respecting the principles of due process and international law presents an ongoing challenge within the evolving legal landscape.

In conclusion, the gaps and challenges in the current legal framework for cybersecurity reflect the intricacies of addressing a dynamic and rapidly evolving digital landscape. The absence of a comprehensive international treaty, difficulties in attribution, jurisdictional challenges, the dual-use nature of cyber capabilities, and the tension between national security and individual privacy rights collectively contribute to a legal framework that struggles to keep pace with the complexities of cyberspace. Addressing these challenges requires sustained international dialogue, cooperation, and a commitment to developing legal mechanisms that are adaptive, inclusive, and responsive to the evolving nature of cyber threats. Only through collaborative efforts can the international community hope to bridge these gaps and establish a robust legal foundation for ensuring the security and stability of the digital realm.

The role of diplomacy in addressing cyber conflicts.

Diplomacy plays a pivotal role in addressing cyber conflicts, offering a nuanced and strategic approach to managing tensions, fostering cooperation, and mitigating the risks associated with malicious activities in cyberspace. In the ever-evolving landscape of international relations, where borders are blurred by the interconnected nature of the digital realm, traditional diplomatic mechanisms are being recalibrated to confront the challenges posed by cyber conflicts. The multifaceted role of diplomacy encompasses preventive measures, crisis management, norm-building, and the facilitation of international cooperation, reflecting the complex and dynamic nature of addressing cyber threats at the global level.

Preventive diplomacy is a cornerstone in the diplomatic toolkit for managing cyber conflicts. By engaging in dialogue and confidence-building measures, states can work to establish norms of responsible behavior in cyberspace, reducing the likelihood of misunderstandings and misinterpretations that could escalate into conflicts. Preventive diplomacy involves fostering a shared understanding of the rules of the road in cyberspace, encouraging states to adopt transparent policies, and promoting the responsible use of cyber capabilities. Multilateral forums and initiatives, such as the United Nations Group of Governmental Experts (UN GGE) and the Open-Ended Working Group (OEWG), provide platforms for diplomatic engagement to shape norms and expectations regarding state behavior in cyberspace.

Crisis management represents another critical dimension of diplomacy in the context of cyber conflicts. As cyber incidents unfold, diplomatic channels become essential for de-escalation and managing the fallout. Establishing communication channels and protocols for incident response allows states to share information, clarify intentions, and prevent misunderstandings that could lead to a dangerous escalation. Crisis management in cyberspace demands a level of agility and responsiveness that is emblematic of the digital age. Rapid diplomatic exchanges, often facilitated through existing communication channels or dedicated hotlines, become essential to ensuring that conflicts triggered by cyber incidents do not spiral out of control.

Norm-building is a core function of diplomacy in the cyber domain. The establishment of norms and principles guides state behavior, fostering a shared understanding of acceptable conduct in cyberspace. Diplomacy plays a crucial role in shaping and promoting these norms through international forums and negotiations. The Tallinn Manual, developed by legal experts, and the Paris Call for Trust and Security in Cyberspace, a political commitment from states and non-state actors, exemplify diplomatic efforts to codify norms that discourage destabilizing cyber activities. The continuous refinement of these norms through diplomatic initiatives contributes to the development of a more stable and predictable cyber environment.

Moreover, the role of diplomacy extends to the facilitation of international cooperation in addressing cyber conflicts. Given the transboundary nature of cyber threats, effective responses require collaborative efforts among states. Diplomacy provides the necessary framework for building partnerships, sharing threat intelligence, and coordinating responses to cyber incidents. Bilateral and multilateral agreements, such as mutual assistance treaties and information-sharing mechanisms, form the basis for diplomatic cooperation in the cyber realm. By fostering collaboration, diplomacy strengthens the collective ability of states to respond to cyber threats, leveraging the diverse expertise and resources of the international community.

International organizations, particularly the United Nations, play a crucial role in diplomatic efforts to address cyber conflicts. The UN serves as a forum for member states to engage in dialogue, negotiate norms, and coordinate actions to enhance cybersecurity. The UN GGE, despite facing challenges in reaching consensus, has played a key role in advancing diplomatic discussions on responsible state behavior in cyberspace. The establishment of the OEWG further reflects the commitment of the international community to addressing the challenges posed by emerging technologies, artificial intelligence, and the evolving cyber threat landscape. Diplomacy within the UN framework allows for the representation of diverse perspectives, fostering a more inclusive and comprehensive approach to addressing global cyber challenges.

Diplomacy also acts as a bridge between the public and private sectors in addressing cyber conflicts. The private sector, which owns and operates critical infrastructure, possesses valuable expertise and resources in cybersecurity. Diplomatic efforts engage with private entities to establish public-private partnerships, sharing information on emerging threats, coordinating incident responses, and developing best practices. The collaboration between states and private entities contributes to a more resilient and secure cyber ecosystem, acknowledging the integral role of the private sector in maintaining the stability of digital infrastructure.

The application of diplomatic tools in addressing cyber conflicts faces several challenges. One of the fundamental challenges is the attribution problem, where accurately determining the source of a cyber attack remains difficult due to the use of sophisticated techniques and the involvement of non-state actors. The lack of clear attribution can hinder diplomatic efforts to hold malicious actors accountable and may result in challenges when seeking to establish norms of behavior. Moreover, the inherent tension between national security interests and the desire for transparency and cooperation poses a diplomatic challenge. States may be reluctant to share information about their cyber capabilities and activities, particularly if those activities straddle the line between traditional espionage and potentially destabilizing actions.

The geopolitical dimensions of cyber conflicts further complicate diplomatic efforts. Cyber operations may be wielded as instruments of statecraft in pursuit of strategic objectives, leading to a blurring of lines between traditional geopolitical rivalries and digital conflict. Diplomacy must navigate these geopolitical complexities, balancing the interests of states and fostering a cooperative environment that transcends political differences. The application of sanctions, diplomatic condemnation, or other punitive measures in response to cyber incidents adds another layer of complexity, requiring careful consideration of potential consequences and unintended escalations.

In conclusion, the role of diplomacy in addressing cyber conflicts is multifaceted, encompassing preventive measures, crisis management, norm-building, and the facilitation of international cooperation. As states grapple with the challenges posed by an increasingly interconnected and digitized world, diplomatic efforts become central to shaping the rules and norms that govern behavior in cyberspace. Despite the inherent challenges, diplomacy remains a critical tool for managing cyber conflicts, offering a strategic and collaborative approach to navigate the complexities of the digital domain and foster a more stable and secure international cyber environment.

Case studies illustrating diplomatic efforts in cybersecurity.

Diplomatic efforts in the realm of cybersecurity are often exemplified through case studies that illuminate the challenges, successes, and complexities of addressing cyber threats at the international level. One notable case study revolves around the Stuxnet cyber operation, a sophisticated piece of malware discovered in 2010 that targeted Iran's nuclear facilities. Attributed to joint efforts by the United States and Israel, Stuxnet marked a significant intersection of cyber operations and diplomacy. The operation sought to disrupt Iran's nuclear program, showcasing the strategic use of cyber capabilities for geopolitical objectives. The diplomatic dimensions unfolded as the international community grappled with the implications of state-sponsored cyber attacks. While the U.S. and Israel neither confirmed nor denied their involvement, the Stuxnet case underscored the challenges of attributing cyber operations to specific states and raised questions about the norms and rules governing state behavior in cyberspace.

In the aftermath of the Stuxnet case, the United Nations became a focal point for diplomatic efforts in cybersecurity. The UN Group of Governmental Experts (GGE) on Developments in the Field of Information and Telecommunications in the Context of International Security played a crucial role in shaping norms and principles for responsible state behavior in cyberspace. The GGE, consisting of representatives from various countries, engaged in multi-year discussions to address the challenges of cyberspace, ultimately producing reports that outlined voluntary norms and confidence-building measures. However, the 2017 GGE failed to reach consensus, signaling a diplomatic challenge in aligning diverse perspectives on issues such as the definition of cyber threats, the applicability of international law, and the role of state responsibility.

The diplomatic landscape in cybersecurity further evolved with the establishment of the Open-Ended Working Group (OEWG) on developments in the field of information and telecommunications in the context of international security. Launched in 2019, the OEWG reflects a renewed diplomatic effort within the UN to address emerging challenges posed by technologies such as artificial intelligence and the Internet of Things. The OEWG aims to provide a forum for inclusive discussions on norms, rules, and principles for responsible state behavior in cyberspace. While the OEWG is still in its early stages, it illustrates ongoing diplomatic endeavors to adapt to the evolving digital landscape and engage in comprehensive discussions on global cyber governance.

Another instructive case study revolves around the 2015 agreement between the United States and China on the avoidance of state-sponsored cyber economic espionage. Against the backdrop of escalating cyber tensions, the two nations engaged in diplomatic negotiations to address concerns related to the theft of intellectual property and trade secrets through cyber means. The agreement represented a significant milestone in diplomatic efforts to establish norms of behavior in cyberspace, focusing on economic espionage. Both nations committed to not support cyber-enabled theft of intellectual property for commercial gain. While challenges remain regarding the enforcement and verification of such agreements, the U.S.-China accord exemplifies how diplomatic engagement can lead to tangible outcomes in mitigating specific cyber threats and fostering cooperation.

In the European context, the General Data Protection Regulation (GDPR) serves as a case study where regional diplomacy intersects with cybersecurity. Enforced in 2018, the GDPR is a comprehensive data protection regulation applicable to entities operating within the European Union (EU) and those handling the personal data of EU residents. The GDPR represents a diplomatic effort to address privacy concerns in the digital age, emphasizing the protection of individuals' rights in the face of increasing cyber threats. The regulation imposes stringent requirements on organizations for data protection, breach notification, and individual consent. While the GDPR primarily focuses on data privacy, it showcases how regional diplomatic initiatives can shape legal frameworks to enhance cyber-security by safeguarding personal information.

The Paris Call for Trust and Security in Cyberspace, launched in 2018, serves as another case study illustrating diplomatic efforts in the private sector. The Paris Call is a non-binding political commitment that seeks to address cyber threats through cooperation between states, international organizations, and the private sector. Signatories commit to promoting principles such as the protection of individuals and infrastructure from cyber threats, the prevention of interference in electoral processes, and the prevention of the proliferation of malicious cyber activities. The Paris Call exemplifies diplomatic initiatives that extend beyond traditional state-centric approaches, acknowledging the vital role of non-state actors, including private companies, in enhancing cybersecurity.

In the realm of NATO (North Atlantic Treaty Organization), the alliance has increasingly recognized the significance of cyber-security as a core component of its collective defense. The 2016 Warsaw Summit marked a milestone where NATO formally recognized cyberspace as a domain of operations alongside land, sea, and air. This diplomatic shift underscored the alliance's commitment to addressing cyber threats collectively. Subsequent summits and initiatives, such as the NATO Cyber Defense Pledge, reinforced the alliance's diplomatic efforts to enhance cybersecurity capabilities, share threat intelligence, and coordinate responses to cyber incidents. The evolution of NATO's approach reflects diplomatic endeavors to adapt to the changing nature of security threats in the digital age.

The SolarWinds supply chain attack, discovered in 2020, offers a case study that highlights the diplomatic challenges in responding to sophisticated cyber operations with transnational impact. The attack, attributed to Russian state-sponsored actors, exploited vulnerabilities in the software supply chain, affecting numerous U.S. government agencies and private sector organizations. The incident underscored the need for diplomatic coordination to attribute the attack, respond effectively, and address the broader implications of supply chain compromises. The SolarWinds case illuminates the complexities of diplomatic engagement in the face of state-sponsored cyber threats that transcend borders, emphasizing the importance of international cooperation and collective response mechanisms.

The NotPetya ransomware attack in 2017, attributed to Russian military hackers, serves as another case study illustrating the diplomatic fallout from a destructive cyber incident. NotPetya, which initially targeted Ukraine but quickly spread globally, affected organizations in various sectors, causing significant financial losses. The attack led to diplomatic repercussions, with Ukraine and other affected countries condemning the cyber aggression and attributing it to a nation-state actor. The case highlights the challenges of attributing cyber attacks with high confidence and the diplomatic implications of destructive cyber operations that cause widespread harm beyond the intended target.

In conclusion, these case studies provide insights into the multifaceted nature of diplomatic efforts in addressing cybersecurity. From state-sponsored cyber operations and international agreements to regional regulations, private sector initiatives, and responses to sophisticated supply chain attacks, these examples illustrate the diverse challenges and opportunities within the diplomatic landscape of cyberspace. As technology continues to evolve and cyber threats become more sophisticated, diplomatic endeavors play a crucial role in shaping norms, fostering cooperation, and adapting to the dynamic nature of cybersecurity in the global arena.

Successful examples of international cooperation in cybersecurity.

International cooperation in cybersecurity has become increasingly crucial as the digital landscape transcends national borders, necessitating collaborative efforts to address complex and evolving cyber threats. One notable example of successful international cooperation is the Budapest Convention on Cybercrime, also known as the Council of Europe Convention on Cybercrime, adopted in 2001. This pioneering treaty established a framework for harmonizing national laws, enhancing international cooperation, and facilitating the extradition of cybercriminals. With its extraterritorial applicability, the Budapest Convention exemplifies successful collaboration among countries to combat cybercrime, offering a comprehensive legal framework that promotes information sharing, joint investigations, and the effective prosecution of cybercriminals across borders.

The INTERPOL Global Complex for Innovation (IGCI) serves as a beacon of successful international collaboration in combating cybercrime. Launched in 2014, the IGCI provides a platform for law enforcement agencies from around the world to work together in addressing cyber threats. Its mandate includes coordinating international investigations, facilitating information exchange, and conducting capacity-building initiatives to strengthen global cybersecurity capabilities. The IGCI underscores the importance of a centralized and collaborative approach to tackling cybercrime on a global scale, acknowledging that effective responses require joint efforts beyond individual national borders.

In the Asia-Pacific region, the ASEAN CERT (Computer Emergency Response Team) Incident Drill, initiated by the ASEAN-Japan Information Security Policy Meeting, exemplifies successful international cooperation in enhancing cybersecurity resilience. The annual drill involves participants from ASEAN member states and Japan, simulating cyber incidents to test and improve the response capabilities of participating CERTs. The exercise fosters collaboration, information sharing, and the development of best practices, demonstrating how regional cooperation can contribute to building collective resilience against cyber threats.

The European Union Agency for Cybersecurity (ENISA) stands out as a successful example of international collaboration within the European Union. Established in 2004, ENISA plays a pivotal role in promoting a high level of network and information security within the EU. It facilitates cooperation among EU member states by providing expertise, coordinating cybersecurity efforts, and supporting the development of cybersecurity capabilities. ENISA's activities extend to fostering collaboration with non-EU countries, international organizations, and the private sector, reflecting a comprehensive approach to addressing cybersecurity challenges through effective partnerships.

The United States and the United Kingdom's joint efforts to indict members of a Chinese hacking group for cyber espionage activities represent a successful example of bilateral cooperation in addressing state-sponsored cyber threats. In 2018, the U.S. Department of Justice unsealed indictments against two Chinese nationals linked to APT10, a hacking group associated with the Chinese government. The indictment, developed in coordination with the UK's National Cyber Security Centre, showcased how allied nations can work together to attribute cyber attacks, publicly denounce malicious behavior, and demonstrate a united front against state-sponsored cyber activities.

The NATO Cooperative Cyber Defence Centre of Excellence (CCDCOE) illustrates successful collaboration among NATO member states in enhancing collective cybersecurity capabilities. Established in 2008 in Estonia, the CCDCOE serves as a hub for research, education, and exercises in the field of cybersecurity. It facilitates international cooperation by bringing together experts from NATO and partner nations to address common cyber challenges, share best practices, and conduct joint exercises. The CCDCOE showcases how military alliances can foster collaborative efforts to strengthen cybersecurity resilience in the face of evolving threats.

The Five Eyes alliance, consisting of the United States, the United Kingdom, Canada, Australia, and New Zealand, represents a long-standing and successful example of intelligence-sharing cooperation. Originally formed for signals intelligence, the alliance has expanded its scope to include cybersecurity. The members share threat intelligence, collaborate on cyber operations, and coordinate responses to cyber incidents. The Five Eyes alliance highlights how close collaboration among like-minded nations can enhance collective situational awareness and bolster cybersecurity capabilities.

In response to the escalating ransomware threat, the Ransomware Task Force (RTF) emerged as a global initiative involving government agencies, international organizations, and private sector entities. Launched in 2021, the RTF focuses on developing a comprehensive strategy to address the ransomware challenge. It brings together experts from various sectors to share insights, propose policy recommendations, and foster collaboration among stakeholders. The RTF exemplifies how diverse entities can unite to tackle a shared cybersecurity concern, demonstrating the effectiveness of a multi-stakeholder approach to addressing complex cyber threats.

The Financial Services Information Sharing and Analysis Center (FS-ISAC) serves as a successful model of information sharing and collaboration within the financial sector. Established in 1999, FS-ISAC enables financial institutions, regulators, and law enforcement agencies to share timely and actionable threat intelligence. The center facilitates collaboration through forums, exercises, and information-sharing mechanisms, enhancing the financial sector's collective ability to respond to cyber threats. FS-ISAC demonstrates how sector-specific collaboration can strengthen cybersecurity resilience by leveraging the expertise and resources of industry stakeholders.

The Paris Call for Trust and Security in Cyberspace, launched in 2018, represents a unique and successful international initiative that goes beyond traditional state-centric approaches. The Paris Call is a non-binding political commitment that encourages signatories, including states, private sector entities, and civil society, to work together to improve the security and stability of cyberspace. Signatories commit to principles such as protecting individuals and infrastructure, preventing interference in electoral processes, and preventing the proliferation of malicious cyber activities. The Paris Call showcases the importance of involving diverse stakeholders in diplomatic efforts to build trust and enhance cybersecurity on a global scale.

In conclusion, these examples highlight successful instances of international cooperation in cybersecurity, spanning legal frameworks, law enforcement collaboration, regional initiatives, and sector-specific partnerships. As the digital landscape continues to evolve, the importance of collaborative efforts becomes increasingly evident. Whether through treaties, alliances, information-sharing platforms, or multistakeholder initiatives, these cases illustrate the diverse strategies and mechanisms that contribute to a more secure and resilient global cyberspace. Addressing complex and dynamic cyber threats necessitates ongoing and adaptive international cooperation, emphasizing the interconnectedness of the digital realm and the shared responsibility of the global community in ensuring cybersecurity.

Barriers and challenges to effective collaboration.

Effective collaboration, whether on a local or global scale, faces a myriad of barriers and challenges that stem from the complex interplay of organizational, cultural, technological, and human factors. One prominent barrier lies in the diversity of organizational structures, objectives, and cultures that characterize potential collaborators. Within any collaborative endeavor, participants often bring with them a range of institutional norms, practices, and priorities, making alignment a formidable challenge. Divergent organizational cultures can hinder seamless integration and coordination, leading to misunderstandings, conflicts, and difficulties in achieving common goals. Bridging these cultural gaps demands not only a commitment to understanding diverse perspectives but also the development of flexible frameworks that accommodate varied organizational dynamics.

The technological landscape introduces its own set of challenges to effective collaboration. Despite the proliferation of digital tools designed to facilitate communication and cooperation, the sheer variety of platforms, applications, and systems can create compatibility issues. Incompatible technologies can impede the smooth exchange of information and hinder collaborative workflows, resulting in inefficiencies and frustration among collaborators. The challenge extends beyond mere technological interoperability to encompass issues such as data security, privacy concerns, and the need for standardized protocols. As organizations increasingly rely on digital platforms for collaborative endeavors, addressing these technological challenges becomes imperative to ensure seamless and secure collaboration.

Geographical dispersion poses another significant challenge to collaboration, particularly in the context of global partnerships. Physical distances introduce time zone disparities, communication delays, and logistical complexities that can hinder real-time interactions and coordination. The emergence of remote work, while providing flexibility, has accentuated these challenges, requiring organizations to grapple with issues of virtual team management, communication gaps, and the need for robust infrastructures to support remote collaboration. Overcoming the barriers of geographical dispersion demands innovative approaches to virtual collaboration, including the strategic use of technology, clear communication protocols, and the cultivation of a shared sense of purpose among geographically diverse teams.

A fundamental human challenge to effective collaboration lies in the realm of communication. Miscommunication, whether due to linguistic differences, varying communication styles, or information overload, can result in misunderstandings and hinder the smooth flow of collaborative efforts. Cultural nuances in communication further compound these challenges, as individuals from different cultural backgrounds may interpret messages differently, leading to conflicts or misalignment of expectations. Effective collaboration requires not only linguistic clarity but also a nuanced understanding of diverse communication styles, fostering an environment where participants feel comfortable expressing their perspectives and seeking clarification when needed.

The issue of trust represents a critical barrier to effective collaboration. Trust is the bedrock upon which successful collaboration is built, and its absence can impede open communication, hinder information sharing, and erode the willingness to collaborate. Establishing trust becomes particularly challenging in environments characterized by competition, power imbalances, or historical conflicts. Overcoming trust barriers necessitates intentional efforts to cultivate transparency, reliability, and mutual respect among collaborators. Organizations and individuals must demonstrate a commitment to ethical behavior, accountability, and the shared values that underpin effective collaboration.

The complexity of collaborative endeavors often introduces challenges related to goal alignment and clarity. When participants have divergent understandings of the overarching objectives, priorities, or desired outcomes, collaboration can become fragmented and less effective. Establishing a shared vision, defining clear goals, and ensuring alignment among collaborators demand deliberate efforts in the planning and initiation phases of collaborative projects. Misalignment challenges are further exacerbated when organizations or individuals harbor hidden agendas, leading to potential conflicts of interest that can undermine the collaborative process.

Institutional inertia and resistance to change pose additional barriers to effective collaboration. Established organizations may be entrenched in traditional ways of working, resistant to adopting new technologies or collaborative methodologies. The fear of disruption, concerns about job security, or a reluctance to relinquish control can create organizational cultures that are resistant to innovation and collaboration. Overcoming this inertia requires a commitment to fostering a culture of adaptability, where organizations actively embrace change, encourage experimentation, and view collaboration as a catalyst for positive transformation rather than a threat to the status quo.

Resource constraints, including financial limitations, time pressures, and competing priorities, represent formidable challenges to effective collaboration. Organizations and individuals engaged in collaborative efforts often face the need to balance competing demands on their resources, making it challenging to allocate the necessary time, personnel, and funding to collaborative initiatives. Resource constraints can compromise the quality and sustainability of collaborative endeavors, hindering the achievement of long-term goals. Addressing these challenges demands strategic resource planning, a realistic assessment of available capacities, and a commitment to prioritizing collaboration as a strategic imperative.

Legal and regulatory complexities can introduce significant barriers to effective collaboration, particularly in cross-border initiatives. Varying legal frameworks, regulatory requirements, and compliance standards can create obstacles that impede the seamless flow of information and the execution of collaborative projects. Issues related to data privacy, intellectual property rights, and liability can become points of contention, requiring careful negotiation and alignment of legal frameworks among collaborators. Overcoming these barriers necessitates proactive engagement with legal experts, the development of clear contractual agreements, and a comprehensive understanding of the legal landscape in which collaborative initiatives operate.

Incentive misalignment presents a challenge when collaborators do not share common motivations or face conflicting incentives. Misaligned incentives can lead to a lack of commitment, uneven contributions, or a divergence of interests among collaborators. Addressing incentive misalignment requires a careful examination of the motivations and goals of each participant, along with the development of mechanisms that align individual and organizational incentives with the overarching objectives of the collaboration. Creating a shared sense of purpose and reinforcing the value proposition for all collaborators can help mitigate the challenges associated with misaligned incentives.

Closely tied to incentive misalignment is the challenge of equitable benefit distribution. Collaborative efforts often involve the pooling of resources, knowledge, and expertise, with the expectation that benefits will be distributed fairly among participants. However, challenges arise when there is a perceived imbalance in the distribution of rewards or when certain collaborators feel that their contributions are undervalued. Ensuring equitable benefit distribution demands transparency, clear communication about expectations, and mechanisms for fair resource allocation and recognition of contributions. Fostering a collaborative environment where all participants feel that their efforts are acknowledged and valued is essential for overcoming this challenge.

In conclusion, effective collaboration faces a multitude of barriers and challenges that span organizational, technological, human, and contextual dimensions. Overcoming these challenges requires a holistic and adaptive approach, encompassing strategic planning, cultural awareness, technological innovation, and a commitment to fostering a collaborative mindset. While the barriers may be formidable, successful collaboration is achievable through intentional efforts to address each challenge and cultivate an environment where diverse stakeholders can work together synergistically to achieve common goals.

Chapter 8: The Future of Cybersecurity: Trends and Projections

Acknowledging the dynamic nature of the cybersecurity landscape.

The cybersecurity landscape is inherently dynamic, marked by continuous evolution, complexity, and relentless innovation. In the digital age, where technology is the lifeblood of virtually every aspect of modern society, the dynamic nature of cybersecurity is not merely a characteristic but a fundamental reality that organizations and individuals must grapple with daily. The landscape is shaped by a perpetual arms race between cybersecurity professionals seeking to fortify digital defenses and malicious actors striving to exploit vulnerabilities for various motives, ranging from financial gain to geopolitical influence. The dynamic nature of cybersecurity stems from the interplay of technological advancements, emerging threat vectors, shifting geopolitical landscapes, and the ever-expanding attack surface presented by the digital interconnectedness of the modern world.

Technological advancements are a driving force behind the dynamism of the cybersecurity landscape. As innovations in computing, networking, and information technologies unfold, new opportunities and challenges emerge simultaneously. The rapid adoption of cloud computing, the proliferation of Internet of Things (IoT) devices, and the integration of artificial intelligence (AI) into various systems exemplify the transformative power of technology. While these innovations bring unprecedented convenience, efficiency, and connectivity, they also introduce novel attack vectors and complexities that cybersecurity must adapt to. The dynamic nature of technology necessitates continuous vigilance and adaptability to stay ahead of potential threats that exploit the latest developments in the digital realm.

The emergence of sophisticated cyber threats is a testament to the dynamic and adaptive nature of adversaries in the cybersecurity landscape. Malicious actors constantly refine their tactics, techniques, and procedures (TTPs) to circumvent evolving security measures. Advanced Persistent Threats (APTs), ransomware attacks, and zero-day exploits showcase the agility and innovation of cyber adversaries. APTs, often state-sponsored, leverage sophisticated techniques to infiltrate and persist within target systems over extended periods. Ransomware attacks, fueled by cryptocurrencies, have evolved to target critical infrastructure and demand higher ransoms. Zero-day exploits, leveraging vulnerabilities unknown to the software vendor, underscore the perpetual race between defenders and attackers. The dynamic nature of cyber threats demands a proactive and adaptive cybersecurity posture capable of detecting and mitigating emerging risks.

The geopolitical landscape significantly influences the dynamics of cybersecurity. Nation-states, driven by political, economic, and strategic interests, engage in cyber operations that transcend traditional boundaries. State-sponsored cyber attacks, cyber espionage, and cyber warfare have become integral components of geopolitical strategies. The attribution of cyber incidents to specific nation-states adds a layer of complexity to the cybersecurity landscape, as states often employ tactics to obfuscate their involvement. The strategic use of cyber capabilities in international relations introduces uncertainties and challenges in establishing norms and rules governing state behavior in cyberspace. The dynamic interplay between geopolitics and cybersecurity necessitates a nuanced understanding of the motivations and tactics employed by nation-states in the digital domain.

The attack surface in cyberspace continues to expand exponentially, contributing to the dynamic nature of the cybersecurity landscape. The increasing digitization of critical infrastructure, the wide-spread adoption of IoT devices, and the integration of digital technologies into daily life create a vast and interconnected ecosystem that presents numerous entry points for potential adversaries. The attack surface extends beyond traditional IT networks to include operational technology (OT) systems, smart cities, healthcare infrastructure, and even consumer devices. Each new connection, device, or application introduces potential vulnerabilities that must be identified, assessed, and secured. The dynamic expansion of the attack surface requires a holistic and adaptive approach to cybersecurity that goes beyond traditional perimeter defenses.

The evolving regulatory landscape adds another layer of dynamism to cybersecurity. Governments and regulatory bodies worldwide are recognizing the need for robust cybersecurity frameworks to protect critical infrastructure, sensitive data, and individual privacy. The implementation of regulations such as the General Data Protection Regulation (GDPR), the California Consumer Privacy Act (CCPA), and sector-specific cybersecurity requirements reflects the global shift toward prioritizing cybersecurity as a regulatory imperative. The dynamic nature of these regulations, often subject to updates and amendments, demands a continuous commitment to compliance and the integration of regulatory requirements into organizational cybersecurity practices.

The cybersecurity workforce plays a pivotal role in navigating the dynamic landscape of cyber threats and technologies. The demand for skilled cybersecurity professionals has surged, driven by the increasing frequency and sophistication of cyber attacks. The shortage of cybersecurity talent poses a significant challenge, as organizations struggle to fill key roles in areas such as threat detection, incident response, and security analysis. The rapid evolution of technology and the dynamic nature of cyber threats necessitate ongoing training and upskilling for cybersecurity professionals to stay abreast of the latest developments in the field. The human element introduces a dynamic aspect to cybersecurity, where the effectiveness of defenses depends on the knowledge, skills, and adaptability of the individuals responsible for securing digital environments.

The collaboration and information-sharing landscape in cybersecurity exemplify the dynamic nature of collective defense. Cybersecurity threats are not confined to individual organizations; they often have broader implications that transcend sectoral, national, and organizational boundaries. Collaborative efforts, such as Information Sharing and Analysis Centers (ISACs), public-private partnerships, and threat intelligence sharing communities, have emerged to facilitate the exchange of timely and relevant information about emerging threats. The dynamic nature of cyber threats demands a shift from a siloed approach to a collaborative and community-driven model, where organizations, industries, and nations share insights and collaborate in real-time to enhance collective cybersecurity resilience.

The integration of AI and machine learning into cybersecurity practices introduces both opportunities and challenges to the dynamic landscape. AI-driven technologies enhance the speed and efficiency of threat detection, enabling security systems to analyze vast amounts of data and identify patterns indicative of potential threats. However, the dynamic nature of cyber threats requires adaptive AI models capable of learning from evolving attack tactics and adjusting their defense strategies accordingly. Adversarial machine learning, where attackers attempt to manipulate AI models, adds a layer of complexity, demanding continuous innovation and vigilance in AI-driven cybersecurity solutions.

The ongoing evolution of privacy concerns and data protection regulations further contributes to the dynamic nature of cybersecurity. Individuals and governments alike are increasingly cognizant of the importance of privacy in the digital age. The introduction of comprehensive data protection regulations, such as GDPR, reflects a global shift toward empowering individuals with greater control over their personal data. The evolving expectations regarding privacy introduce complexities in how organizations collect, process, and store data. The dynamic landscape of privacy requires cybersecurity strategies that not only safeguard sensitive information but also align with evolving regulatory frameworks and societal expectations.

In conclusion, the dynamic nature of the cybersecurity landscape is a multifaceted reality shaped by technological innovations, emerging threats, geopolitical dynamics, regulatory shifts, workforce challenges, collaborative initiatives, and the integration of advanced technologies. Navigating this landscape demands a proactive, adaptive, and holistic approach that encompasses continuous learning, collaboration, and innovation. Organizations and individuals must recognize that cybersecurity is not a static goal but an ongoing process of resilience-building, one that requires a deep understanding of the ever-changing dynamics inherent to the digital realm. Embracing this dynamism enables a more effective response to emerging challenges, ensures the relevance of cybersecurity practices, and ultimately enhances the overall security posture in the face of an evolving and complex threat landscape.

The importance of anticipating and preparing for future challenges.

Anticipating and preparing for future challenges is paramount in navigating the complex and dynamic landscape of our interconnected world. The acceleration of technological advancements, geopolitical shifts, environmental changes, and societal transformations underscores the need for foresight and proactive planning. The importance of anticipation lies in the ability to identify emerging trends and potential disruptions before they manifest fully, allowing individuals, organizations, and societies to position themselves strategically and respond effectively. As the future remains inherently uncertain, foresight becomes a compass, guiding decision-makers in charting resilient paths forward.

One crucial aspect of anticipating future challenges is understanding the rapid evolution of technology and its pervasive impact on various facets of our lives. Innovations in artificial intelligence, quantum computing, biotechnology, and other fields hold immense promise, but they also present ethical, security, and socio-economic challenges. By anticipating the trajectory of technological developments, stakeholders can prepare for the ethical considerations surrounding the use of emerging technologies, address potential cybersecurity threats, and navigate the societal implications, ensuring that the benefits of innovation are maximized while mitigating the associated risks.

Geopolitical dynamics play a central role in shaping the future, influencing global stability, economic landscapes, and international relations. Anticipating geopolitical shifts involves assessing the impact of geopolitical events on a wide range of areas, from trade and security to diplomatic relations. As alliances evolve, new actors emerge on the world stage, and power dynamics undergo transformations, those who are vigilant in their anticipation of geopolitical changes can position themselves strategically to adapt to shifting landscapes, forge beneficial partnerships, and navigate potential challenges arising from geopolitical uncertainties.

Environmental sustainability is a critical consideration for the future, given the ongoing challenges posed by climate change, resource depletion, and environmental degradation. Anticipating the long-term consequences of these challenges is essential for formulating effective mitigation and adaptation strategies. Proactive measures can include transitioning to renewable energy sources, implementing sustainable practices in industries, and developing resilience against the impacts of climate change. Anticipation allows communities and nations to prepare for and mitigate the potential consequences of environmental challenges, fostering a more sustainable and resilient future.

Societal transformations, driven by demographic shifts, cultural changes, and evolving values, are integral components of the future landscape. Anticipating these shifts is crucial for policymakers, businesses, and communities alike. An aging population, increasing urbanization, and the digitalization of daily life are among the factors shaping the societal landscape. Understanding these trends enables the development of policies that address the needs of diverse populations, the creation of sustainable urban environments, and the adaptation of education and healthcare systems to meet the evolving requirements of society.

In the realm of healthcare, anticipating future challenges is of paramount importance, as the dynamics of global health are constantly evolving. Emerging infectious diseases, the rise of antimicrobial resistance, and the increasing burden of chronic illnesses are challenges that demand proactive measures. By anticipating these health challenges, countries can invest in robust healthcare systems, research and development of new therapies, and international collaborations to address global health threats effectively. The COVID-19 pandemic serves as a stark reminder of the importance of anticipatory preparedness in the face of unforeseen health crises.

Economic landscapes are subject to continual change influenced by factors such as technological disruptions, market fluctuations, and global economic interdependencies. Anticipating economic challenges allows businesses and policymakers to prepare for potential recessions, market shifts, and disruptions to supply chains. By developing adaptive strategies, fostering innovation, and investing in workforce development, entities can position themselves to weather economic uncertainties and capitalize on emerging opportunities.

In the realm of cybersecurity, anticipation is foundational to maintaining the integrity and security of digital ecosystems. The ever-evolving nature of cyber threats demands continuous vigilance and preparation. Anticipating potential cyber threats, understanding new attack vectors, and investing in robust cybersecurity measures are essential components of a proactive defense strategy. As technologies such as artificial intelligence and quantum computing advance, anticipating the implications for cybersecurity becomes crucial to stay ahead of potential vulnerabilities and risks.

Anticipating future challenges also plays a vital role in the domain of education. The skills required in the future workforce are evolving rapidly, influenced by automation, artificial intelligence, and changing job markets. Educational institutions that anticipate these shifts can adapt their curricula, incorporate technology-driven learning approaches, and foster the development of critical thinking and adaptability in students. Anticipation in education is not only about preparing individuals for specific jobs but instilling a lifelong learning mindset that enables them to navigate the uncertainties of a dynamic future.

In the context of global governance and international cooperation, anticipation is indispensable for addressing transnational challenges. Issues such as pandemics, climate change, and cyber threats transcend national borders, necessitating collaborative and anticipatory approaches. International organizations and agreements that anticipate and prepare for such challenges contribute to global stability, resilience, and the equitable distribution of resources. Anticipation fosters a collective understanding of shared risks and responsibilities, enabling nations to work together to address global challenges.

Crisis preparedness is a tangible outcome of effective anticipation, ensuring that individuals, communities, and organizations are ready to respond to unexpected events. Whether natural disasters, public health emergencies, or geopolitical crises, anticipating potential crises allows for the development of robust contingency plans, early warning systems, and coordinated response mechanisms. The ability to mobilize resources swiftly and implement well-thought-out plans is a testament to the efficacy of anticipation in crisis management.

Anticipation is closely tied to innovation, as both concepts involve looking ahead and envisioning possibilities. Innovators and entrepreneurs who anticipate future trends and consumer needs are more likely to create products and services that resonate with evolving demands. By fostering a culture of anticipation within organizations, leaders can inspire creativity, encourage forward-thinking, and position their teams to embrace change and drive innovation.

In conclusion, the importance of anticipating and preparing for future challenges cannot be overstated in a world characterized by rapid change and complexity. From technological advancements and geopolitical shifts to environmental sustainability and societal transformations, the ability to anticipate and proactively respond is a hallmark of resilience and adaptability. Anticipation empowers individuals, organizations, and societies to navigate the uncertainties of the future with foresight, agility, and a commitment to building a more sustainable, secure, and equitable world. As the dynamics of our interconnected world continue to evolve, those who embrace anticipation as a guiding principle are better positioned to shape a future that is both responsive to challenges and rich with opportunities for growth and progress.

Projected advancements in AI and automation for cyber defense.

The projected advancements in artificial intelligence (AI) and automation within the realm of cyber defense promise to revolutionize the way organizations safeguard their digital ecosystems. As technology continues to evolve at an unprecedented pace, the integration of AI-driven solutions is anticipated to play a pivotal role in enhancing the efficiency, effectiveness, and adaptability of cyber defense mechanisms. One notable area of advancement is in threat detection, where AI algorithms are poised to surpass traditional signature-based methods. Machine learning models, trained on vast datasets containing diverse threat scenarios, have the ability to identify anomalous patterns indicative of cyber attacks. This proactive approach enables organizations to detect and respond to emerging threats in real time, minimizing the window of vulnerability and mitigating potential damages.

The application of AI in threat intelligence represents another significant advancement, with the potential to transform the landscape of cyber defense. AI-driven threat intelligence platforms can analyze massive volumes of data from diverse sources, including open-source intelligence, dark web forums, and incident reports. By harnessing natural language processing and machine learning, these platforms can distill actionable insights, helping cybersecurity professionals stay ahead of evolving threats. Predictive analytics powered by AI enable organizations to anticipate potential cyber threats, understand the tactics of adversaries, and fortify their defenses strategically. The synergy between AI and threat intelligence is expected to provide a dynamic and proactive defense posture against sophisticated cyber adversaries.

Automation, in conjunction with AI, is poised to streamline and accelerate incident response in cyber defense. The traditional manual processes of identifying, analyzing, and mitigating security incidents are time-consuming and resource-intensive. However, automated response mechanisms driven by AI can significantly reduce the response time to cyber incidents. Through the use of playbooks and predefined response actions, organizations can orchestrate automated workflows that address common threats without human intervention. This not only enhances the efficiency of incident response but also allows cybersecurity teams to focus on more complex and nuanced aspects of cyber defense, such as threat hunting and strategic planning.

The evolution of AI-driven threat hunting is expected to be a game-changer in cyber defense strategies. Instead of relying solely on reactive measures, organizations can leverage AI to proactively seek out potential threats within their networks. AI algorithms, equipped with the capability to analyze vast datasets and identify subtle patterns indicative of malicious activities, empower cybersecurity analysts to conduct targeted and efficient threat hunting operations. This shift towards proactive threat hunting aligns with the growing recognition that advanced threats often operate stealthily within networks before triggering alarms. AI-driven threat hunting enables organizations to identify and neutralize threats before they escalate, enhancing the overall resilience of cyber defense postures.

One of the key challenges in cyber defense is the overwhelming volume of security alerts generated by various monitoring tools. The integration of AI and automation in security orchestration, automation, and response (SOAR) platforms addresses this challenge by automating the analysis and response to security alerts. AI-driven SOAR platforms can correlate and prioritize alerts based on their severity and relevance, allowing organizations to focus their resources on the most critical incidents. Automated playbooks, guided by AI algorithms, facilitate the execution of predefined response actions, ensuring a swift and coordinated response to security incidents. The seamless integration of AI and automation in SOAR platforms is anticipated to enhance the overall efficacy of security operations, enabling organizations to manage the complexity of modern cyber threats more effectively.

In the context of identity and access management, AI is expected to play a crucial role in augmenting authentication and authorization processes. Traditional methods of username and password-based authentication are increasingly vulnerable to sophisticated attacks such as phishing and credential stuffing. AI-driven authentication systems leverage behavioral biometrics, device recognition, and contextual information to establish more robust and adaptive authentication mechanisms. Machine learning algorithms can analyze user behavior patterns and detect anomalies that may indicate unauthorized access. Additionally, AI-based systems can continuously learn and adapt to evolving user behaviors, ensuring a balance between security and user experience in access management.

The concept of self-healing cybersecurity ecosystems, empowered by AI and automation, is emerging as a visionary goal for the future of cyber defense. In a self-healing system, AI algorithms continuously monitor the network, identify vulnerabilities, and automatically apply patches or configuration changes to mitigate potential risks. Automation plays a central role in executing these remediation actions swiftly and accurately. The vision of a self-healing cybersecurity ecosystem represents a paradigm shift from reactive defense measures to a proactive and autonomous approach. While this vision may still be in its infancy, the projected advancements in AI and automation suggest a trajectory towards more adaptive, self-aware, and resilient cyber defense architectures.

The integration of AI and automation extends beyond traditional cybersecurity measures to include the domain of deception technologies. Deception technologies involve the deployment of decoy assets within a network to confuse and mislead attackers. AI-driven deception platforms can dynamically adapt to the evolving tactics of adversaries, creating realistic decoys that mimic authentic assets. By leveraging machine learning to analyze adversary behaviors and predict potential attack paths, deception technologies can proactively identify and divert attackers away from critical assets. This not only provides organizations with valuable insights into adversary tactics but also serves as an active defense mechanism that disrupts the traditional cyber kill chain.

The convergence of AI and the Internet of Things (IoT) introduces new dimensions to cyber defense challenges and solutions. As the number of IoT devices proliferates, so does the attack surface and the potential for new threat vectors. AI-driven anomaly detection and behavior analysis become critical in securing IoT ecosystems, where traditional signature-based approaches may fall short. Automation in managing and securing IoT devices, including patching vulnerabilities and enforcing security policies, becomes imperative to prevent large-scale compromise. The anticipated advancements in AI and automation for IoT security aim to provide comprehensive solutions that address the unique challenges posed by the interconnected nature of IoT environments.

The human factor in cyber defense remains indispensable, and AI is poised to augment the capabilities of cybersecurity professionals rather than replace them. AI-driven tools, such as cognitive threat analytics, can assist analysts in processing vast amounts of data, identifying patterns, and making informed decisions. Automation in routine tasks allows human experts to focus on strategic aspects of cyber defense, such as developing and implementing robust security policies, conducting in-depth threat analyses, and formulating adaptive response strategies. The symbiotic relationship between AI and human expertise is anticipated to create a force multiplier effect, enhancing the overall resilience and effectiveness of cyber defense teams.

In conclusion, the projected advancements in AI and automation for cyber defense herald a transformative era in how organizations protect their digital assets. From proactive threat detection and predictive analytics to automated incident response and self-healing ecosystems, AI is poised to revolutionize the cybersecurity landscape. The integration of automation complements AI by streamlining operational workflows, accelerating incident response, and managing the complexity of security operations. While challenges such as ethical considerations, adversarial machine learning, and the need for human oversight persist, the trajectory indicates a future where AI and automation play pivotal roles in fortifying cyber defenses against the evolving and sophisticated threats of the digital age. As organizations embrace these advancements, they stand to benefit from a more adaptive, efficient, and resilient cybersecurity posture in the face of an ever-changing threat landscape.

The integration of AI into offensive cyber capabilities.

The integration of artificial intelligence (AI) into offensive cyber capabilities represents a paradigm shift in the landscape of cyber warfare, introducing unprecedented complexities and challenges. As AI technologies advance, nations and malicious actors are leveraging these capabilities to enhance the effectiveness, efficiency, and sophistication of offensive cyber operations. One of the primary areas where AI is being integrated into offensive cyber capabilities is in the realm of cyber espionage. AI-driven tools can sift through vast amounts of data to identify valuable intelligence targets, analyze patterns, and tailor espionage efforts with a level of precision that was previously unattainable. The ability to process and analyze massive datasets enables adversaries to gain insights into critical infrastructure, military operations, and strategic planning, amplifying the potency of cyber espionage as a tool for information warfare.

In the context of offensive cyber operations, AI is increasingly playing a central role in automating and optimizing the process of identifying and exploiting vulnerabilities in software systems. Automated vulnerability scanners, powered by AI algorithms, can systematically analyze codebases, identify potential weaknesses, and exploit them at scale. This integration of AI-driven tools into the offensive toolkit accelerates the reconnaissance and weaponization phases of cyber operations, providing adversaries with the ability to exploit vulnerabilities swiftly and efficiently. The use of AI in vulnerability discovery and exploitation heightens the speed at which attackers can compromise systems, making defensive measures more challenging for organizations and governments to implement effectively.

AI is also being integrated into the domain of weaponizing malware and creating sophisticated cyber attack payloads. Adversarial machine learning techniques enable attackers to develop malware that can adapt and evolve in response to changing defensive measures. AI-driven malware can dynamically alter its behavior, evade detection by traditional security solutions, and autonomously adjust tactics based on the evolving security landscape. This level of adaptability makes AI-powered malware a potent tool for offensive cyber operations, as it can persistently exploit vulnerabilities and maintain a persistent presence within targeted networks.

The integration of AI into offensive cyber capabilities extends to the domain of social engineering and manipulation. AI-driven tools can analyze vast amounts of data from social media, online platforms, and public records to create highly targeted and convincing spear-phishing campaigns. By synthesizing information about individuals' preferences, behaviors, and relationships, attackers can craft personalized and contextually relevant phishing messages that increase the likelihood of success. The use of AI in social engineering tactics enhances the precision and effectiveness of phishing attacks, enabling adversaries to compromise individuals or organizations with a higher degree of success and subtlety.

AI is increasingly being employed in the development of advanced persistent threats (APTs), which are sophisticated, long-term cyber campaigns often associated with state-sponsored actors. Machine learning algorithms enable APTs to adapt to the unique characteristics of targeted networks, blend into the normal patterns of network traffic, and evade traditional signature-based detection methods. The integration of AI into APTs enhances their ability to remain undetected, persist within compromised networks, and gather intelligence over extended periods. As a result, APTs augmented by AI capabilities pose a formidable challenge to defenders, requiring advanced threat detection and response mechanisms to counteract their stealth and persistence.

The use of AI in automating the decision-making processes of cyber operations introduces a new dimension to offensive capabilities. AI-driven autonomous agents have the potential to make realtime decisions during cyber attacks, adapting their strategies based on evolving circumstances. This level of autonomy could enable AI-driven cyber weapons to dynamically select targets, adjust tactics, and respond to defensive measures without direct human intervention. The integration of AI in autonomous decision-making introduces ethical and strategic considerations, raising questions about the potential for unintended consequences, escalation dynamics, and the accountability of autonomous cyber entities in the context of international norms and laws.

The concept of swarm intelligence, inspired by collective behavior observed in natural systems like insect colonies, is influencing the development of offensive cyber capabilities. AI-driven swarms of cyber agents can collaborate and coordinate their actions to overwhelm and bypass defenses. This approach leverages the parallel processing capabilities of AI to conduct distributed and synchronized attacks across multiple vectors. The use of AI-driven swarms introduces a level of unpredictability and complexity that challenges traditional defense strategies, as the swarm can dynamically adapt its tactics based on the responses of defenders, making it difficult to anticipate and counteract.

AI is increasingly integrated into the manipulation of information and the conduct of influence operations, marking a new frontier in offensive cyber capabilities. Adversaries can leverage AI to analyze public sentiment, manipulate social media algorithms, and create targeted disinformation campaigns. AI-driven algorithms can optimize the spread of false narratives, exploit existing divisions within societies, and amplify the impact of influence operations. The use of AI in information warfare introduces challenges for defenders in distinguishing between authentic and manipulated content, as well as mitigating the societal impacts of orchestrated disinformation campaigns.

The integration of AI into offensive cyber capabilities extends beyond traditional digital domains to include the manipulation of physical systems in the emerging field of AI-enhanced cyber-physical attacks. Adversaries can leverage AI to analyze the vulnerabilities of interconnected systems, such as industrial control systems (ICS) and critical infrastructure. The use of AI in cyber-physical attacks enables sophisticated and targeted disruptions to physical processes, potentially causing damage to infrastructure, disrupting essential services, or even posing risks to human safety. The convergence of AI and cyber-physical attacks introduces a new dimension of complexity and potential consequences, necessitating a holistic approach to securing both digital and physical domains.

The evolution of AI-powered autonomous agents in offensive cyber capabilities raises profound ethical and legal considerations. The lack of clear norms and regulations surrounding the use of AI in cyber warfare poses challenges for the international community. Questions about accountability, attribution, and the potential for unintended consequences become central to discussions on the ethical use of AI in offensive cyber operations. The integration of AI introduces the potential for faster, more adaptive, and unpredictable cyber attacks, challenging the traditional paradigms of conflict and necessitating a reevaluation of existing international norms and agreements.

In conclusion, the integration of AI into offensive cyber capabilities signifies a transformative shift in the landscape of cyber warfare, introducing unprecedented challenges and complexities. From automating vulnerability exploitation to enhancing social engineering tactics, leveraging swarm intelligence, and influencing information landscapes, AI-driven offensive capabilities mark a new era of sophistication and adaptability for malicious actors. As the international community grapples with the ethical, legal, and strategic implications of AI in cyber warfare, the urgency to establish norms, regulations, and collaborative frameworks becomes paramount to ensure the responsible and accountable use of these technologies in the evolving landscape of cyber conflict.

Predicting future trends in cyber threats.

Predicting future trends in cyber threats is a complex endeavor shaped by the relentless evolution of technology, the dynamic strategies of malicious actors, and the intricate interplay of geopolitical, economic, and societal factors. One notable trend that is anticipated to persist is the escalation of ransomware attacks. The pervasive use of ransomware, wherein malicious actors encrypt valuable data and demand ransom payments for decryption keys, is expected to continue and evolve in sophistication. Future ransomware variants may employ advanced evasion techniques, target critical infrastructure, and exploit emerging technologies like the Internet of Things (IoT), posing severe challenges for organizations and governments in safeguarding against these financially motivated attacks.

Another significant trend in future cyber threats is the rise of nation-state-sponsored cyber operations. State-sponsored actors are increasingly leveraging cyber capabilities for geopolitical influence, espionage, and strategic advantage. The blurred lines between traditional espionage and cyber operations make attribution challenging, and nation-states are likely to intensify their use of advanced persistent threats (APTs) and sophisticated cyber tools in pursuit of political, economic, and military objectives. The geopolitical landscape is expected to witness an uptick in cyber-espionage campaigns targeting critical infrastructure, defense systems, and intellectual property, with potential repercussions for international relations and global stability.

As the digital transformation accelerates across industries, the attack surface for cyber threats is expanding, giving rise to a trend in targeting supply chain vulnerabilities. Cybercriminals are recognizing the interconnected nature of supply chains, where compromising one entity can have cascading effects on multiple organizations. Future cyber threats are likely to exploit weaknesses in supply chain ecosystems, with attacks ranging from software supply chain compromises to manipulation of hardware components. Securing the end-to-end supply chain will become paramount, requiring collaborative efforts and enhanced cybersecurity measures to mitigate the potential fallout from supply chain-focused cyber attacks.

The proliferation of Internet of Things (IoT) devices presents a fertile ground for future cyber threats. The increasing prevalence of connected devices in homes, businesses, and critical infrastructure introduces a vast attack surface vulnerable to exploitation. Future trends may see a surge in IoT-based attacks, including unauthorized access, data exfiltration, and the use of compromised devices for large-scale distributed denial-of-service (DDoS) attacks. As IoT ecosystems become more intertwined with daily life, the potential impact of cyber threats targeting these devices could extend beyond the digital realm to affect physical systems, amplifying the need for robust security measures in the IoT landscape.

Cyber threats are expected to leverage artificial intelligence (AI) and machine learning (ML) in increasingly sophisticated ways. While AI has shown promise in enhancing cybersecurity defenses, its application in offensive tactics is a concerning trend. Future cyber threats may involve AI-driven attacks that can autonomously adapt, learn, and evade traditional security measures. Adversarial machine learning, where attackers manipulate AI models, could become prevalent, challenging the effectiveness of AI-based defense mechanisms. The use of AI in crafting convincing social engineering attacks, automating phishing campaigns, and optimizing malware behavior is likely to be a key feature of future cyber threats.

Social engineering tactics are anticipated to evolve with greater intricacy, targeting human vulnerabilities to a higher degree. Future cyber threats may involve highly personalized and contextually relevant social engineering attacks that leverage AI-driven analysis of individuals' online behaviors, preferences, and relationships. Deepfake technology, capable of creating realistic audio and video impersonations, could be employed in phishing campaigns, disinformation, and business email compromise attacks. The convergence of AI and social engineering poses challenges for individuals and organizations in discerning between genuine and manipulated communications, necessitating heightened awareness and countermeasures.

The gaming industry, with its massive user base and virtual economies, is poised to be a prime target for future cyber threats. As in-game assets and currencies gain real-world value, cybercriminals may exploit vulnerabilities in gaming platforms for financial gain. Future trends may witness attacks targeting user accounts, stealing valuable in-game items, and compromising virtual currencies. Additionally, the integration of blockchain technology in gaming ecosystems introduces new attack vectors, such as smart contract vulnerabilities and token theft. The multifaceted nature of the gaming industry makes it an attractive target, requiring enhanced security measures to protect both players and the virtual economies they participate in.

The advent of 5G technology brings both opportunities and challenges, and future cyber threats are likely to exploit the vulnerabilities inherent in this next-generation infrastructure. The increased speed and connectivity offered by 5G networks create a more expansive attack surface, with potential targets ranging from IoT devices to critical infrastructure. Threat actors may capitalize on the distributed nature of 5G architecture to launch sophisticated attacks, including man-in-the-middle attacks, eavesdropping, and the compromise of network slices. As the deployment of 5G networks becomes more widespread, securing these infrastructures against cyber threats will be paramount to ensuring the reliability and integrity of communication systems.

The convergence of cyber and physical security is a trend that is expected to gain prominence in the future threat landscape. Cyber threats with the potential to cause physical harm to individuals or disrupt critical infrastructure pose a new dimension of risk. Threats such as ransomware targeting healthcare systems, attacks on autonomous vehicles, or the compromise of smart city infrastructure exemplify the fusion of cyber and physical risks. Defending against these hybrid threats requires a holistic approach that integrates cybersecurity with physical security measures, underscoring the interconnected nature of the digital and physical worlds.

Future cyber threats are likely to exploit the expanding attack surface presented by cloud computing environments. As organizations increasingly migrate their infrastructure and services to the cloud, threat actors will focus on exploiting misconfigurations, vulnerabilities, and insecure application programming interfaces (APIs) within cloud platforms. The shared responsibility model inherent in cloud computing necessitates robust security practices from both cloud service providers and the organizations utilizing their services. Threats such as data breaches, unauthorized access, and cloud-specific malware are expected to escalate, emphasizing the importance of comprehensive cloud security strategies.

The evolving regulatory landscape and the increasing emphasis on data privacy are anticipated to shape future trends in cyber threats. As more stringent data protection regulations come into effect, threat actors may intensify their efforts to circumvent these measures. Future threats could involve the unauthorized access, exfiltration, and manipulation of sensitive personal data, leading to regulatory non-compliance and reputational damage for organizations. The convergence of cybersecurity and privacy concerns highlights the need for a unified approach in safeguarding data against both traditional cyber threats and the regulatory implications of data breaches.

The scarcity of skilled cybersecurity professionals is expected to persist, creating a trend where threat actors capitalize on the shortage of talent. Future cyber threats may involve more sophisticated and targeted attacks that exploit vulnerabilities for more extended periods before detection. The use of advanced persistent threats (APTs) by well-funded and organized cybercriminal groups is likely to increase, requiring organizations to invest in workforce development, threat intelligence sharing, and collaborative approaches to bolster their defenses against persistent and adaptive adversaries.

In conclusion, predicting future trends in cyber threats is a complex endeavor influenced by a myriad of factors, including technological advancements, geopolitical shifts, societal changes, and the evolving strategies of malicious actors. The trends outlined here underscore the need for a proactive and adaptive cybersecurity posture that recognizes the interconnected nature of digital ecosystems and the dynamic landscape of cyber threats. As organizations and governments navigate the evolving threat landscape, staying abreast of emerging trends, investing in robust cybersecurity measures, and fostering collaboration within the cybersecurity community will be essential in mitigating the impact of future cyber threats.

The emergence of new threat vectors and attack methods.

The emergence of new threat vectors and attack methods in the ever-evolving landscape of cybersecurity poses formidable challenges to individuals, organizations, and governments. One prominent threat vector gaining prominence is the exploitation of artificial intelligence (AI) and machine learning (ML) technologies by malicious actors. As AI becomes more integrated into various aspects of our digital lives, threat actors are leveraging these technologies to develop sophisticated and adaptive attack methods. Adversarial machine learning, wherein attackers manipulate AI models to evade detection or produce false results, introduces a new dimension to cyber threats. This method can be employed in evasion tactics, making it harder for traditional security measures to discern between malicious and legitimate activities. The use of AI-driven attacks represents a paradigm shift, requiring defenders to develop advanced techniques for securing AI systems and mitigating the risks posed by adversarial machine learning.

Another emerging threat vector is the exploitation of supply chain vulnerabilities. As organizations increasingly rely on interconnected supply chains for software development, hardware manufacturing, and service delivery, threat actors are targeting these complex ecosystems to infiltrate and compromise their targets. Cyber attacks that compromise the integrity of the supply chain can have cascading effects, impacting multiple organizations downstream. This vector introduces a level of interconnected risk, as a breach in one entity can lead to widespread compromise. Future threats in the supply chain may involve the injection of malicious code into software updates, manipulation of hardware components, or compromise of third-party service providers, highlighting the need for robust supply chain security measures.

The integration of the Internet of Things (IoT) into our daily lives presents a burgeoning threat vector as the number of connected devices continues to proliferate. IoT devices, ranging from smart home appliances to industrial sensors, often lack robust security measures, making them attractive targets for malicious actors. Future threats in this vector may involve the compromise of IoT devices to create massive botnets for distributed denial-of-service (DDoS) attacks, unauthorized access to sensitive data collected by IoT sensors, or the manipulation of critical infrastructure systems. The decentralized and diverse nature of IoT ecosystems introduces challenges in standardizing security measures, requiring a concerted effort to establish comprehensive security standards and practices for IoT devices.

The expansion of cloud computing introduces a new threat vector as organizations migrate their infrastructure and services to cloud platforms. Cloud environments offer numerous benefits, but the shared responsibility model between cloud service providers and their clients introduces potential vulnerabilities. Threat actors may exploit misconfigurations, insecure application programming interfaces (APIs), or vulnerabilities in shared infrastructure to compromise cloud-based systems. Future threats in this vector could include data breaches, unauthorized access to cloud resources, or cloud-specific malware targeting virtualized environments. As organizations continue to embrace cloud computing, ensuring the security of cloud-based assets becomes imperative in mitigating the risks associated with this evolving threat vector.

The convergence of cyber and physical security introduces a multifaceted threat vector with potential consequences for both digital and physical realms. Attacks that target cyber-physical systems, such as industrial control systems (ICS) and critical infrastructure, pose a unique set of challenges. Malicious actors may seek to disrupt essential services, cause physical harm, or manipulate systems that bridge the gap between the digital and physical worlds. Future threats in this vector could involve sophisticated attacks on smart cities, energy grids, or autonomous vehicles. The interconnectedness of cyber-physical systems requires a holistic approach to security that addresses the vulnerabilities inherent in both digital and physical components.

One of the emerging attack methods that amplify the impact of cyber threats is the use of deepfake technology. Deepfakes, which involve the creation of realistic audio and video content using artificial intelligence, have the potential to deceive individuals and manipulate public discourse. Threat actors can leverage deepfakes for disinformation campaigns, impersonate individuals in phishing attacks, or create fraudulent content that undermines trust in media and communication. The use of deepfakes introduces challenges in discerning between authentic and manipulated content, requiring advancements in detection techniques and awareness among individuals and organizations to mitigate the risks associated with this deceptive attack method.

The targeting of critical infrastructure represents a persistent and evolving threat vector with significant implications for national security and public safety. Threat actors, including nation-states and cybercriminal groups, may seek to exploit vulnerabilities in essential services such as energy grids, transportation systems, and water supply networks. Future attack methods against critical infrastructure could involve the use of sophisticated malware, ransomware, or coordinated cyber-physical attacks that disrupt operations and compromise the integrity of these vital systems. As societies become more dependent on interconnected infrastructure, defending against attacks on critical systems becomes paramount, necessitating robust cybersecurity measures and collaboration between public and private sectors.

The integration of blockchain technology, heralded for its security features in ensuring the integrity of transactions, also introduces new threat vectors and attack methods. While blockchain provides a decentralized and tamper-resistant ledger, threat actors may exploit vulnerabilities in blockchain implementations, smart contracts, or consensus mechanisms. Future threats in this vector could include attacks on cryptocurrency platforms, manipulation of decentralized applications (DApps), or the compromise of blockchain networks through novel attack methods. As blockchain technology continues to evolve and gain widespread adoption, securing these decentralized systems against emerging threats becomes crucial in maintaining trust and reliability.

Phishing attacks, a longstanding and prevalent threat vector, continue to evolve with increasing sophistication and effectiveness. Beyond traditional phishing emails, threat actors employ tactics such as spear-phishing, whaling, and business email compromise to target individuals and organizations. Social engineering techniques, coupled with extensive reconnaissance using publicly available information, enable attackers to craft personalized and convincing phishing campaigns. Future trends in phishing attacks may involve the use of AI to automate the generation of convincing phishing messages, deepening the challenge of distinguishing between genuine and fraudulent communications. Enhancements in phishing detection mechanisms, user awareness training, and multi-factor authentication are essential components in mitigating the risks associated with this enduring threat vector.

As organizations embrace remote work and digital collaboration tools, a growing threat vector is the compromise of virtual meeting platforms and communication channels. Malicious actors may exploit vulnerabilities in video conferencing software, conduct eavesdropping attacks, or compromise user credentials to gain unauthorized access to virtual meetings. Future threats in this vector could include the manipulation of audio and video content during virtual meetings, creating opportunities for disinformation and social engineering attacks. Securing digital communication platforms against emerging threats becomes crucial in maintaining the confidentiality, integrity, and availability of virtual collaboration tools that have become integral to modern work environments.

The expansion of 5G technology introduces a new threat vector as the increased speed and connectivity of 5G networks create a more expansive attack surface. Threat actors may leverage 5G networks to conduct man-in-the-middle attacks, eavesdrop on communications, or exploit vulnerabilities in the distributed architecture of 5G infrastructure. Future threats in this vector could involve attacks on IoT devices connected to 5G networks, the compromise of network slices, or the manipulation of communication protocols. As 5G technology becomes ubiquitous, securing these high-speed networks against emerging threats becomes imperative in ensuring the reliability and security of next-generation communication systems.

In conclusion, the emergence of new threat vectors and attack methods underscores the dynamic and multifaceted nature of the cybersecurity landscape. From the exploitation of AI and supply chain vulnerabilities to the convergence of cyber and physical security, each evolving threat vector presents unique challenges that demand innovative and adaptive security measures. As organizations and individuals navigate this complex terrain, a holistic approach to cybersecurity that integrates advanced technologies, collaboration, and awareness becomes indispensable in mitigating the risks associated with emerging threats. The proactive identification and response to these evolving threat vectors are essential in building resilient and secure digital ecosystems in the face of an ever-changing cyber threat landscape.

The adoption and evolution of zero-trust security models.

The adoption and evolution of zero-trust security models mark a paradigm shift in cybersecurity, challenging traditional notions of trust and emphasizing a proactive and comprehensive approach to safeguarding digital assets. Zero trust, as a concept, rejects the default assumption that entities within a network are inherently trustworthy, regardless of their location or past behavior. This departure from the traditional perimeter-based security model becomes increasingly relevant in a landscape characterized by mobility, cloud computing, and a dynamic threat environment.

Historically, cybersecurity models relied on the notion of a trusted internal network separated from an untrusted external network by a well-defined perimeter. However, as organizations increasingly embraced cloud services, mobile devices, and remote work, the traditional perimeter dissolved, creating new attack surfaces and rendering the perimeter-based trust assumptions obsolete. The zero-trust security model addresses this shift by asserting that trust must be continuously validated, and no entity, whether inside or outside the network, should be granted implicit trust.

Key to the evolution of the zero-trust model is the principle of "verify, never trust, always verify." This principle emphasizes the need for continuous authentication and authorization of users, devices, and applications, irrespective of their location or network proximity. Multi-factor authentication (MFA), device posture assessment, and continuous monitoring are integral components of the zero-trust approach, ensuring that only authenticated and authorized entities can access sensitive resources.

One of the pillars of the zero-trust model is micro-segmentation, a strategy that involves dividing the network into small, isolated segments to contain potential breaches and limit lateral movement by attackers. This granular segmentation enhances the overall security posture by restricting unauthorized access, reducing the attack surface, and preventing lateral movement within the network. Micro-segmentation aligns with the zero-trust philosophy by assuming that even within the internal network, trust is not implicit, and access permissions must be explicitly defined and continuously validated.

The evolution of zero trust extends beyond network access to include the concept of "zero trust for endpoints." Traditional security models often relied on the assumption that devices within the network could be trusted once they passed through the perimeter. However, the proliferation of mobile devices, Internet of Things (IoT) devices, and remote work scenarios challenged this assumption. Zero trust for endpoints entails treating every device as untrusted until proven otherwise. Continuous monitoring of device behavior, regular security assessments, and the enforcement of security policies on endpoints are critical components of this evolving approach.

The integration of identity as a core component of zero trust reflects a growing recognition that user identities are a primary target for attackers. The principle of least privilege, where users are granted the minimum level of access necessary for their roles, aligns with the zero-trust model. Implementing least privilege access reduces the potential impact of a compromised account and limits lateral movement by attackers. Continuous authentication and adaptive access controls, guided by user behavior analytics, contribute to the evolving sophistication of identity-centric zero-trust strategies.

As organizations increasingly adopt cloud services and migrate their infrastructure, the zero-trust model extends its principles to cloud security. Zero trust in the cloud assumes that no entity, whether originating from inside or outside the organization, should be inherently trusted. Identity and access management (IAM) becomes a crucial aspect, ensuring that users, applications, and services are granted the appropriate level of access based on continuously validated permissions. The dynamic nature of cloud environments, where resources scale up or down based on demand, aligns with the adaptive and continuous nature of the zero-trust philosophy.

The application of artificial intelligence (AI) and machine learning (ML) in zero-trust security models represents a significant evolution in response to the complexity and scale of modern cybersecurity challenges. AI-driven threat detection, anomaly detection, and behavioral analysis contribute to the continuous monitoring and assessment of the security posture. These technologies enable organizations to identify patterns indicative of malicious activities, detect deviations from baseline behavior, and respond in near real-time to potential threats. The use of AI and ML aligns with the dynamic and adaptive nature of zero trust, providing a more proactive defense against evolving cyber threats.

Zero trust is not confined to the boundaries of an organization but extends to the interconnected ecosystems of partners, suppliers, and third-party entities. The zero-trust approach recognizes that external entities should not be automatically trusted based on their affiliations but, instead, should be subject to the same rigorous verification and validation processes. This evolution addresses the reality that supply chains and business ecosystems are potential vectors for cyber threats, and a breach in one entity can have cascading effects on others.

The evolution of the zero-trust model is reflected in the increasing importance of continuous monitoring and threat intelligence. Continuous monitoring ensures that the security posture of an organization is actively assessed, and any deviations from normal behavior trigger immediate response mechanisms. Threat intelligence, informed by global and industry-specific insights, enhances the organization's ability to anticipate and proactively defend against emerging cyber threats. The integration of threat intelligence into the zero-trust framework reinforces the model's adaptive nature, allowing organizations to stay ahead of evolving threat landscapes.

Zero trust aligns with the principles of least privilege and just-in-time access, emphasizing the need to restrict access permissions to the bare minimum required for specific tasks and only for the duration needed. Just-in-time access minimizes the window of opportunity for attackers, reducing the risk of unauthorized access or privilege escalation. This approach reflects the evolving emphasis on proactive risk reduction and containment within the zero-trust framework.

The concept of "assume breach" embodies the proactive mindset of the zero-trust model. Rather than operating under the assumption that the perimeter defenses will prevent all breaches, organizations adopting zero trust acknowledge that breaches are inevitable. This assumption guides the implementation of security controls and measures to contain and mitigate the impact of a breach promptly. The evolving zero-trust mindset recognizes that security is an ongoing process of adaptation and response rather than a static state.

The evolution of zero trust is also reflected in its integration with Security Operations Centers (SOCs) and Incident Response (IR) processes. The zero-trust model emphasizes the importance of rapid detection, investigation, and response to security incidents. Continuous monitoring, real-time analysis of security events, and automation in incident response contribute to the efficiency and effectiveness of the zero-trust approach. The integration with SOCs ensures that the zero-trust model is not just a theoretical framework but a practical and operational security strategy.

Zero trust, as an evolving security paradigm, embraces the principles of resilience and adaptability. The recognition that cybersecurity is a dynamic and ever-changing landscape, coupled with the understanding that trust should be continually validated, positions zero trust as a proactive and future-ready approach. The model's evolution involves a holistic consideration of network security, endpoint security, identity management, cloud security, and threat intelligence, reflecting a comprehensive and adaptive strategy in the face of emerging cyber threats.

The emergence of zero trust as a holistic and adaptive security model underscores its relevance in addressing the challenges posed by the evolving cybersecurity landscape. The model's evolution from a focus on network security to a comprehensive approach encompassing endpoints, identities, cloud environments, and external entities reflects a nuanced understanding of the interconnected and dynamic nature of modern cybersecurity. As organizations continue to grapple with sophisticated cyber threats, the adoption and evolution of the zero-trust model provide a roadmap for building resilient, proactive, and adaptive security postures in an ever-changing digital landscape.

Benefits and challenges associated with implementing zero-trust.

Implementing a zero-trust security model brings forth a spectrum of benefits and challenges, reflecting the complexity and transformative nature of this cybersecurity approach. The primary advantage lies in the enhanced security posture it provides by dismantling the traditional assumption of trust based on network location. One of the key benefits is the proactive defense against evolving cyber threats. Unlike traditional security models that rely on a defined perimeter, zero trust assumes that threats may already be present within the network, prompting a continuous validation of user, device, and application trustworthiness. This proactive stance enables organizations to identify and respond to potential threats in real-time, reducing the dwell time of attackers and minimizing the impact of security incidents.

A crucial benefit associated with the implementation of zero trust is the principle of least privilege, which ensures that users and entities are granted only the minimum level of access required for their specific roles and tasks. This granular approach reduces the attack surface and limits the potential damage that can be caused by compromised accounts. By adhering to the principle of least privilege, organizations can mitigate the risks of unauthorized access and privilege escalation, aligning security controls with the core tenets of the zero-trust model.

Another notable advantage of zero trust is its adaptability to the dynamic nature of modern IT environments. With the increasing adoption of cloud services, remote work, and mobile devices, the traditional perimeter-based security model has become obsolete. Zero trust, on the other hand, is well-suited for these dynamic scenarios, as it focuses on continuous authentication and validation regardless of the user's location or the network they are accessing. This adaptability supports the flexibility and scalability required in today's interconnected and distributed IT landscapes.

Zero trust promotes a holistic approach to security by encompassing various dimensions, including network security, endpoint security, identity management, and cloud security. This comprehensive strategy addresses the interconnected nature of cyber threats, ensuring that security measures are implemented across all facets of the organization. The integration of security controls within a unified framework enhances visibility and control, allowing organizations to effectively manage and monitor their security posture. This holistic perspective is particularly valuable in an era where cyber threats can exploit vulnerabilities across diverse attack vectors.

Identity plays a central role in the zero-trust model, and one of its benefits is the elevation of identity-centric security. By focusing on continuous authentication, adaptive access controls, and least privilege principles, zero trust strengthens the protection of user identities. This is especially crucial given the increasing prevalence of identity-related attacks, such as credential theft and unauthorized access. The elevation of identity-centric security aligns with the evolving cybersecurity landscape, where user identities are prime targets for malicious actors seeking to exploit vulnerabilities and gain unauthorized access.

Furthermore, the integration of artificial intelligence (AI) and machine learning (ML) technologies enhances the efficacy of zero trust in threat detection and response. AI-driven threat analytics can analyze vast datasets, identify patterns indicative of malicious activities, and automate response actions in near real-time. This proactive and intelligent approach is well-aligned with the continuous monitoring and adaptive nature of the zero-trust model, providing organizations with the ability to detect and respond to threats with greater speed and precision

While the benefits of implementing zero trust are substantial, organizations also encounter challenges in adopting this transformative security model. One of the primary challenges is the complexity of implementation, especially for enterprises with existing infrastructure and legacy systems. Transitioning to a zero-trust architecture requires a thorough understanding of the organization's current IT landscape, careful planning, and strategic deployment to avoid disruptions to ongoing operations. The complexity of integrating zero trust into established environments often necessitates a phased approach, wherein organizations incrementally implement components of the model to minimize disruptions.

Another challenge lies in the cultural and organizational shift required to embrace the zero-trust mindset. Traditional security models often instill a sense of trust based on network location, and transitioning to a zero-trust paradigm demands a shift in mindset and a reevaluation of established security practices. This cultural shift involves fostering a cybersecurity awareness that assumes breaches are inevitable and emphasizes a continuous validation of trust. Overcoming resistance to change, educating stakeholders, and instilling a zero-trust culture across the organization are crucial components of successfully implementing this model.

The granularity of the zero-trust model, while beneficial for security, can also pose a challenge in terms of complexity and management. Implementing and maintaining the various components, such as micro-segmentation, continuous monitoring, and adaptive access controls, requires a comprehensive understanding of the organization's assets, user roles, and data flows. The management overhead associated with maintaining these granular security controls can be substantial, requiring skilled personnel, robust processes, and effective security automation tools.

Integration with existing security tools and technologies is another challenge organizations face when adopting a zero-trust model. Many enterprises have invested heavily in traditional security solutions that are designed around the concept of a trusted perimeter. Integrating these legacy systems with the principles of zero trust may require significant customization, reconfiguration, or, in some cases, the adoption of new security technologies that align with the zero-trust paradigm. Achieving seamless interoperability between existing security infrastructure and zero-trust components is an ongoing challenge in the implementation journey.

Zero trust also introduces considerations related to user experience and operational efficiency. The continuous validation and authentication mechanisms inherent to zero trust may, at times, create friction for end-users. Striking a balance between robust security controls and a seamless user experience is essential to prevent user resistance and ensure the practical viability of the zero-trust model. Organizations must prioritize user education, provide user-friendly authentication methods, and implement adaptive access controls that align with business needs while maintaining a high level of security.

The dynamic nature of zero trust, while beneficial for adapting to evolving threats, introduces challenges in terms of ongoing maintenance and updates. The continuous monitoring of user behavior, device posture, and network activities requires constant vigilance, and organizations must remain agile in responding to changes in their IT environments. Regular updates to security policies, access controls, and threat intelligence integrations are essential for maintaining the effectiveness of the zero-trust model over time. The challenge lies in sustaining this dynamic approach without overwhelming security teams or causing disruptions to business operations.

Moreover, the implementation of zero trust requires a clear understanding of the organization's data and its criticality. Identifying and classifying sensitive data, understanding data flows, and implementing data-centric security measures are integral to the success of the zero-trust model. The challenge lies in organizations' ability to effectively categorize and protect their data, especially in environments with large volumes of diverse data types and storage locations.

The scale and scope of implementing zero trust across large, multinational organizations with diverse business units and geographical locations present additional challenges. Coordinating the deployment of zero-trust components, ensuring consistent security policies, and managing the cultural shift across a globally distributed workforce require a strategic and coordinated approach. Organizations must consider regional regulations, compliance requirements, and the unique cybersecurity landscapes in different locations when implementing a uniform zero-trust strategy.

In conclusion, the adoption and evolution of the zero-trust security model offer substantial benefits in enhancing cybersecurity resilience, adapting to dynamic IT environments, and mitigating the impact of evolving cyber threats. However, organizations must navigate the challenges associated with complexity, cultural shifts, granular management, integration with existing infrastructure, user experience considerations, ongoing maintenance, and the global scale of implementation. Successfully implementing zero trust requires a strategic, phased approach that balances security requirements with operational efficiency, user needs, and the dynamic nature of the cybersecurity landscape. As organizations continue to prioritize cybersecurity in the face of persistent threats, the journey towards zero trust remains a transformative and essential endeavor for building resilient and adaptive security postures.

Anticipated changes in cybersecurity regulations.

Anticipated changes in cybersecurity regulations are poised to reshape the legal landscape governing digital security, reflecting the evolving nature of cyber threats, technological advancements, and the increasing interconnectedness of global digital ecosystems. One prominent trend is the expected strengthening of data protection and privacy regulations. With a growing awareness of the importance of safeguarding personal information, jurisdictions around the world are likely to enact or enhance regulations to provide individuals with greater control over their data. Anticipated changes may include stricter requirements for data breach notifications, enhanced consent mechanisms, and expanded rights for individuals to access, correct, or delete their personal information. As data breaches continue to pose significant risks to individuals and organizations, regulators are expected to emphasize proactive measures and stringent compliance to fortify data protection frameworks.

The evolving threat landscape is driving anticipated changes in regulations pertaining to critical infrastructure protection. Governments and regulatory bodies are recognizing the increasing vulnerability of essential services, such as energy, transportation, and healthcare, to cyber attacks. Anticipated regulations may mandate enhanced cybersecurity measures for critical infrastructure operators, including robust risk assessments, regular security audits, and the adoption of specific cybersecurity frameworks. Collaboration between public and private sectors is likely to be emphasized, with regulations encouraging the sharing of threat intelligence and best practices to fortify the resilience of critical infrastructure against sophisticated cyber threats.

The anticipated surge in regulations related to supply chain security reflects the interconnected nature of global business operations. As organizations increasingly rely on complex and globalized supply chains, regulators are expected to introduce measures to mitigate the risks associated with third-party vulnerabilities. Anticipated changes may include requirements for thorough supply chain risk assessments, due diligence on third-party cybersecurity practices, and the establishment of contractual obligations for suppliers to adhere to specified security standards. The goal is to ensure that the weakest link in the supply chain does not become a gateway for cyber attacks that can have cascading effects on multiple organizations.

The integration of emerging technologies into various sectors is driving anticipated changes in regulations to address the associated cybersecurity challenges. Artificial intelligence (AI), the Internet of Things (IoT), and blockchain technologies are becoming integral parts of modern business operations, but their adoption introduces new vulnerabilities. Anticipated regulations may focus on ensuring the security-by-design of these technologies, mandating adherence to cybersecurity standards, and establishing guidelines for responsible AI and IoT development. Regulators are likely to collaborate with technology stakeholders to strike a balance between innovation and security, acknowledging the need for regulations that evolve in tandem with technological advancements.

The anticipated convergence of cybersecurity and financial regulations reflects the critical role of the financial sector in global economic stability. Financial institutions are prime targets for cybercriminals seeking financial gain or destabilization, necessitating robust regulations to safeguard the integrity of financial systems. Anticipated changes may include enhanced cybersecurity requirements for financial institutions, stricter guidelines for incident reporting, and measures to bolster the cybersecurity resilience of payment systems. Regulators are expected to prioritize the detection and mitigation of financial cyber threats, potentially requiring organizations to undergo regular cybersecurity assessments and adhere to industry-specific best practices.

Cross-border data flows are integral to the functioning of the global digital economy, and anticipated changes in regulations aim to address the complexities surrounding data sovereignty and international data transfers. With privacy concerns at the forefront, regulators may introduce measures to ensure that the transfer of personal data across borders aligns with stringent data protection standards. Anticipated changes may involve the negotiation of international agreements on data transfer mechanisms, such as data adequacy decisions or the use of standardized contractual clauses. As the regulatory landscape evolves, organizations engaged in cross-border data processing are likely to face increased scrutiny and may need to implement additional safeguards to navigate the intricacies of global data protection regulations.

The anticipated rise in regulations related to incident response and breach disclosure underscores the growing importance of transparency and accountability in the aftermath of cyber incidents. Regulators are expected to emphasize the need for organizations to have well-defined incident response plans, including clear protocols for identifying, containing, and mitigating cybersecurity incidents. Anticipated changes may include stricter timelines for reporting data breaches, requirements for providing affected individuals with timely and accurate information, and potential consequences for organizations that fail to meet disclosure obligations. This trend reflects a global shift toward enhancing transparency in the face of escalating cyber threats and the increasing impact of data breaches on individuals and businesses.

With the growing recognition of the cybersecurity risks associated with the Internet of Things (IoT) devices, anticipated changes in regulations may focus on establishing minimum security standards for IoT manufacturers. As the number of connected devices continues to proliferate, regulators are expected to address the inherent vulnerabilities in IoT ecosystems that can be exploited by malicious actors. Anticipated regulations may mandate secure-by-design principles, periodic security updates for IoT devices, and measures to prevent unauthorized access and data breaches. The goal is to create a baseline of cybersecurity protections for IoT devices, fostering a more secure and resilient IoT landscape.

The anticipated regulatory emphasis on consumer protection in the context of cybersecurity reflects the increasing impact of cyber incidents on individuals. With the rise in cyber threats targeting personal data, regulators are expected to introduce or enhance regulations that prioritize the protection of consumers' digital identities and sensitive information. Anticipated changes may include measures to empower individuals with greater control over their personal data, enhanced transparency requirements, and avenues for seeking redress in the event of data breaches. This consumer-centric approach aligns with the broader trend of prioritizing privacy and security in the digital age.

As the digital transformation accelerates across industries, anticipated changes in regulations may focus on promoting a cybersecurity culture within organizations. Recognizing the critical role of human factors in cybersecurity, regulators may emphasize the need for organizations to invest in cybersecurity awareness programs, employee training, and measures to mitigate the risks of insider threats. Anticipated regulations may encourage a proactive approach to building a cybersecurity-aware workforce, potentially involving incentives for organizations that demonstrate a commitment to fostering a strong cybersecurity culture.

The anticipated evolution of cybersecurity regulations is closely intertwined with the broader trends shaping the digital landscape. Regulators are expected to navigate the delicate balance between fostering innovation and ensuring robust cybersecurity practices, recognizing the need for adaptive and responsive regulations that evolve alongside emerging technologies and cyber threats. Organizations, in turn, must stay vigilant, anticipate regulatory changes, and proactively adapt their cybersecurity strategies to align with the evolving legal landscape. The anticipated changes in cybersecurity regulations underscore the imperative for a holistic and collaborative approach, involving governments, regulatory bodies, industry stakeholders, and cybersecurity professionals working together to create a secure and resilient digital future.

The impact of regulatory shifts on organizations.

The impact of regulatory shifts on organizations is profound, shaping the way businesses operate, manage data, and secure their digital assets. Regulatory changes in areas such as data protection, cybersecurity, and privacy have become increasingly common as governments worldwide respond to the evolving threat landscape and the rapid pace of digital transformation. One of the significant impacts of regulatory shifts is the increased burden of compliance on organizations. As regulations become more stringent and comprehensive, businesses are compelled to invest significant resources in understanding, implementing, and maintaining compliance measures. This includes adapting internal policies, enhancing cybersecurity protocols, and establishing robust data protection frameworks to align with the evolving regulatory landscape.

The financial impact of regulatory shifts cannot be overstated. Organizations often face increased compliance costs, including expenses related to cybersecurity infrastructure upgrades, hiring specialized compliance personnel, and conducting regular audits to ensure adherence to regulatory requirements. The need for ongoing training and awareness programs to keep employees abreast of compliance measures further adds to the financial burden. Smaller businesses, in particular, may find it challenging to allocate the necessary resources, potentially leading to increased operational costs and a reallocation of budgetary priorities.

Regulatory shifts also influence the strategic decision-making process within organizations. Executives and boards must consider compliance as a strategic imperative, impacting business plans, technology investments, and overall risk management strategies. The dynamic nature of the regulatory environment requires organizations to maintain agility and flexibility in their strategies, anticipating changes and proactively adjusting their operations to remain compliant. This strategic recalibration often necessitates a closer integration of legal, IT, and risk management functions within organizations to ensure a cohesive and comprehensive approach to compliance.

The impact of regulatory shifts extends beyond internal operations to external relationships, particularly in supply chain management. Organizations are increasingly held responsible for the cybersecurity practices of their third-party vendors and partners. Regulatory changes often mandate that organizations assess and ensure the cybersecurity posture of their suppliers, creating a ripple effect across supply chains. This can lead to additional due diligence, renegotiation of contracts, and, in some cases, a reassessment of the overall supply chain structure. The interconnectedness of businesses in today's global economy means that regulatory shifts in one jurisdiction can have cascading effects on organizations operating across borders.

Regulatory changes in data protection and privacy, such as the implementation of the General Data Protection Regulation (GDPR) in the European Union, have had a profound impact on how organizations handle personal information. The enhanced rights of individuals and the stringent requirements for obtaining and processing personal data have forced organizations to reevaluate their data management practices. The need for explicit consent, transparent data processing policies, and the right to be forgotten have compelled businesses to implement more robust data governance frameworks. The impact on marketing practices, customer engagement, and data monetization strategies has been particularly significant, requiring organizations to find a delicate balance between utilizing customer data and respecting privacy rights.

Moreover, the impact of regulatory shifts is not limited to specific industries; it permeates across sectors, influencing businesses ranging from healthcare to finance, from technology to manufacturing. For example, in the healthcare sector, regulations such as the Health Insurance Portability and Accountability Act (HIPAA) mandate strict standards for the protection of patient data, impacting the way healthcare providers, insurers, and technology vendors handle sensitive health information. In the financial sector, regulatory changes, such as those introduced by the Dodd-Frank Wall Street Reform and Consumer Protection Act, have reshaped risk management practices, financial reporting, and executive compensation structures.

The reputational impact of regulatory shifts is a critical consideration for organizations. Non-compliance with regulations can result in public scrutiny, damage to brand reputation, and loss of customer trust. High-profile data breaches and privacy scandals have demonstrated the potential for severe reputational damage, leading organizations to prioritize compliance as a means of safeguarding their brand image. Ethical considerations and corporate social responsibility now intertwine with regulatory compliance, as customers, investors, and the public increasingly expect businesses to operate ethically and responsibly in the digital realm.

Organizations also face the challenge of navigating a patchwork of regulations and standards across different jurisdictions. As regulatory frameworks evolve independently in various regions, multinational companies must contend with a complex web of compliance requirements. Harmonizing internal policies and practices to align with diverse regulatory expectations becomes a logistical challenge, requiring legal expertise, cross-functional collaboration, and a nuanced understanding of the legal landscapes in each operating jurisdiction. The impact of this complexity is often felt most acutely by organizations with a global footprint.

Furthermore, the impact of regulatory shifts on innovation and technology adoption cannot be overlooked. While regulations aim to enhance cybersecurity, protect privacy, and ensure data integrity, they can inadvertently create barriers to the adoption of cutting-edge technologies. Organizations may face challenges in experimenting with emerging technologies, such as artificial intelligence, due to regulatory uncertainties and concerns about compliance. Striking a balance between fostering innovation and adhering to regulatory requirements becomes a delicate task, with organizations needing to navigate the regulatory landscape while embracing technological advancements.

The impact of regulatory shifts extends to the legal liability and accountability of organizations. Regulators increasingly hold companies accountable for the protection of sensitive information and the management of cybersecurity risks. Legal repercussions for non-compliance can include hefty fines, legal actions, and, in severe cases, restrictions on business operations. The legal landscape surrounding cybersecurity and data protection is evolving, and organizations must stay vigilant to ensure that they are meeting their legal obligations, including reporting incidents, addressing vulnerabilities, and demonstrating due diligence in safeguarding sensitive information.

Regulatory shifts can also impact the competitive landscape within industries. Organizations that proactively embrace and exceed compliance standards may gain a competitive advantage by differentiating themselves as trustworthy custodians of customer data. Conversely, companies that lag behind in implementing necessary cybersecurity measures may face increased scrutiny, lose market share, and struggle to compete in an environment where customers prioritize data security and privacy. The impact on competitiveness underscores the strategic importance of compliance as a business differentiator in today's digital economy.

The impact of regulatory shifts is not static; it evolves over time as regulations mature, new threats emerge, and technologies advance. Organizations must adopt a forward-looking approach to compliance, anticipating regulatory trends, and staying abreast of developments to ensure their cybersecurity measures remain effective and aligned with legal expectations. As regulatory frameworks continue to evolve, organizations that view compliance as an integral part of their business strategy, rather than a mere obligation, are better positioned to navigate the complex landscape, mitigate risks, and build trust with stakeholders in an era where data protection and cybersecurity are paramount concerns.

www.ingramcontent.com/pod-product-compliance
Lightning Source LLC
Chambersburg PA
CBHW071104050326
40690CB00008B/1109